Then Sings My Soul

My Mother's Song

JELENE KIRKLAND

Printed in the United States of America

ISBN - 978-0-578-50446-9

For my sweet mother

ACKNOWLEDGEMENTS

Writing this book was like squeezing frosting out of the smallest Wilton frosting tip. Some days the words flowed smoothly and tasted sweet and some days no matter how hard I squeezed the words would not come. Finding the words to share the story of a woman like my mother and the life she lived was not easy and brought many tears of joy and sadness.

As I get closer to my mother's age, that is, what I used to think was old, I wonder about my own legacy. I think we all come to a place in our journey where we wonder if anyone will remember us when we are gone. Will our lives have meant anything? I want my mother to know that hers did. She means everything to me.

There's not a day that goes by that I don't think of Mother. Whenever I hear piano music or one of the hundreds of songs she taught us, I choke up a little. I'm an old woman, but I still hear her scold me when I drink a coke, make bread with white flour instead of whole wheat or take more than two pieces of toilet paper. I feel her beside me every Sunday when my husband and I sit down to listen to the Mormon Tabernacle Choir. And every time I see an American Flag waving in the breeze I hear her say, "Oh, how I love that flag."

I want to thank my siblings for going on this lively adventure with me and sharing their stories and helping me with the details of this book. My sweet sisters, whom I love so dearly and who have been there for me with love and encouraging words.

My cousins, Val Hemming, Sharon Keele and Clayne Pearson for the hours we spent together remembering my younger, ambitious talented Father. And my uncle Ronald for sharing stories from my mother's younger days.

I want to thank Marie Tollstrup, my first writing teacher, years ago, for her encouraging words when I wrote my first story called "Mama's Cow" not knowing that it would someday become part of this book.

I want to thank Dustin Crawford, my son-in-law and English professor at Utah State University, for editing some of my stories.

I want to thank Becky Jackson, Marilyn Richardson, Lydia Jeppson, Pam Jensen, my cousin, Margaret Munoz, my sister Donna, and my daughters Kaylee and LeAnna for being my friends, readers and editors. I want to thank Sheila Kinneer Rob for her help with the Kindle Direct Publishing website.

I want to thank my daughter, LeAnna for her patience and love, while spending hours with me at the computer making files, Documents and downloads. I want to thank my son Brian for stopping by my house every day to make me laugh and for pushing a button on the computer whenever I needed him to. I can't leave out my other beautiful daughters and cute daughter-in-law, who loved listening to my stories and kept asking, "Mom, when is your book coming out?"

I want to thank my husband, who is the hardest worker I have ever met, for never missing a rent payment, for feeding and clothing all of us, but most of all for loving me for the last, almost fifty years.

I was most blest the day I met Dorothy Allred Solomon,

author of "In My Father's House" who became my coach, teacher and friend over the past three years as we met every week to get my story written and ready to publish. It never would have happened without you, Dorothy and I thank you from the bottom of my heart for your patience and perseverance.

I have chosen to change some names for privacy reasons.

There are parts of this book where I have taken the liberty to create dialogue to keep the story interesting and fluid. The stories I tell are mine, from my life. Everyone has a different story to tell.

So if you are ever inclined to write your story, I will gladly and lovingly encourage you to, "Get your own tube of frosting and start squeezing!"

TABLE OF CONTENTS

The Little Black Book

Little did we know that an innocent knock on the front door of our tiny farmhouse in Monteview, Idaho would take our family down a rabbit hole of deception, heartache, and regret. It would be a hole that would take some of us many years to emerge from and some of us would not climb out at all.

Father and the hired man had just come in from the fields to eat lunch on that fateful day. Mother, who had her yellow apron tied around her waist, shooed us all to our places at the table that was quickly becoming too small. With two hot pads holding two hot pans, she brought over her mainstay meal when she had to make a little go a long way-- mashed potatoes and hamburger and milk gravy-- and set it in the middle of the table. Cheryl, who was ten and the oldest of our clan, helped the little boys, Roger and Lee to their places on the bench. Janice, a year younger than Cheryl sat on the other side of them to help put food on their plates. Bart was eight and spent most of his time in the fields with Father but in the house, he was swiftly setting himself up as the boss of us five little kids. Bart pushed

Keith into place beside Kay and I on another small bench and planted himself in a big chair next to the hired man, directly across the table from Father.

"You're not the boss," I hissed at Bart.

"Jelene, be nice to your brother," Mother said, turning from behind the refrigerator door with two pitchers of milk. "Now let us pray."

Father was just scooping the last forkful of food into his mouth, when he heard the knock. He leaned toward Mother who had finally sat down to eat and gave her a kiss.

"Thanks for the food, dear." He scraped his chair back from the table and walked to the front door. I poked Kay with my elbow.

"Move. Let's go see." All eight of us ran, tripping over each other to beat Father to the door. People rarely knocked on our door clear out here on the farm. Who could it be?

A small man stood in the doorway. He looked to be around forty, but was dwarfed by my father, who was a six-foot wall of vitality and muscle, with shoulders of steel that we took turns riding every morning as he went to milk the cows and do chores. Shoulders that chucked big bales of hay, changed tractor tires and levitated Mother off the ground when he wrapped her in his warm embrace.

Alongside Father, the man in the wrinkled brown suit seemed harmless as a child. The glasses hanging off his nose made him look like a little professor. He stuck out his hand.

"Hello. My name is Horace Knowlton. I am with Freedom Insurance Company. Could I have a minute of your time?

"Sure. Come on in. I can tell you right now that I won't be buying any of your insurance. Don't have the money. But you're welcome to come in and give me your spiel. I need a nap."

Father laughed, shook Horace Knowlton's hand and led him to the living room. Mr. Knowlton sat down on the overstuffed floral chair grandma had passed down to us when she got her new red sofa. He spread his papers across the coffee table and began talking numbers. The boys started poking each other the minute we sat down. Father shooed them out to play and Kay ran after them. I was the only one left on Father's lap. I sat very still, his big arm wrapped around me. I could feel his voice vibrating in his chest when he spoke.

"Well, I'd love to be able to afford some insurance but there just isn't a dollar to spare right now," Father said. "You can always check with the Beans down the road. They've had a good year with their alfalfa.

"This is beautiful country. I've often thought how great it would be to have a farm up here." Horace said.

"Yes, it's this rich, black Idaho soil. Just too bad it's so hard to make any money farming. We just lost our haystack and barn in the lightning storm the other night and that hay was our security for the next year. So unless we get a miracle, we will be losing this place."

"Oh, I'm sorry to hear that."

Horace leaned over the table to gather up his papers to leave, "You folks Mormons?"

"Isn't everybody?" Father laughed.

"Well, maybe you would call me a Mormon," the man said. "But I'm more like an old fashioned Mormon."

"I don't see a long beard or a wagon outside. What do you mean?"

Horace sat out on the edge of the chair and lowered his voice. "Have you ever heard that Joseph Smith had more than one wife?"

"I might have heard that. But the church doesn't talk about it much."

"No, they don't. Did you know that an angel came to the Prophet Joseph Smith three times with his sword drawn and told him he must live the law of Celestial Marriage or the angel would take his life?" Horace lowered his voice even more. "Joseph Smith did live polygamy. In fact he had many wives."

"Well, that was a long time ago and it's certainly not part of the Mormon Church today." Father said, lowering his voice to match Horace's.

"Yes, I know, but if I told you that there are people secretly living the principle of plural marriage right now, today, would you be surprised?"

"Yes, I would be surprised." Father leaned back in his chair and I felt his big chest expand with a sharp, quick breath.

"The saints who are living polygamy today believe that the church was wrong in signing the Manifesto in 1890 and doing away with the commandment from God to live the Principle of Plural Marriage."

"But Prophet Wilford Woodruff signed the Manifesto. So it must have been a revelation from God." Father sounded more like he was asking a question than making a statement. Horace reached into his brief case and brought out a little black book and handed it to Father.

"Here, read this. I will stop by again in a couple of months and we can talk about it."

Looking down at the tiny book in his hand, Father seemed anxious or excited. I couldn't tell which. He pulled me in tighter to his chest.

"Just read that book. I think you will find it very interesting." Horace got up to leave. Father pushed the small book between the cushion and the side of the couch, took my hand and we walked Horace to the door.

The next morning I was in mother's bedroom when she

found the small booklet on the night stand and picked it up, read the title and opened it to the middle.

"*Michael Our Father and Our God.* Where did you get this book?" She frowned at Father.

"Oh, it's just a little book that insurance fellow gave me to read.

Mother read aloud. "When Father Adam came into the Garden of Eden, he came into it with a celestial body, and brought Eve, one of his wives, with him."

"One of his wives?" Mother looked shocked.

"Did you know that Joseph Smith and Brigham Young believed that Adam was our Father and our God? He wasn't just Adam. He was God. I have never heard that before."

"Are you sure you should be reading books like this? You heard the bishop just last Sunday, telling everyone not to delve into the mysteries. We need to trust the prophet of today and his counselors." Mother opened the nightstand drawer and tucked the book out of sight. Father came around behind her and reached into the drawer and took the book out. He held it to his chest.

"Don't you want to know the teachings of all our prophets, including the old prophets?"

"You mean the early history of the Church?" Mother asked.

"Yes, the teachings of Joseph Smith and Brigham Young."

Mother ducked under Father's arm, her lips pressed into a fine, straight line. She shooed me along as she walked down the hall, Father following at her heels.

"Heck, I've never even read the Book of Mormon all the way through," he said. "Maybe we could start there."

Mother took her apron off the hook by the pantry and tied it around her waist. "Well, if you're going to read it then you have to share everything you read with me. You have a tendency to get very excited about things and go a little overboard. We're a team. You see all these little children?" Mother waved her spatula at her children gathered around the table. "They are part of the team too. Everything we do affects them. And," she stopped and brought her spatula up to Father's chest. "You can't go around telling everyone what you are reading. This has to stay here, in this house, just between us! "

"We're just reading. That's all, nothing more." Father reassured her. She didn't look convinced.

Nothing more turned into much more. That tiny book turned Father and Mother's whole world upside down. It made reference to a set of books called the *Journal of Discourses*. Father went to the bookstore and bought the whole set. In those books they read the old prophets passionately preaching the restored gospel. Brigham Young, Heber C. Kimball and John Taylor taught the saints about the blessings of the New and Everlasting Principle of Plural Marriage, a principle they believed in with all their hearts and would give their lives for. These prophets spoke of mansions in heaven, populated by many wives and children, kingdoms where they reigned as Gods on thrones with power and dominion and a warning that those refusing to accept this new principle would go to Hell.

By 1844, Joseph Smith's newly established Mormon Church had become so large that its members could swing an election in the state of Illinois, where they built the beautiful city of Nauvoo out of the swamplands bordering the Missouri river. When rumors began circulating that the Mormons were living "The Principle of Plural Marriage" the people of Illinois were outraged. A mob of vigilantes forced the Prophet Joseph Smith and his Brother Hyrum into the Carthage Jail where two days later they were murdered. Brigham Young stepped up as their leader and when the mobs came again with the message, either leave or be exterminated, the saints were forced to leave their beautiful city with its temple on the hill. In February of 1846, they loaded their covered wagons with everything they could carry and crossed the ice-covered Missouri River to begin the heroic trek to the Rocky Mountains. My ancestors were among those brave saints, who sacrificed everything for their religion.

"Listen to this." Father said. Each night at supper, he read to us from the little black book, holding it softly and carefully like a valued treasure. "Here it says, 'Let us here observe, that a religion that does not require the sacrifice of all things never has power sufficient to produce the faith necessary unto life and salvation. It was through this sacrifice, and this only, that God has ordained that men should enjoy eternal life.'"

The wrinkles etched into Mother's forehead and the tired look in her eyes showed that she was tired of sacrifice already. Weren't they already giving ten-percent of their income for tithing to their church? Didn't they fast and pray the first Sunday of every month in remembrance of the Atonement of Christ? As a Mother in Zion, didn't she give her body to build the kingdom of God by bringing as many souls to the earth as she could?

Later in my life as a married woman, my heart ached for my mother. I imagine her worries stacked up like a grey, cinder block wall, separating her from the only life she had ever known. How could she leave the beloved Church of her youth? If she and Father continued down this path, the life she knew and loved would be gone forever. Her kind, loving parents would be devastated. Her brothers and sisters would never understand. She had spent almost as much time in Mormon Church buildings as she had at home--singing in choirs and playing the piano for primary class, sacrament meeting and anywhere else she was needed.

When my parents began reading section 132 of *the Doctrine and Covenant* in which the Prophet Joseph Smith's revelation states that Celestial Marriage is a commandment of God, I'm sure Mother wondered how she could give her husband, the man she loved with all her heart, another wife. Yes, it might be nice to have another hand to help around the house, but another woman in Father's bed? Would the new wife have children? How could they afford more mouths to feed?

Father became the missionary Mother begged him not to be. He grabbed his sword of truth with both hands and wielded it with the same enthusiasm he gave to everything else in his life. He began telling his brothers and sisters and all the neighbors about the Adam God Doctrine and the blessings of plural marriage. He couldn't hold back. The truth must be told. Every where he went he took *The Doctrine and Covenants,* and the 132nd section with him so he could stop and read it to any and all who would listen.

One summer afternoon, after a day spent shopping in Rexburg, we stopped by to visit Grandpa and Grandma Pearson. None of us kids really liked going to Grandma Pearson's because we had to sit perfectly still and silent on her red velvet couch and chairs listening, while the adults visited. A beautiful winding staircase went up to the bedrooms, but we didn't ever ascend to explore because Grandma told us there were rats upstairs. That was enough to keep our butts securely planted on the couch. Staring into her glass curio cabinets filled with small statues of Victorian Ladies and china from China, we couldn't help jiggle our feet and poke each other. When Grandpa could see that we had had enough grown up talk, he said, "Who wants to go see my garden?" We jumped up, excited to escape the museum to help him pick fresh peas and corn.

On the ride back home, Kay and I sat with bags of peas on

our laps, opening each shell and sharing the delightful green morsels with Roger and Lee. We were almost home when Father took a detour and pulled into our neighbor, Mr. Sullivan's yard.

"Why are you stopping?" Mother looked exhausted. "We have tired kids. Let's just go home. If you're going to start in with your *Doctrine and Covenants* again like you did at your mother's, I will choose to stay in the car. You've turned everyone in the county against us because you insist on preaching."

I remembered the loud discussion of just an hour earlier that Father had had with Uncle Lee and Aunt Dorothy, who had also stopped in to visit Grandpa and Grandma just as we were leaving. Father had told them that every couple was commanded by God to bring forth as many souls as they possibly could because there were spirit children up in Heaven just waiting for a body and the chance to come to Earth and hear the words of the Prophets. He said that by using birth control you were denying these spirits bodies and therefore you were living in sin.

Aunt Dorothy told Father he had no right to tell other people how many children they should have. Uncle Lee came to his wife's defense and said that the life and health of the mother should be their first priority. Father disagreed, asking them that when they stood before God on Judgment Day, would God be pleased or would he line some beautiful spirits in front of them and say, "These are the children you could have had?" Aunt Dorothy began to cry. Mother hustled us out to the car as fast as she could.

"Don't worry, I won't bring it up again," Father assured Mother. "I've been meaning to stop by and ask Jack about that tractor he has for sale. We won't be long. Let's just go in for a minute and visit."

Mrs. Sullivan answered the door with a smile and invited us in.

Jack shook Father's hand and gestured for him to sit in one of the chairs around a small table. They began talking about farm equipment and the price of hay. Mother asked Caroline if she was ready for the Primary program coming up the next Sunday. Kay and I sat together in an overstuffed chair in the corner of the living room. I poked her with my elbow and pointed to the beautiful baby grand piano in the opposite corner. She nodded her head. I wondered why they could have such nice things. They were just farmers like us. Then we heard Father ask Mr. Sullivan if he could read something to him from the *Doctrine and Covenants*. "I left my book in the car. Can I read from yours?"

"Of course." Jack reached up into the bookcase behind him and brought out his *D&C*. I could tell by the scowl Mother was sending in Father's direction that she was not happy. Father opened the book.

"I'm starting with verse 61 in the 132 section:

> *"And again, as pertaining to the law of the priesthood if any man espouse a virgin, and desire to espouse another, and the first give her consent, and if he espouse the second, and they are virgins and have vowed to no other man, then is he justified."*

Mother's face was red from the neck up. I took Kay's arm, ready for our exit. Mother stood and began to gather up her children. Father read on:

> *"For they are given unto him to multiply and replenish the earth, according to my commandment, and to fulfill the promise which was given by my Father before the foundation of the world and for their exaltation in the eternal worlds, that they may bear the souls of men."*

Mother exited the house with eight children in tow. Kay and I were the last ones out the door and I heard Father say, "Just thought you might like to know about this revelation given to the Prophet Joseph." Father snapped the book closed and handed it to Mr. Sullivan. "Thanks for the visit." As soon as Father was in the car, Mother turned to him.

"Why did you do that? You said you wouldn't," she hissed.

"I just want everyone to have the same blessings that I want for us," Father said.

"They don't want those blessings. Didn't you see the expression on Caroline's face when you were reading? She'll be on the phone to the bishop before we get home. You are just making it more difficult for us," Mother said. She sounded angry, sad and tired.

Father was driven by big dreams and big ideas. He believed everyone needed this information about the Principle of Plural Marriage so they too could go to the highest kingdom in heaven. He was motivated by visions of himself as a sort of savior of the poor souls who didn't know better and who seemed content to lead mediocre lives.

Word of his proselytizing got back to our bishop, who called Father into his office and gave him a warning. He ordered Father to stop reading books that weren't sanctioned by the Church because they were just causing him to be misinformed. The bishop urged Father to trust the Prophet and his Counselors. He told him to go home and repent. Father opened *the Doctrine and Covenants* to the 132 Section. "Have you read the 132 section of this book you profess to believe in?" Father asked.

"Of course I have." The bishop said indignantly.

"Well, maybe you should read it again. Because you have to decide if you really want to believe every revelation that the Prophet Joseph Smith received from God or if you want to pick and choose the ones you want to live. Ilene and I have decided we will live every commandment of God not just the ones that are easy."

"Brother Pearson, you go home and pray to God for repentance and a change of heart. I will pray for you, too. I hope that you come to your senses and don't forgo all the blessings of the Priesthood because of your carelessness. Come back and report to me in one month. Hopefully we can place you in good standing beside your brethren in the Church."

For Father there was no turning back. He had gone too far down the hole. He would have to come all the way through and out the other side. He didn't check back with the bishop in one month and he didn't stop preaching to family, friends and neighbors. On February 24, 1960 Father received a letter from the Rigby Stake Presidency informing him of his excommunication from the Church of Jesus Christ of Latter-day Saints. Mother was never excommunicated because her father, David Archibald, was a patriarch in the Church and he made sure she was not going down to Hell with Father.

The Brethren

A few months before Father's excommunication, Mother's brothers rallied together to save her and her little family from hell and damnation. We kids didn't know what the special trips Uncle Robert and Uncle Don made to our house were all about; we were just glad to see them.

One Saturday we waited impatiently for Mother to finish making one of our favorite treats; raisin filled cookies. We sat on the bench at the table and watched her stir the sweet dough, roll it out and cut it into small circles. Then she brought over the cooled boiled raisin filling and spooned it onto the circles. She made us wash our hands so we could help her put the top circles over the filling. Then, dipping her fork in water so it wouldn't stick to the dough, she pressed down gently around the circle, to keep the filling from coming out. She slid a sheet of cookies into the oven when Roger came running into the house.

"Uncle Don and Uncle Robert are here!"

Mother smiled and wiped the flour off her hands onto her apron. "Cheryl, watch the cookies in the oven and put these in when the first batch is done."

Mother hurried up the stairs and into the summer afternoon. Scrambling from the bench, Kay and I followed her, trying to be the first ones out the door.

Uncle Don, Uncle Robert and three of their boys climbed from their car, along with the biggest, blackest bird dog we had ever seen. Janice, Kay, Roger, Lee and I all tried to hide behind Mother's skirt. We peeked around to see Bart and Keith bravely petting and talking to the dog; they didn't seem to be bothered by all the slobber coming out of its mouth.

"Jelene, run in the house and tell Cheryl to bring everyone a cookie." I ran inside and helped Cheryl count out just enough for everyone to have one.

"I want to carry it," I said, as I reached for the heavy plate.

"Don't be silly. You'll drop it and then there won't be any for anyone." Cheryl said. I pouted as I followed her outside. She passed the cookies out to the uncles and their boys and then she gave one to each of us kids, leaving the plate empty.

Three-year-old Lee brought his cookie up to his nose, closed his eyes and smelled it. He loved Mother's raisin cookies more than just about anything in the world. He opened his mouth to take the first delicious bite and in came the bird dog, snatched it out of his hand and swallowed it in one big gulp. I think the dog had surveyed our little group and picked out the littlest kid to steal from. But that dog had picked on the wrong kid. He must not have known about the things little brothers learn from big brothers. With his prized cookie gone, Lee stood in shock and surprise for a few seconds, then he let loose.

"You damn dog!" He grabbed that bird dog with both hands and bit down hard on its ear.

Now it was the dog's turn to be surprised. The mutt let out a howl as loud as a train whistle and went running for the car; he jumped through the open window and didn't come out again.

Uncle Don and Uncle Robert laughed till they had tears rolling down their cheeks.

When he got his breath back, Uncle Robert asked Mother, "We were hoping to catch Wayne today. Is he home?"

"Yes. I'll have Bart ride the horse out to the field and tell him you are here."

She welcomed Uncle Robert and Uncle Don into the house where they sat comfortably talking and munching raisin cookies. Upon Fathers arrival they set out their church books like a gourmet dinner on the kitchen table. Their main course came from the *Book of Mormon*, Jacob, chapter 3, verse 5:

> *"The Lamanites, your brethren, whom you hate, are more righteous than you; for they have not forgotten the commandment of the Lord, which was given unto our fathers---that they should have save it were one wife, and concubines they should have none and there should not be whoredoms committed among them."*

Father and Mother listened respectfully. Then Father brought out his equally delicious 132nd section of the *Doctrine and Covenants* and read Joseph Smith's revelation:

> *"And as pertaining to the new and everlasting covenant, it was instituted for the fullness of my glory; and he that receiveth a fullness thereof must and shall abide the law, or he shall be damned, saith the Lord."*

Uncle Don wasn't done yet. He picked up his *Book of Mormon* and read again in Jacob:

> *"Behold, David and Solomon truly had many wives and concubines, which thing was abominable before me, saith the*

Lord. For there shall not any man among you have save it be one wife; and concubines he shall have none."

They talked back and forth discussing doctrine until finally the uncles looked at each other in resignation, packed up their books and said goodbye.

Years later I would read in Uncle Robert's diary: "We have been going out to Wayne and Ilene's place, trying to teach them the gospel. I don't think we can ever touch them. They have gone too far into this Fundamentalist junk." In a later entry he said: "This is our last lesson. They ate up our lessons but when they started talking about their new religion, we couldn't believe how cold they turned. It just breaks our heart to see them so interested in some other faith. All we could do was bear our testimonies to them and leave."

Mother told me years later that after one of her brothers teaching sessions she walked them to their car and they offered to rent her a house in town if she would leave Father. But when she went to her mother for advice, her mother told her that she had made her bed and that she should lie in it. I think that's when she decided to stay and commit the rest of her life to her husband. She wrote in her journal, "I could never find another man who would love my children as much as their Father did".

Mr. Horace Knowlton came back to retrieve his little book. He and Father discussed religion and business. Horace invited Father and Mother to Salt Lake City to meet President LeRoy Johnson, who was now our new prophet and Marion Hammon and Guy Musser, who were two of Johnson's seven counselors. The brethren welcomed my parents with open arms and invited them to come to The Fundamentalist Latter-Day-Saints meetings so they could gain counsel and instruction from the Lord.

As their religious views merged, Father and Horace decided they wanted to go into business together and they filed a claim with Desert Land Entry on one thousand acres of raw farmland covered in tall sagebrush just up the road from where the haystack had burned down. Father talked his Father, John Axel, and his brother Lee into giving him one more chance at farming. They could each homestead two-hundred and fifty acres for $1.25 an acre if they could prove they were making improvements on the land. It was agreed that Father would run the farm; Horace would finance the development of the farm. Then, at the end of the harvest, each investor would get their share of the profits from the sale of the crops.

Horace built a beautiful new brick house on the farm. He moved one of his polygamist families into the top part of the house and we moved into the basement apartment. Mother was excited to pick out the cabinets and the linoleum for the floors. Her parents gave her the six-foot long table that Grandpa had made when his kids were young. Father and Cheryl lifted it off the truck and carried it down the stairs into our new house. They placed its long narrow bench along the kitchen wall and pushed the table up to it. Now we had a new home and a gathering place to feed body, mind and spirit.

Horace invited three other families he knew from the 'FLDS Group' (Fundamentalists Latter Day Saint) to come to Idaho to help Father build and run the farm: two brothers, Bill and Sam Roundy and their families, Lynn and Viola Hunter and their four kids. Sam Roundy pulled a small camp trailer up beside our house and plugged a big red cord into the outside electric outlet on our back porch for electricity. Bill and Barbara Roundy rented a farmhouse up the road. The Hunters moved upstairs with Horace and his family until they could find a house to rent. Their children became our friends and classmates.

One day Horace knocked on our door at the top of the stairs. Father walked to the bottom of the steps and yelled, "Come in." Horace told Father he had invited the Prophet Leroy Johnson and his Counselors to come to Idaho and visit with the small group of saints that were living and working on their farm. I saw Father's chest expand. "Well, that's great. We're about to harvest the wheat in the south forty. I'm pretty proud of what we've accomplished."

I remember sitting at the table, wiggling with excitement on the bright Sunday morning our new prophet came to see us.

"Sit up here and we will have our mush and toast and then I want you all to get dressed into your Sunday clothes. Today is a very special day. Your hair has to be combed and your shoes clean." Mother moved from the table to the stove and stirred the oatmeal. "Keith, say a blessing on the food." We bowed our heads. Keith was the speediest blessing-giver in the family.

"Bless the food. Thank thee for it. Amen."

"All I can hear is slurping," Mother said, standing over us at the table. "You put the spoon in your mouth and take the food off with your lips. You don't put the spoon to your lips and slurp it into your mouth." She gave us that look. "I am not raising a bunch of hillbillies."

She took the cod liver oil bottle from the cupboard and picked up a spoon from the pile on the table. "Okay, everyone open up and let's get our cod liver oil for the day." Three-year-old Lee started crying the minute he saw the bottle.

"Since today is a special day, maybe we could skip the cod liver oil." I said as sweetly as I could. Mother carefully filled a tablespoon of the vile smelling stuff and we opened our mouths and swallowed as she went around the table. I scrunched my face up and shuddered as the fishy oil slid down my throat. Mother fixed me with that look.

"If you big kids wouldn't make such faces then Lee wouldn't

make such a fuss." Lee was still too little to realize that you couldn't and shouldn't fight Mother. She got him mid-scream and closed his mouth around the spoon and he swallowed. He came up for air, spitting and choking and screaming even louder. How long would it be before Lee realized that things went along a lot smoother if you just did what Mother said when she said it? She didn't put up with any sassing or fighting. There would be no name calling. She taught us to treat each other with kindness and love. She reminded us that we were family and that we would never find better friends than we had right next to us at our table.

"Cheryl and Janice, get the little ones dressed while I clean up the kitchen. Roger, run out to the barn and get your father and Bart. Tell them breakfast is getting cold. As soon as everyone is dressed, we'll practice."

"Practice what?" Roger asked.

"President Johnson and his Counselors are coming today. We are going to sing for them at the meeting. Remember?"

Kay and I put on our best Sunday dresses and took our socks and shoes to the living room and put them on.

"So is President Johnson the Prophet and the President?" Keith asked Mother as he was tying his tie. "How do you get to be a Prophet? Does God tell you to be one and so then you are one?"

"Something like that." Mother laughed, opening the music book. "You know your parts really well, so let's just go over it a few times and we'll be good. There won't be a piano upstairs in the meeting so I will sit in front of you and lead you. Just follow me and you will do great." She smiled with confidence.

It was a beautiful thing, watching her hands going up and down the piano, our voices ringing out together. I had no way of knowing how important music would be in holding our family together. I just assumed every family was like ours. After we left the Mormon church Mother's children became her church. All the time she had spent playing the piano for other people was now spent on us. We were the benefactors of this wonderfully talented lady. Now that she wasn't playing for sacrament meeting, choir and every soloist in our Mormon ward, she had the time to concentrate on us and teach us how to sing and play the piano.

"That sounds beautiful." Father had just come in from doing chores and stood in the doorway listening. "The Prophet will love it." He turned to us children. "You know, it's a real privilege to have the Priesthood brethren come all the way up here to visit us. I think they are going to be impressed with the beautiful farm and with this beautiful family. Don't you?" He winked at Mother.

We knew from what our parents said that these men were important people in the building up of the kingdom of God and in teaching others to live the Law of Celestial Marriage. We felt special to be counted among God's Chosen Ones.

Father said, "Let's play a game called, 'How to Use Your Best Manners When the Prophet Comes to Visit' ". In Father's game, we each had to pretend we were Brother Johnson, the Prophet.

"Jelene, you go first." Father waved me forward with his hand.

"Hello, President Johnson." Father said in a small girl's voice as he reached out to shake my hand.

"Now, you say something," whispered Father.

"Hello. How are you today?" I said in my manly voice. The other kids snickered at our game.

"Very fine, thank you," Father said, in his little girl voice. Keith laughed out loud. "Okay Keith, you get to go next." Then Bart and Kay took their turn practicing their manners. "Always remember to be polite and never speak unless you are spoken to," Father said, finishing his lesson.

Kay and I were wiping our hands after washing the dishes when we heard a car roll up into the driveway and the sound of children running past our basement windows.

"Mother, they're here," I said excitedly. "Can we go outside and see what they look like?"

"Yes, you may. Use your manners." We ran to join the crowd that had gathered.

President LeRoy Johnson, his counselors, Marion Hammon, and Carl Holms and three young women stepped out of two shiny Lincoln Town cars and onto the dirt driveway. All the adults gathered around to welcome these three men who were different sizes and shapes but all wearing identical dark suits, white shirts and navy ties.

"They look rich," I whispered to Kay.

We stood in a neat row beside Mother who had come outside to make sure we were behaving. President Johnson came over to us and started down the row, shaking each of our hands. "Look at these polite children," he said smiling at Mother. When he reached out to shake my hand I noticed that his pinky finger was bent in half and stuck straight out like it was broken in two. His second finger was also deformed and bent in the opposite direction. I was trying to be polite and not stare, when Roger, who was standing next to me said, "What's wrong with your fingers, Mister?" I felt Mother's body jerk sideways toward Roger and her face looked like a red Christmas light against her brown hair.

"Oh, my fingers decided they didn't like each other. So this one went this-a-way and this one went that-a-way." He laughed and tousled Roger's mop of blonde hair.

Mother hurried us inside the house to finish getting ready

for the meeting and I overheard her say to Father, "Are those girls their wives? They are all so young and pretty. I just can't imagine you having a young, beautiful wife like that."

Father took her in his arms and pulled her up tight. "You know you will always be my true love. I could never love anyone as much as I love you."

The chairs for the meeting were already set in rows covering every available inch of Horace's living room. There were three chairs at the front of the room facing the congregation for our Prophet and his counselors. The Brethren and their wives were welcomed with glasses of water. They drank as they waited for everyone to take their seats. The meeting was opened with a prayer.

I sat beside mother and felt her lean forward, catching every word, looking for nuggets of gold to hold onto, treasures to tuck away and rub against her doubts. She wanted some reassurance that she had done the right thing by leaving her Mormon Church behind to join these few faithful saints who were living the true and everlasting principles of the gospel the way Joseph Smith had taught them. Anyone could see that she was filled with the sincere desire to be a faithful polygamist wife.

I know she loved my father. After I married, I realized that she wanted desperately to please him and if that meant living the Principle of Plural Marriage she would do it. But at that moment, looking over at the young, pretty wives of the Priesthood Brethren and envisioning Father bringing another woman home, I imagine all her good intentions left in a hurry. Maybe she even doubted if she was enough.

Polygamy gave a husband permission to look at single women as potential wives, women he could have families with. Wives that would help him build his kingdom. Mother must have felt she was not only losing her church and her family, she was also losing her husband.

Perhaps she considered retracting some of her love. Maybe it would be easier to let him have another wife if she didn't love him quite so much. But no matter how much she fought with her emotions it always came back to the 132nd section of the *Doctrine and Covenants*: how can you believe in Joseph Smith and not believe all the revelations God gave him?

On this special Sunday the Brethren spoke to us with passion in their voices, reminding us of the importance of the restored Gospel given to Joseph Smith by God the Father and His Son. The Priesthood had been restored by Christ's disciples, Peter, James and John to Joseph Smith by the laying on of hands. If a man didn't have this special Priesthood, he couldn't pass it on to the next generation and he couldn't expect to be blessed by the Lord when he performed healings or marriages.

When the Prophet finished his talk he brought a piece of paper up close to his glasses, "It looks like we have a special musical number from the Pearson family."

Mother stayed in her seat and gathered us in front of her, gesturing with her arms trying to get us into our places. She took a deep breath and we did too. Then she sang a note and we hummed together. Our eyes were on her and no one else. She opened her mouth and started singing and we followed.

> *"Praise to the Man who communes with Jehovah.*
> *Jesus anointed that Prophet and Seer.*
> *Blessed to open the last dispensation,*
> *Kings shall extol him and nations revere."*

Our young voices harmonized in praise for our Prophet. After we sang for the Brethren, we sat back in our seats and I looked over at mother. She glowed with pride.

When the last speaker finished, Mother walked to the front of the room to lead the closing song. She stood erect and stately in front of the small congregation, her pretty white crocheted collar falling down the maroon fabric and over her shoulders. I thought of the conversation I had overheard earlier when Mother had commented to Father about the prophet's pretty wives. They didn't even compare to her.

There were only a few hymnbooks scattered throughout the group so Mother chose a song she thought everyone would know. Sitting in the front row, I gestured with my hands and shook my head, trying to tell her that I didn't have a hymnbook and what in the world would I do without one? Mother looked right at me and moved her lips to say, "Watch my lips and follow me."

She chose, "*Come, Come Ye Saints.*" Our voices rang out, giving new meaning to the word saints, announcing that we were brave enough to live our lives the way we felt the Lord had commanded us… even if it went against the whole world. I watched Mother's lips pronounce each word from the song and I sang out. Who needed a book when they had a mother like mine?

Our Beginnings

By the time I made my entrance into this big, beautiful world, there were already five little monkeys jumping on Father and Mother's double bed. That's probably why there are only three entries in my baby book, written in Mother's beautiful cursive penmanship sometime between a diaper change and supper dishes. The first entry says: "I wanted to pick a name as near mine (Ilene) as possible and yet different enough so we wouldn't get them confused." And the second: "She is the sweetest baby.... always so happy and cheerful. The hired man asked me if she ever cried. I believe I have enjoyed her more than any of the babies because she is so sweet." With six kids under six, Father and a hired hand to feed three meals a day, all the washing, cleaning and cooking going on, I'm surprised Mother found time to enjoy me at all.

If you were lucky like me, you were born right after a sister who would be your best friend for life. Just eighteen months older, Kay was my partner, my constant companion and playmate. We shared our bed, our dolls and our underwear, until I turned eight and things like pink underwear became important.

Being the sixth child in a big family was like being part of a large organism, each cell moving in rhythm, all led by Mother. Her morning piano concerto signaled everyone up, time to eat breakfast. The stories she read to us each night signaled that it was time to sleep. All was orchestrated to keep some semblance of order if that was at all possible.

The third entry in my baby book written two and a half years later, states: "At two and a half, she has a lovely singing voice. She gets the tune just right." I'm sure my singing voice made Mother happy but it couldn't have surprised her. Father and Mother sang to us continually and I sang alongside my brothers and sisters, just happy to be part of the party.

Whenever I read the few precious words in my baby book, I'm reminded of my mother's ability to find joy and beauty everywhere she looked. She was always pointing out the orange sunsets or the way the wheat fields swayed in the wind or the tiniest flower sticking its head from under a rock. "God made a beautiful world. You just have to look around you to see it," she told us.

The treeless flat lands of Central Idaho held the rich soil of prosperity and wealth that Father longed for. My brothers and Kay and I played hide and seek in the golden wheat fields that stretched out for miles. Every morning we raced each other to the haystack next to the corrals where we climbed up and down, sticking our hands in every hole, hunting for the eggs the chickens thought they could hide from us.

But let me start at the beginning with my brave pioneer ancestors who came across the plains with the Mormons to escape persecution and find a safe home in the West. One of these hardy pioneers was my father's great-grandfather, Thomas E. Ricks, who eventually had five wives and 43 children. My father grew up listening to stories about how Thomas E. was shot by the Indians and left for dead while crossing the plains on the Mormon trek to Utah and how his father rode out to find him and saved his life. The three bullets lodged in his kidneys and back from the incident were never removed and he walked with a limp the rest of his life.

Thomas was one of the men who rode their horses through the snow to help rescue the Willy Handcart Company, when they were trapped in the Wasatch Mountains by an early snowstorm.

In 1883, when Brigham Young asked Thomas to establish a settlement in the Snake River Basin, one of the families he asked to go with him was that of Robert Russell Archibald, my mother's grandfather. These industrious pioneers built the city of Rexburg, Idaho and Ricks College, which is now BYU Idaho.

My father's mother, Margaret Ricks was Thomas E's granddaughter. Her father, Joseph Ricks, had two wives. Margaret learned to keep a spotless house, cook large pots of soup, and heal scraped knees. She also drilled truth and righteousness into everyone around her, especially the nine children she had with her husband, John Axel Pearson, a tall, skinny, soft-spoken man from Sweden, who celebrated his fourth birthday on the ship coming to America. However, she had run low on righteous fervor by the time Wayne, who would be my father, came along. Margaret was forty-five years old when Wayne was born and he weighed fifteen pounds. I don't think she liked him too much after that. His nine-year-old sister, Alice, who was an epileptic and not allowed to leave the house for fear she would have a seizure in public, became his baby-sitter. She helped him with his chores and gave him anything he wanted. As the baby of the family, he got away with things his older siblings didn't.

Wayne grew strong and athletic. Horrible at spelling and

reading, he could beat everybody at marbles. He spent every extra hour he had throwing a baseball against the side of the barn, where he had made a small black circle with some soot from the fire. There was hardly a day during the summer months when he wasn't standing on the pitchers mound playing ball somewhere. One of his daily chores was feeding the pigs the extra potatoes from the fall harvest. Instead of dumping the potatoes in the trough, Wayne used the pigs for targets. One morning his father came into the house and told Margaret, "I have the strangest pigs. Usually pigs are happy to see you and come running when you pour the slop in the trough. Mine run for the shed as fast as they can go."

After chores, Wayne gathered his friends and his cousins Mark and Joseph Ricks, who lived up the road, to play football or to ski on their homemade ski jumps in the winter. Mark was in a seminary class with Wayne and told me: "I don't know if Wayne talked too much in class or what happened but on several occasions the teacher would single him out and say, "Come here, Wayne. I want to talk to you." So he would come up to the front of the class and they would head over to the Principal's office, which was just across the street. I'm sure the teacher's intention was to put Wayne in a different class. But before they got over to the high school, my good buddy Wayne, would always talk the teacher into not going any further with his idea and back they would come again. This happened three or four times during that school year."

Wayne learned to play the clarinet in sixth grade and loved to listen to Tommy Dorsey and his band on the new Victrola his parents had bought for Christmas. In his junior year of high school he started his own swing band and they earned money playing for church and community dances.

It was at one of those dances, a few years later, he had the good fortune to meet the lovely and talented Ilene Archibald, my mother. She was at the dance playing the piano for her brother, Keith, who was singing a solo, "Asleep in the Deep" in his rich bass voice. When Wayne saw this tall, graceful girl in her green and white polkadot dress walk across the stage and sit at the piano, he fell in love. He learned that they were both attending Ricks College and wondered why he had never seen this beauty before. He set down his saxophone and told the guys they could play the next one without him. He walked over to ask Ilene to dance, held out his hand and she took it. As they danced around the floor it was like they had been dancing together forever.

Wayne called Ilene the next week to ask her on a date, but her schedule was full. She was attending Ricks College to earn a major in teaching and a minor in music. She was busy playing the piano for operettas, school plays, and church on Sunday. She practiced three hours on the piano and one hour on the organ every day. In addition to her classes, she was student-body vice-president, sang in the choir and played the clarinet in the school orchestra.

Ilene was the seventh child of David Watson Archibald and Lillie Isabelle Stallings, a devoutly religious couple who lovingly taught their children right from wrong. The day Ilene was born, December 30, 1924, was cold and snowy and the road to the house was impassable. Grandpa hitched the horses to the sleigh and went to get the doctor. I'm sure Grandma was expecting to have another black haired, brown eyed boy to add to the six she already loved. Instead, a beautiful, blonde, blue-eyed baby girl surprised her. When she gathered her little ones around her to meet their baby sister, she said to Grandpa, "It's a good thing we had her at home. If we had been in the hospital, I would have thought they gave us the wrong baby."

Ilene thrived in this loving, industrious family. They worked hard and sang as they worked. She spent her childhood in the garden with her mother and brothers picking raspberries, strawberries and corn. They bottled everything they could raise so they would have food through the winter. During those long winter nights they practiced their instruments and the piano. When one of the "sisters" at Church asked their bishop why the Archibalds were always the ones doing the special number in Sacrament Meeting he said, "Because, they are always ready."

When Ilene was eight years old, her mother realized she had taught her daughter all she knew and Ilene needed a more advanced piano teacher. Every Wednesday, when Mr. Gunthery came to the house to give Ilene piano lessons, her mother went out to the chicken coop, killed, plucked, and gutted a chicken to pay for Ilene's lesson.

On Sundays the family went to Sacrament Meeting. On Tuesday they had Primary; a class for ages four to eleven. On Wednesday they went to Mutual, the religious class for the teenagers. There were always lessons to prepare, new songs to learn, hair to be cut and combed, clothes to be cleaned and ironed. They raised eleven children through the Great Depression. When I asked Mother if her family suffered during that time, she told me that they hardly noticed it because they raised all their own food. The only noticeable difference before and during the Depression was that there was not as much money changing hands so they traded goods and services with the farmers around them.

Many times Ilene helped her brothers out in the fields when they needed extra hands. Her brother Blair wrote the following story:

"Raising a large field of sugar beets kept us busy from the time school was out in the spring until Thanksgiving. First we had to walk down each row and thin the beets so that a single beet plant was left every twelve inches. When that job was finished it was time to walk each row again and get the weeds out. The weeding job went all through the summer until it was time to loosen the big mature beets with a lifter plow. This loosened the beets so they could be picked out of the ground with a pick, attached to the end of a large topping knife. The beet was held in one hand while the other hand wielded the knife that chopped the green top off the beet, without chopping off any precious fingers or thumbs. Next we tossed six rows of topped beets into one row, so that when the horses pulled the beet wagon down the rows the beets could be thrown onto the wagon. Some of the beets became mighty heavy to lift, especially after the ground became frozen and the black mud clung to them.

One fall, arrangements were made to have Will Harris, a neighbor, come with his new model A International truck to haul our sugar beets the five miles to the beet factory in Sugar City, which would be a lot faster than driving the horses with a full load. The clouds over-head were threatening snow and we still had several days of work left. We wanted to get all the topped beets on this load as there wouldn't be time for another trip and the beets would freeze if they were left on top of the ground over the weekend.

Twelve-year-old Ilene felt small next to her six older brothers but every hand was needed that day. We walked down each row heaving the beets into the truck. The sun was just setting and we had about one hundred yards to go when suddenly Ilene came running around from the drivers side of the truck, shouting, "Come quick! Mr. Harris is dead!" Everyone ran around the truck just in time to see Mr. Harris, with his hat caved in, slowly rising to his hands and knees. He wasn't dead but he had been struck in the head and was stunned and visibly shaken. Shaking his head a few times and straightening his hat, he let us know in no uncertain terms, “If that happens again, I am taking my truck and going home, and you will have to haul your stupid beets to the factory with your horse and wagon!” Fortunately we got all the beets onto the truck and Mr. Harris on his way to the beet factory without further mishap.

On the way home we tried to figure out who had struck the near fatal blow. Someone suggested it could have been Ilene since she was the youngest and not as coordinated as her brothers. Maybe she could have thrown the beet straight up into the air like she did when we tried to have her play ball with us but after giving it further thought, it was decided that it couldn’t have been Ilene. To strike with that much force the beet had to have been launched from the other side of the truck and with more muscle than our little sister possessed.

The next morning at church, Brother Harris stood before us, arms raised, ready to lead the congregation in song, a great big goose egg on his head. He announced the opening song, “Rise Up, Oh Men of God.” My brothers and I sang with much gusto, trying not to laugh out loud, when we sang the last phrase, “Rise up! Rise up! Rise up!”

Like most girls going off to College, Ilene dreamed of meeting the love of her life. And she did. After that first dance, Wayne was not going to let Ilene’s rejection for a first date slow him down. He just kept asking her until she found an opening in her schedule. In truth, she was excited to accept a date with this handsome young man. Away from home for the first time and free from the ever-present eyes of her mother, she was ready for a new chapter in her life.

Wayne had a car so he would pick Ilene up in Rexburg where she was living with her older brother and his wife and take her back to his farm so he could get his chores done. Then they would head back to town for a movie and a milk shake. Sometimes they stayed at the farm long enough to take out his clarinet or saxophone and she would sit at the piano and accompany him in a solo. The love they shared for music was a dangerous weaving of two souls.

In Ilene's diary she wrote, "I played a piano solo at a Relief Society Tea and accompanied a trio" and "Wayne called". On the next day, "Wayne rang up. We went to the movies. Sure had fun." They talked or saw each other almost every day.

Another entry reveals, "I bore my testimony in church today. I wish Wayne was more religious." Even though he went to church with her almost every Sunday from the time they met, she knew it was probably just to please her and this worried her. When Ilene went home for the summer months, Wayne made sure he was not forgotten. He drove ten miles from his house out to Salem, Idaho to spend time with her and her family.

Ilene's parents begged her not to get serious about Wayne. They said he wasn't religious enough and he had wild, impossible dreams. Grandfather David Archibald was serious about his children marrying people with the right bloodlines. And although Wayne's mother was of "Royal Rexburg blood", being a Ricks, some of Wayne's older brother's smoked and drank and had given up the blessings of faithful members of the Mormon Church.

Ilene's parents were hoping and fervently praying that she would wait for Norman Ricks (a distant cousin to Margaret) to come home from his mission and marry her. He was a much better match for their intelligent, talented daughter. Perhaps they also feared that Wayne's crazy dreams would lead to a life of poverty and worst of all that he would lead her away from their beloved Mormon Church.

Wayne was handsome, strong and fun. He worked hard and played hard and was always trying to invent a faster, better, easier way to do things. Ilene's life had consisted of work, music and her piano, and although these things brought her great satisfaction and joy, meeting Wayne had given her a taste of spontaneity and excitement she had never known before.

When Ilene went back to college in the fall of 1943, Wayne got the courage to go to her parents and ask for her hand in marriage. How nervous he must have been as he sat across the living room from my grandparents. Squeezing Ilene's hand so tight it hurt, he said, " I would like your permission to marry your daughter." I don't imagine that he ever expected them to say no --- people didn't often tell Wayne no --- but they did.

Their rejection hurt Wayne's feelings, but it didn't stop him from courting Ilene. Nothing was going to keep him from her.

By the spring of 1944, five of Ilene's brothers had gone to war. The world was full of anxious mothers and fathers, wives and girlfriends. The list of fallen soldiers hung on the bulletin board at the courthouse, where families could find out if their world had come to an end or if there was still hope that their sons would come home. Wayne joined the Navy and went to San Francisco for training. Ilene had watched her brothers go off to the war and now she was losing her man too.

During his first furlough home, Wayne took Ilene in his arms and asked her to marry him again. She said yes. They were married by Bishop Powell, in his home on October 23, 1944 and even though her parents didn't approve of the match they were kind enough to attend and show their support. According to my grandmother Lillie Isabelle's journal, "Ilene looked beautiful, a pink corsage pinned to her gold satin dress." And that day when they joined their hearts together forever, they became Father and Mother.

After a short honeymoon in Boise, Idaho, Father returned to San Francisco and Mother went back to her teaching job in Ammon, Idaho. When Father's parents planned a trip to San Francisco for Christmas they invited Mother to accompany them. She was so happy to see her sweetheart, she called the principal of the school where she was teaching and asked if he would replace her so she could stay with her husband. He agreed. Mother was ready to start life as a married woman.

The war was coming to an end and the whole country was filled with excited anticipation for the future. Mother and Father were ready to start a family of their own. They would use their talents to bless their church and community. They were certain that all their dreams would come true.

In September 1945, Mother was six months pregnant when she was diagnosed with appendicitis. The operation put her into labor and her baby boy, Carl, was born weighing only three pounds. Mother wrote in her journal: "We prayed like we had never prayed before." Father called in some priesthood brethren from their church and they gave the tiny baby a name and a blessing so that he could be sealed to them in the eternities. Carl lived for four days.

The young couple was heartbroken. Mother wrapped her baby up in a blanket, nestled him in the tiny casket at the end of her hospital bed. She was not allowed to leave her bed for two weeks, so Father loaded the small box in his car and drove alone to Rexburg where he buried their first baby in the Archibald Family plot. Both families were there to hug the grieving daddy as he gave his baby to the earth. Alone in her hospital bed in Shoemaker, California, Mother cried tears of sadness and tried to process her first real heartache. But this was just the beginning of her discovery of how brave she could be.

World War II ended in 1945 and in March of 1946, Father

was discharged from the Navy and with Mother beside him, they headed home to Rexburg, Idaho. Father went through one job after another. He ran a sandwich shop, sold insurance and sold cars. He was full of restless energy and inventive ideas. In 1952, the year I was born, his brother Theo died of cancer, leaving a wife with ten children, to run a farm in Mudlake, Idaho. Father's family decided that he should go out and run Uncle Theo's farm. Grandpa Pearson and his sons would help with the finances. His brother's untimely death made Father realize that he needed to get closer to his God and Savior. He began opening his scriptures at night around the supper table and reading to his family. The bishop of their new Mormon ward in Mudlake asked Father to be ward chorister and Mother to be the pianist. There was never a more enthusiastic chorister. Father's beautiful tenor voice could be heard throughout every room in the building. He sang the songs of Zion with a renewed fervor. With each song he was pleading for the Lord to save his soul.

Father dug his feet into the rich black Idaho soil and dreamed of riches and alfalfa. He had been raised on a farm but perhaps he wasn't meant to be a farmer. Farmers need patience and prudence, two virtues Father didn't have.

But he didn't lack passion. Especially for the two things he loved most in this world, my mother and baseball. He worked hard and fast all week so he could play ball on the weekends. He recruited a bunch of farmers and they were good enough to make it to Pocatello to play in the All-Church Softball Tournament. Father pitched underhand and was famous for his drop ball and riser. I can still hear him telling the story we heard at least one hundred times.

"For five years in a row we beat every team in Southern Idaho.

In the Western Idaho Division there was a team from

Pocatello with four brothers. They were the best batters I had ever come up against. One year they beat us fifteen to nothing. They hit so many home runs we had to quit playing ball cause we ran out of balls to play with. Every year they would send us home and they got to go down to Salt Lake City to play in the finals. It had always been my dream to play in the All-Church Softball Finals in Salt Lake City.

On our way down to Pocatello the sixth year, I rode with my manager and we knew we had to come up with a new strategy so we could beat the brothers. I figured in order for us to win, I would have to walk the four brothers and strike out everyone else. I told my manager, I think they'll stagger the brothers so if someone gets a hit the brothers will knock them in. Maybe if we are lucky, one of them will get injured. I'm going to pull my left fielder in and put him behind the catcher. I know it's unheard of, but it's not illegal. Then there's no way the ball can get lost at the backstop.

The game started and sure enough they staggered the brothers, one brother then two players. So I walked the first brother, struck out the next two players, walked another brother, struck out the next player. The second inning one of the brothers got up and got a hit. The ball went flying, clear out into the outfield but my guy scooped it up and threw hard to third base. The brother rounded third and headed for home. Third baseman threw it home; the brother went back to third. Catcher threw it back to third and the brother headed home again. Sure enough, he came sliding in home, hit the catcher's foot and sprained his ankle and one brother was out of the game. Now, we have a chance, I told myself. I just have to concentrate. Every pitch has to be exactly right to win. This is my chance to beat these brothers.

The games were only supposed to be seven innings but the

score stayed zero to zero and I was pretty tired when I picked up my old bat in the fourteenth inning and walked up to the plate. The first pitch looked good, I hit the ball hard and sent it up over the fence. We had won the first game, one to nothing. But there was no time to cheer. It was double elimination. Somehow, we had to win one more game.

We took a thirty-minute break and then started the second game. This time they put the three brothers in a row and I walked them all. The bases were loaded. Then I proceeded to strike out the next three players. Fifth, sixth, seventh innings came and went. I was sweating like a workhorse, drinking a quart of water every time I got a break between innings. But the score stayed zero to zero. Only a little while longer, I told myself. Wayne, you can do this. You just have to hang in there and stay with the plan. Fourteen innings went by and I was one tired boy. I had just pitched twenty-eight innings. As I walked up to the plate the last time I felt like I had to physically pick up my arm where it lay limp and ragged on the bench. My manager handed me my old lucky bat. The first pitch was good and I swung hard. I could tell by the sound of the ball on the bat that I had knocked another home run. Wow! We had just created a miracle. We had finally beaten the brothers and we were jumping for joy. Those brothers were not happy.

We got to go to Salt Lake City but only played two games. We got beat bad by the Arizona Mesa team. He was a left-handed pitcher. We couldn't even see his ball. But I had lived my dream and kept the promise I had made to myself when I was a boy."

As a farmer, Father did some rather impulsive things like the day his tractor broke down and he brought his brand new Cadillac out into the field and hooked it up to the plow. It would have to do until he got the tractor fixed. The land didn't care if it was plowed by a Cadillac or a tractor and by the end of the first year Father had a beautiful stack of hay standing next to the barn.

One night Mother was startled awake by a loud clap of thunder. She went to the window and looked out at the hard rain coming down. Suddenly there was a flash and another clap. She closed her eyes and jumped. When she looked again, she saw flames coming from the haystack. Father was already in his clothes, headed for the door.

"Oh, glory be." Mother whispered. That haystack was the only thing between them and bankruptcy. She watched as the haystack and the barn burned to the ground. The cattle had already been sold to buy new equipment. The money Grandpa had put in the bank to use on the farm was gone.

How would Father ever elevate himself to the status of his Ricks ancestors? He had dreamed of being a successful farmer with visions of huge fields of wheat stretching on for miles. His land. His success. There were no vast plains to trek, no Indians to fight, but there was still land to conquer and plant and harvest. What he didn't know was that soon he would meet someone who would open a whole new world of challenges to him and that this new world would pose the biggest challenge of his life.

Two weeks later Horace Knowlton knocked on the door of our little farmhouse in Monteview, Idaho.

Back row: Janice, Father, Cheryl, Mother, Bart

Front row: Keith, Jelene, Lee, Roger, Kay

Growing up in the Fifties

Like any other child growing up in the Cold War Fifties, I was frightened by words like Atom bomb, smallpox, polio and a thousand other things I didn't understand about the big world out there. But it was the things going on inside my own little world that scared me even more. Thank goodness I was blessed with a mother who brought a sense of calm and loveliness to a world of confusion and fear.

Mother bathed her children in music from conception. She started singing to Cheryl, her oldest, when she was a baby. By the time I was three, Cheryl could sing the lead with four-year-old Kay, and Mother would sing alto with me. At the age of eight, the same year we were emerged in water at Church, we were baptized in 88 black and white keys. We weren't asked if we wanted to learn to play the piano -- to Mother it was part of growing up. She sat on a chair beside the piano usually bouncing a baby on one knee. "Sit up straight. No slouching. Wrists up, fingers bent, thumbs meet middle C." Of course, she had all our pieces memorized, so if she wasn't sitting beside us and we missed a note, she would sing out from anywhere in the house, "Sharp!" or "Flat!"

Standing at the sink doing dishes every day we sang in three-part harmony: *Love at Home, America, the Beautiful,* and *My Country tis of Thee*. Mother loved patriotic songs. Father and Mother both loved songs from the war years, like *Don't Fence Me In, Over There* and *Boogie Woogie Bugle Boy*. We learned songs from the Twenties and Thirties, including the songs Mother's parents sang to each other, like *Silver Threads among the Gold* and hymns like *Have You Done Any Good in the World Today?* We sang as we made our beds and cleaned the toilets. We sang as we ventured out to play, and we sang as we came home for dinner. There was always a song stuck in my head and stayed there throughout the day making me sing it over and over. Anytime we were in the car together, Father would start singing one of his favorites, *Cherry Blossom Lane.* Cheryl's vibrant voice would take over the lead, Father would switch to second soprano and Mother sang alto.

We were all expected to keep up. Every part was important. Every child's voice was special. On trips into town to see Grandma and Grandpa, Father and Mother were training our ears to hear the intervals between the harmonies. Later, I realized they were giving us memories we would never forget while training our hearts to love each other. Through music we learned to rely on each other for the most intimate of tasks; to sing the part of the song that wouldn't be the same if you weren't there. And getting the boys to sing was the only way to keep them from killing each other.

Mother was somewhat of a harmony snob. She believed that if there were three people up on stage singing, there better be three parts coming out of their mouths. Otherwise, it was just a waste of a person and a good song. When Mother had a new song she wanted us to learn, she gathered us around her at the piano and plunked each part out for us a few times. Then she played all the parts together and we followed along, reading the music. The piano lessons became useful in more ways than one, connecting the notes to the part we were singing.

Father had a crystal clear, but overbearing tenor voice. When I told my own children I thought his tombstone should read, "He sang too loud in church", they said, "No, Mom. That should be on *your* tombstone!"

By contrast, Mother's voice was smooth and sweet, with very little vibrato. We rarely got to hear her lovely singing voice, because it was always mingled with ours. But when she sang the duet, *Oh, Divine Redeemer* with Father, it was like hearing her for the first time. Father's robust tenor voice drowned hers out a little, but I sat mesmerized. *Wow.* I remember thinking. *She doesn't even need us to sing with her. She sounds good all by herself.* I can still hear her voice going up the scale, in a crescendo, almost like she was begging God to, *"Have Mercy. Protect thou My Soul."* Even today, it makes me cry just thinking about it.

My parents were two people who never had to compete for the same virtues. Mother was steadfast, honest and loyal to a fault. Father was spontaneous, impetuous and driven to do something important with his life. Their love for music bonded them together like glue and no matter how many things Father did to screw up their lives Mother stuck by him. When she heard him singing with his children she saw the goodness in her man's heart and forgave him his trespasses. And when his trespasses seemed too big to forgive, she went to her piano and let her frustrations leave through her fingers.

But there was no way Mother and her music could compensate for atom bombs and polio, neither could she contain the unpredictability of Father. Because of him, we learned that life was fragile and we were never fully prepared for what he might throw at us next.

One day he used his backhoe to dig a large hole south of the house. We kids stood around watching the hole get bigger and bigger. When we ask about the hole he told us that the Russians were coming with bombs so powerful they could blow the whole state of Idaho to smithereens so he was building us a shelter. We listened to Father and Mother discuss what they needed to have in the bomb shelter so we could survive inside that deep dark hole. We soon realized that Father wasn't crazy after all because the very next day at school we started practicing getting under our desks in case our enemies attacked with nuclear weapons.

Soon after we learned that we were going to all be blown to bits by the Russians, our dog, Taffy had puppies...thirteen of them! We loved on them for a week and then one morning they were gone. Father told us there were too many puppies for Taffy to take care of so he had taken them away. My childish mind imagined that "away" meant he had given them away. That night, my brother Bart, was whittling something that looked like a small dog, his head was turned down. I pestered him to tell me where the puppies were, until he confessed that father had put every single one of those thirteen puppies in a gunnysack and threw them in the canal.

"The puppies drowned, Jelene. Now, don't ask about it ever again." He looked up at me, just long enough for me to see his red, sad eyes.

The huge canals that carried water to the fields, made the alfalfa and wheat fields look lush and green, but I always stayed away from the water because I hadn't learned to swim. Not far from our farm, was a covered community swimming pool with a diving board. We had gone there a few times and it had been great fun. One Saturday afternoon Cheryl and Bart asked

Father if we could go swimming. Mother decided she would keep the babies at home and the rest of us grabbed our bathing suits and jumped in the car.

I was six years old and in first grade, so I thought I was pretty grown-up. I was having a great time splashing in the shallow end of the pool when Father decided it was time I learned to swim. Since I hadn't taken the initiative to teach myself, he decided he would help me along. He took me by the hand and led me to the deep end of the pool; he looked down at me with a sweet smile, picked me up and threw me in. I went down screaming and came up screaming.

He ran along the side of the pool, yelling, "Paddle your arms and legs! SWIM!" His voice seemed far away, his words shouted down a tunnel. I could see him swinging his arms up and over his head and shouting. I went down again and came up gasping for air; he was still standing there, waving his arms up and down.

"Paddle harder. I'm not coming in for you."

Down I went again. I knew I was going to die. Why was he doing this to me? Just the night before, he had bounced me on his knee, singing 'Trot My Pony'. We had laughed together because my legs were getting too long to play the game and I had to hold them up off the floor. Now he was letting me drown.

As I sank under again, I remembered what Bart had told me: Father had drowned the puppies. Maybe there were too many of us. Nine kids is a lot of kids. Was that too many? Was this how the puppies felt, their mouths and noses filling with water, the weight of their bodies pulling them down? I kicked hard to the surface, gasping in terror.

Father reached in and grabbed me. He set me down on the side of the pool. I shook with fear, sobbing, drawing away from him.

Father sighed in disgust. "Watch this." He bent his arms into a point, arched his back and lifted off with his feet. He glided across the pool, with the ease and grace of an athlete. He kicked off the other side and came back to me. "See how easy that is. You're making it way too hard. Now go practice." I got to my feet, still trembling, and ran down to the shallow end, where Kay put her arms around me to comfort me.

"I'm sorry," she said. "I should have come to save you but then both of us would have drowned. I'm so sorry."

"It's okay," I said, wiping an arm across my dripping nose. I knew that there was nothing anyone could do to save me. Not even Mother could save me.

In the 1950s the government launched a campaign to get every child immunized. The schools were set up as clinics; the first Saturday of the month school buses picked up the kids at their homes and took them to the school for their shots. One Saturday, when I was six, Mother sent me on the bus with Cheryl to get my smallpox shot. As I watched the other kids cry and carry on, my resolve to stay strong faltered. The closer I got to the nurse, the more scared I got. When it was my turn, I let the nurse take my arm. I closed my eyes so I couldn't see the needle, but it didn't keep me from feeling the sting as it bit into my arm, two tears sneaked out and spilled down my face. Determined not to cry out like those other kids, I bit my bottom lip.

"All done," the nurse said. I opened my eyes and smiled at her through my tears. She unwrapped a pink bandage and stuck it over my shot and handed me a sucker. "That's for being such a good girl." I grabbed Cheryl's hand and rushed toward the door.

By the time the bus dropped us off at home, my arm had stopped hurting, the sucker was long gone and I was happy again. I skipped down the dirt road. I could hear the water running down the canal.

"Oh, look. A baby bird!" I ran along the ditch bank to get a better look.

"Don't get too close. It's probably still learning how to fly." Cheryl put a hand on my shoulder, to slow me down.

"I'm going to save her from the water. Look how cute she is. We should take her home. She can be my pet bird." The tiny bird skipped up the road. I trotted right behind her. She ran faster. I ran faster and suddenly she stopped and I didn't. When I lifted my foot, she was flat. Squished. Dead. I looked back in horror. Cheryl shook her head at me and I started crying.

"Well, why did you do that, silly? I told you to stay back." She leaned over the baby bird to inspect the damage. "She's dead, alright."

"I didn't mean to step on her." I wailed. "Oh, my poor baby bird. This is just awful. First I had to get that awful shot and now this."

"Well, let's get her buried." Cheryl said, walking to the side of the ditch. She dug a hole in the soft dirt with her fingers. "Pick her up and bring her over here."

I gently picked up the tiny bird and placed her in the hole. "Sorry, baby." I wiped my tears.

Cheryl covered her with some dirt. "Aren't you going to pray?" I asked, sniffing.

"Sure. I'll pray. Fold your arms. 'God bless this bird. Amen'. Now let's get home. I'm sure there's a stack of dishes to do when we get there."

At home, I ran to find mother to tell her about getting my shot and the tragedy of the baby bird. She would understand my sadness more than Cheryl. Mother knew all about babies: how to birth them and how to bury them.

After losing their first baby, Carl, Father and Mother were overjoyed when Cheryl was born eleven months later. She was robust and healthy with lots of thick black hair and she was friendly and out going...everything she needed to take on the challenge of being the oldest child. One Sunday at their Mormon Ward, when Cheryl was one and a half years old, she had on a brand new pair of red ruffled panties. Father was leading the congregation in song; Mother was playing the piano when Cheryl escaped her baby-watcher. She strutted up onto the stage and pulled her dress up and showed off her red panties right in the middle of "More Holiness Give Me". Mother was horrified. Father laughed, walked over and picked up his little show-off and held her in his arms while leading the rest of the song. Cheryl became our kind, loving big sister and Mother relied on her for everything from holding crying babies to cooking morning mush, to cleaning up messes. Mother was always saying, "Cheryl, I don't know what I would do without you."

Janice was Mother and Father's third child. She was born one month premature with porcelain skin and bright red hair but because of insufficient oxygen during the birthing process, Janice would be handicapped all her life. Mother told me that she knew from the first day that something was wrong with her new baby, who was sickly and wouldn't suck a bottle so Mother used an eyedropper. When Janice was six months old she began holding her breath until she passed out whenever she cried. Mother would kneel beside her and breathe into her mouth, until Janice gasped for air and came back to her.

I've often wondered what kind of contract Mother and Janice made with each other when they were in heaven. I wonder if Janice came to Mother and said, "I'll come to you as your daughter. I will teach you all about patience and love and humility. Because of me, you will teach the other children who come to you to be kind and loving to the less fortunate souls they find in the world. I will live with you my whole life and never leave you. I will be your constant companion. I will never speak like others. I will never have a voice like others. You will be my voice and my interpreter. You will try all your life to understand me. You will breathe for me when I cannot breathe. You will speak for me when I cannot speak. You will fight for me when I cannot fight. You will love me and you will hate me. I will be your teacher; you will be my savior." And I imagine that in the face of all these valuable lessons, Mother said to Janice. "Yes, my friend, you will teach me more than I could ever teach you. I will be and do all those things and more because I love you."

When Janice didn't begin talking like a normal child by the time she was three, Grandma Lillie, Mother's mother, took her to her house to give her some special attention. Grandma had Janice repeat sounds and words over and over. She took her to every doctor she could find who might have a solution. But no one could figure out why Janice couldn't talk. Well, actually she could talk but it was hard to understand her. Her family could understand her because we lived with her and her strange language became articulate to us. Sometimes it took a few minutes to figure out what she was saying. We would say what we thought she was saying and if we were right, she would smile and nod her head up and down and say, "Uh, huh." If we were wrong, she would frown in disgust at us for not being smart enough to figure out the small, simple thing she had said! She'd shake her head. "No, no, no."

Mother never treated Janice any differently than her other children. She was just another member of the family. Janice did her chores and we expected her to keep up with us. And she did. We forgot there was anything different about her until we went to town and someone would ask us why she couldn't talk. I remember thinking, *'She can talk. You're just not smart enough to understand her.'*

At the drugstore one day, I saw some boys pointing to Janice and I heard them say the word retarded. When we got back in the car I asked Mother, "What's retarded?"

"It means slow, but I don't like that word and you will never say it." So we didn't.

But just because Janice couldn't talk didn't mean we didn't get mad at each other once in awhile.

One night Janice and I slept together on the bottom bunk. We woke up the next morning to a giant wet spot in the middle of the bed. I started yelling at Janice. "Why did you pee the bed?"

"No, me." Janice fired back.

"Well, it wasn't me. Six year olds don't wet the bed. So it must have been you!" I hollered.

"No, uh, uh, me!" Janice defended herself, her hands on her hips.

Mother stopped by our bedroom with her arms full of washing. "You girls stop fighting and get the sheets and blankets off your bed and put them by the washer. Hurry now, it's time for breakfast."

Mother wanted Janice to feel accepted and as capable as possible. She sent her to school with Cheryl and Bart for a while. But the boys at school called her retarded and Bart was constantly getting into fights trying to protect her from the bullies. So Mother took her out of school and Janice became her helper. She kept Janice busy doing the wash, folding clothes, and doing dishes. Janice loved to take care of the babies, changing diapers and getting them dressed. At our house there was never a shortage of work to do or babies to love.

Mother taught Janice how to print and spell. Mother would print some words neatly on a piece of paper and Janice would copy them on another piece of paper. Then she would help her send out thank-you cards and birthday cards to Grandma. Janice still sends everyone in the family a card on their birthdays, Valentine's Day and Christmas. Valentine's Day is her favorite. She loves to make her own heart shaped cards with lots of stickers and doilies. I smile whenever I go to the mailbox and see an envelope with her childlike handwriting on it.

Janice loved to sing. "Janice, you follow Cheryl's voice and sing along." Mother told her. Even though you couldn't understand most of the words she said, she didn't seem to care and neither did we. Now when we get together to sing and visit, we ask Janice what she wants to sing and she always says, "Sugar!" Her favorite song:

Sugar in the mornin'
Sugar in the evenin'
Sugar at suppertime.
Be my little sugar and love me all the time.

If Janice was hard to understand, Father and Mother's next child, Bart, compensated by making his intentions perfectly clear. Bart was born sixteen months after Janice, sporting lots of beautiful red hair. When we looked through the photo album and saw Bart's two-year-old picture with long red curls, we asked, "Who is that?" Mother said, "That's Bart. I just couldn't bring myself to cut them off. Those curls were too beautiful!"

When Bart was three, he escaped Mother and walked down to the Mercantile, just a block from their little house in Rexburg and helped himself to the red wagon on display out in front of the store. He came into the house and told Janice to come out and get in for a ride. As soon as she was perched in the wagon and smiling happily, he called Mother outside and then proceeded to walk back and forth in front of the house, demonstrating how useful this wagon could be. Mother took note of his expert salesmanship, set her two youngest on her hips and walked him and the wagon back to the store, explaining to him why he couldn't keep the wagon. He was not a quitter and he stole that wagon more than once, hoping Mother would eventually change her mind, but she never did.

In the fall of that same year, Bart fell off the horse and broke his arm. The doctor told Father and Mother that his elbow was broken so badly that it would never heal normally and he would be crippled. When Mother told Grandma Lillie what the doctors had said Grandma told Mother to bring Bart to her after the cast came off and not to listen to those old doctors. The day the cast was removed, Mother took Bart to stay with Grandma. Grandma gave him a small bucket to carry in his injured hand as they went for a walk and every day she would go to the sand pile and add more sand to the bucket. Soon his arm began to move lower and lower until he could move it freely. The day he could throw her a ball, she took him to the store and bought him a red wagon.

In my baby book when Mother says she enjoyed me more than any of her other babies I'm pretty sure it was because there was only one of me. Eighteen months before my birth, she was surprised by twins. Kay made her entrance first. There were smiles all around until the doctor said, "Oh, my! We have another baby coming." Mother started to cry. She already had two babies at home in diapers. Cheryl was potty trained and turning four in three days. Janice was two and Bart was one. How in the world could she handle twins? But the doctor was announcing, "It's a boy! Look at him being a gentleman, and letting the little lady come first." Mother cried harder.

Father was running a gas station at the time and he decided to do a "Name the Twins Contest" for his customers. Every time they filled their gas tank they could enter the contest by writing down their favorite twin names and putting them in the jar. If their names were chosen they got a free tank of gas. When they drew the names Keith and Kay out of the jar Mother was delighted because she had an older brother named Keith, whom she dearly loved and the name Kay was perfect for her little girl.

And then there was me, with blue eyes and lots of curly blond hair, the cutest baby ever born. If only I could have kept my good looks and not turned into a child only a mother could love by the time I was twelve. For a whole eighteen months after I was born, I was famous for being the first baby in my family born in the new Rexburg Hospital. But my claim to fame was soon shot all to pieces by my little brother's dramatic entrance.

Roger takes the family prize for being born in the most unusual place. It was a cold December night and the first snow of the year was covering the ground and making the roads slick as Father and Mother sped toward Rexburg in the new Cadillac. Mother was in the back seat trying to breathe through her contractions. Father was driving as fast as he dared. Suddenly, through the fog they saw a herd of cattle in the road. There was no way Father could stop the car in time. So Mother prayed. The cattle parted right in front of them, creating an opening just wide enough for them to pass through.

Moments later, they were crossing the Snake River Bridge when Roger decided it was time to enter the world. Father pulled off the road and helped Mother wrap the baby in the towels she had grabbed as she rushed out the door. By the time they arrived at the hospital, the rough, line-dried towels had irritated the baby's tender skin so severely that the nurses thought he had some horrid skin disease and quarantined him. Mother just laughed at them. She knew he was fine and she was proud of her adventurous little guy.

While visiting the new baby, both grandmothers made a fuss about Mother giving birth in the car. One year and fifteen days later when my brother Lee was born they talked her into going to the hospital and getting a shot to start labor. Mother vowed she would never repeat that painful experience. The natural way had been a lot less painful and would be her choice from then on.

Birth and death were a regular part of farm life. With eight children, birth was a familiar celebration in our home. But one day, death came inside....just waltzed right in and sat down to stay awhile.

It was a cold wintry February 3, 1957, when baby brother James was born. Like Janice he came one month too early and couldn't fill his tiny lungs with life-giving air. Mother explained to us when she got home from the hospital, "He struggled so hard to breathe, he finally just got so tired he quit." Her eyes were red and puffy. She hugged her throbbing, swollen breasts, and grimaced down at them. Father saw her distress and wrapped his arm around her shoulders, leading her down the hall to their bedroom. Cheryl, Janice, Kay and I followed and watched as Father pulled back the blankets and helped Mother into bed. Two-year-old Lee started crying, reaching his arms out to Mother. She pulled the covers back open and pulled him up and snuggled him against her. Father shooed the rest of us out of the room.

"We need to let Mother sleep now. You all find something to do that doesn't make any noise." Kay and I went to our room and sat on our bed.

"Poor Mother." I said, trying not to cry.

Kay couldn't talk. Tears were falling onto her lap and I put my arm around her. "I wonder who he looked like. I bet he was really cute." I said.

Three days later we stood around a deep hole at the Salem City Cemetery, trying to stay warm in our winter coats. Mother's brothers lowered the tiny casket into the ground. With my arm looped through Kay's, we said goodbye to our baby brother and prayed for Mother.

Three months later Mother was pregnant again.

One Saturday morning in November, Cheryl got some warm soapy water ready in the kitchen sink preparing to scrub and wax the kitchen and living room floors. After Cheryl had thoroughly washed the floor, Kay, Roger, Lee and I jumped from one couch to the other playing the shark game while we watched Cheryl squirt the wax from a plastic bottle and spread it all over with the sponge mop. After the floors were dried, our favorite thing to do was to have Cheryl pull us around on the crocheted rug that normally sat minding its own business in front of the kitchen sink. We took turns sitting on one end, while she grabbed the other end and pulled. We were sliding and screeching with laughter when Mother, who was seven months pregnant, came around the corner and stepped on the sliding rug. Her feet went out from under her and she crashed to the floor. We gasped and ran to her. She lay in a stunned heap; Cheryl went around her and grabbed her under the arms and helped her up.

"Mother, I'm so sorry! Are you alright?"

Mother held her pregnant belly, stretching her back, checking for damage. "I'll be fine. I'm sure everything is fine. Let's get back to work."

That night mother went to the hospital and had her baby two months early. He lived only long enough to take a single breath. Father held the tiny, perfect body in the palm of his hand and blessed him, giving him the name John, after Grandpa Pearson.

Again we stood beside another tiny casket, in a cruel kind of déjà vu, mourning for the second time that year. I was wearing the same pink dress with daisies I had worn that cold day in February when we had buried James. My shoes were getting tight, but my feet were so cold in the November snow that I didn't care. All I could think about were the tears rolling down Mother's cheeks.

Before the babies died, Mother's music had filled the whole house, drifting down the hall into our rooms and our hearts, sounding the time of day and the meaning of life. *'Time to sleep'*, whispered Rachmaninoff's *Concerto in C# minor*. *'Time to wake up'*, rang out Chopin's *Deux Polonaises.* Mother had memorized these pieces in high school and college; she told us she had to play them often to help her remember them.

The music in our house came to a complete stop after the second baby was buried. It seemed strange not to wake up to Mother practicing her scales. I had a hard time falling asleep without a Brahms Lullaby. I lay wide-awake, listening to Kay breathe beside me. How would I ever fall asleep without the music?

But even during the quiet months, joy sometimes got mixed in and around the sadness. One of those times was when the gasman came once a month to fill the huge tank that stood on stilts, like a giant spider, out by the tractors, plows and seeders. We would run out to meet him because we knew he had brought each one of us a big round sucker with the chocolate middle. He always had a funny joke to make us laugh, something we didn't do too much anymore. He knew each of us by name. "For Keith, for Jelene, for Kay, for Roger and for Susie."

"Hey, I'm not Susie." Three-year-old Lee protested. The gasman smiled and winked as he went down the row, handing us our treats. We laughed at him. Our uncles had a hard time remembering our names but the gasman always remembered.

One Saturday morning it dawned on me that Mother was wearing the same flowered blouse she had worn when she was pregnant with babies James and John. I sat beside Kay at the table and whispered in her ear, "Mother is wearing her baby shirt." Kay looked at Mother and then at me, a worried look on her face.

"It'll be fine this time. Don't worry so much." I whispered.

At breakfast Mother scooped the hot steaming oatmeal mush into small bowls and set one in front of each of us as we slid across the bench next to each other. She took a spoon from the stack, put a tiny bit of honey on it and stuck it in each bowl.

Mother brought the toast over from the oven on a plate to butter it. She put some butter on her knife and scraped it across the toast she had in her hand, trying not to leave any butter. I honestly didn't know why she bothered. You couldn't taste it anyway.

"Father and I have to go to town for my doctor's appointment," Mother said. "Please be obedient and listen to Cheryl. She is in charge." Mother gathered her purse and her youngest, Lee. She never left the baby home, it was just one of her rules. Babies need their mothers.

With light hearts, Kay and I slurped our oatmeal mush, and hurried outside to meet our friend Lizzie, who lived upstairs, for another day of baking mud pies, cakes and cookies.

We had taken over the old chicken coop Mother had abandoned when Father built her a new one. It became the perfect playhouse. Kay and I fancied up the place by hammering any scrapes of fabric, canvas and tinfoil we could find to hold up the remaining walls and ceiling. The two sawhorses we found in the shed made a perfect table with a few boards from the broken down fence laid across them.

The mud pies from the day before were neatly lined up on a two-by-four baking in the warm sun. I went straight to our collection of second-hand high-heels, scarves, and dresses that over flowed the box in the corner of the playhouse and started dressing up in case we decided to go to pretend town or visit pretend neighbors. Mother had given us some old dresses from the box of clothes Aunt Lola had sent us, after she had carefully gone through and picked out everything she and Cheryl could wear. I put on the blue and purple flowered dress, stuffed another dress underneath and tied the pink scarf under my big belly to keep it all in place so I could be pretend pregnant like Mother. I found the blue patent-leather high heels and slipped them on my feet. I was ready for the day.

"I'll go down to the ditch and get some good dirt for our pies," Kay volunteered. The rich dark earth lining the irrigation canals made especially smooth mud pies.

"I'll get some clean water." I took the two pork-n-bean cans we had retrieved from the trash and walked over to the corral to fill them with water from the cow's trough. Heading back, I could hear Lizzie and Kay arguing.

"It's my turn to use the red spoon today," Kay declared, her hand held out toward Lizzie. "You got to use it yesterday. Give me the spoon."

"No. It's my turn," Lizzie yelled back, holding the spoon high out of reach. "You can use the little one. And besides, I stir better than you do."

"I'll show you better," yelled Kay. She reached over and grabbed the spoon out of Lizzie's hand and clunked her over the head with it.

It took Lizzie a minute to recover from the shock that mild-mannered Kay had done such a horrible thing. Jelene did such things, but never sweet Kay. Then the pain registered on Lizzie's face as the goose egg began to swell. She let out a scream the devil could hear. She stopped screaming long enough to grab the nearest bowl and chucked it at me. "You girls are just horrid!" She began screaming even louder and ran toward the house, holding her head.

"I think I'm in big trouble," Kay said, looking at me as she set the spoon down. She grabbed my hand and ran, dragging me behind her, toward the house.

"Wait! Not so fast," I yelled, holding my big pregnant belly. "I'm going to lose my baby and my high heels."

Cheryl was standing at the kitchen sink, arms elbow deep in dishes. "What was that screaming all about?" she asked, wiping her hands on her apron.

"We were making mud pies and Lizzie wouldn't let me have the red spoon, so I took it away from her and clunked her over the head with it." Kay rushed to tell her story. "Lizzie's mother is going to kill me!"

Just as soon as the words were out of her mouth, we heard a loud knock on the door. Cheryl shoved Kay behind her and whispered, "Be still. Don't move." I sidled up to Cheryl to build a wall of defense. Horace's wife and Lizzie's mother, Vera, all two hundred and seventy five pounds of her, came stomping down the stairs, into our house without an invitation.

"Where's Kay?" She shouted at Cheryl.

"I don't know," Cheryl lied, trying to keep her voice strong and big.

"That little brat hit Lizzie over the head with a spoon and gave her a goose egg. You tell her when I find her, she is in deep trouble." She turned her big self around and stomped out, her hips and arms jiggling with each step.

Kay waited until she heard the door slam. Then she came from behind Cheryl and wrapped her arms around her. She breathed a big sigh. "You just saved my life."

"Yeah, I did. And don't you forget it." Cheryl laughed. "Did you see how red her face was?" She laughed again.

"Let's go play." I grabbed Kay's arm.

"Are you kidding? I can't go anywhere until she calms down." Kay pointed her finger upstairs. "I could die."

"But I'm wearing high heels," I said. "Look at me. I'm all dressed up and ready to go."

"Kay, you make the beds. Jelene, you clean the toilet," Cheryl called from the kitchen.

"Now, look what ya done!" I scowled.

"Did." Kay corrected me.

When Mother got home that evening she asked Cheryl, "So, how were the kids today? Were they good? Did they mind you?"

Cheryl looked over at Kay and I said, with a wink, "Yes, those two even cleaned the toilet and made the beds, without saying a word. They were quite happy to stay inside and help me all afternoon."

"Well good. I'm glad that everything was calm and peaceful while I was gone."

'A whole summer day and not even one mud pie made.' I thought to myself. *'What a waste.'*

As mother's belly grew bigger, I knelt beside my bed each night and prayed that this baby would grow big and strong in Mother's stomach and that she would play the piano again very soon. I was getting tired of playing the pieces in my head every night to put myself to sleep.

Early one morning before it was light, I heard Father come into our room and wake Cheryl up. "I'm taking Mother in to the hospital to have the baby," he whispered. "You are going to have to stay home with the little kids and get the others off to school."

"Yes, yes, okay. Got it," Cheryl said, sitting up in her bed and rubbing her eyes. I poked Kay, who was sleeping next to me in the side and smiled. She smiled back. Then deep down in my stomach I worried. Would Mother finally bring home a baby in her arms?

Father came home that evening and told us we had a new baby sister. But Mother had to stay in the hospital for three days, which seemed like an eternity. The first day, Kay and I rushed to the door, making sure we were the first ones off the bus after school. Maybe, just maybe, Mother and the baby had come home early. We ran up onto the back porch, looked around the side of the house to see if the car was there. If the car was there, Mother would be home with the new baby girl. No car. No baby. Maybe tomorrow.

The next day after school, we pushed and shoved past the boys and ran as fast as we could and looked around the house. Dang. Still no car. No baby. That nagging thought started to come up again. I sure hope everything is okay. I was worried.

The next morning I woke up excited. "Today is the day!" I shouted, scaring Kay awake. "Finally, Father and Mother and the baby will be here even before we get out of school."

"I sure hope so." Kay said, as we shivered into our school clothes. "I can't wait another minute. I can't believe we have a baby sister."

After school, Kay and I ran as fast as we could up onto the porch and looked around the house. The car.

"They're here!" We shouted in unison. Crashing through the door we pounded down the stairs. Mother met us at the bottom with her finger pressed up to her lips.

"Shush," she whispered. "Be very quiet. She is over in the bassinet. You can go peek at her."

We tiptoed across the room and peered inside the bassinet. There before us was the most beautiful baby in the whole world. She had fat cheeks and fair white skin. Her head was cover with bright red hair. She rolled her head from side to side in her sleep and stuck out her miniature tongue.

"Wow. Did you see that? She stuck her tongue out." I giggled. "She really is something, isn't she?"

"Yea, she really is. And she's all ours." Kay whispered.

Mother and Father named her Helen. We took turns holding her, smelling her and kissing her. We spoiled her the best we could. This baby would be a new beginning. Now there were nine of us. Things could get back to the way they were.

And sure enough about a week later we woke to Rachmaninoff and I knew the spell of bad luck was broken. As I lay in bed snuggled up to my sister, warmth ran through me that I hadn't felt for a long time.

Mother's beautiful piano pieces still play in my head today and when they do, I don't just hear them. I see Mother sitting at the piano, her long graceful fingers running up and down the keys, and joy fills my heart. How do you sing Chopin? I don't know. But I make myself hum the whole piece clear to the end so I will never forget.

The Bus Ride Home

Growing up on a thousand acre farm with the rich black volcanic soil of Idaho between our toes should have made for a perfect childhood. I woke up every weekday to the sounds of Mother playing Chopin on the piano and every Saturday morning she made the best pancakes in the world. She did her best to make all of her children feel safe, nurtured and loved. We were also blessed with Father, a man with an ego the size of Idaho and a little voice in his head always reminding him he would never be good enough.

My oldest brother Bart was a lot like Father. Both had thick red hair, strong bodies, and quick, inventive minds. Bart shared a memory with me from when he was five. He remembered looking up at Father when he was beating the hell out of him and thinking to himself, '*This man is crazy*'. Father's eyes would glass over and all Bart could do was wait until Father came to his senses and put down the stick, which became a two-by-four as Bart got older. Between the beatings for things like not stripping enough milk from the cow's bag, running the horse too hard, or not driving the truck fast enough, Bart spent every waking minute that he wasn't in school learning from Father.

He was with Father when he bought Dart, a rodeo horse that spooked at everything and everyone. The day they brought Dart home in the back of the pick-up, tied to the sideboards, he got loose and jumped over the cab of the truck and bashed in the windshield. The horse raced through the neighbor's fields and along the ditches, places the truck couldn't go. Father and Bart took chase but every time they got close Dart took off again. When they finally had the horse in the corral at home that night, Father tied Dart up to the fence and turned to Bart, "This horse gets nothing to eat for three days. Do you hear me?" Father let out a streak of curse words and walked to the house.

Bart stood beside Father when he used the transit to level a thousand acres of Idaho earth and make fifteen miles of ditches that would bring water from an artesian well to our farm. Father decided it would be a waste of time and dirt to make a two-sided ditch, so he used one side of another farmer's ditch until he came to the place where he needed it to turn south. Then he ran eight-foot culverts under the other farmer's ditch, finishing with a two-sided ditch that led to our farm—all without the other farmer's consent. Father's motto was, "It's easier to ask forgiveness than get permission." There was not a rule invented that was meant for him. I'm quite sure the controversy resulting from the one-sided ditch was one of the fifteen lawsuits on file at the Jefferson County Courthouse involving my father and other unfortunate folks who came in contact with him between 1954 and 1960.

But I was only six and all I wanted to do was go to school and be happy.

"The bus will be here in ten minutes," Mother called down the hallway. She sat down on her chair at the kitchen table where I was waiting for her to hurriedly run the brush through my hair. The brush caught on some tangles at the nape of my neck. She lifted my hair to reveal a solid row of twisted knots.

"Why are you twisting your hair back here?" she asked.

"Because, Mrs. Douglas makes me nervous."

"Did she find out about us....the way we believe?"

I stared up at her, trying to understand. "Oh, because we don't go to the Mormon Church anymore? No, she makes me nervous because she whacks the boy's fingers with her ruler when they misbehave. It scares me so bad I have to twist my hair to keep my stomach from hurting." I shrugged. "I don't like her. Why does she have to be so mean?"

"Is she mean every day?" Mother asked.

"Well, the first day of school she was nice. But ever since then she makes one of the boys cry every day, so I close my eyes and twist my hair."

Mother sighed. "I can't have you afraid to go to school." She gently drew the brush through the last knot. "School should be a happy place for six year olds."

"What can I do about it?" I looked up at Mother, believing she would have an answer. She was the smartest person I knew.

"Well, maybe it will get better soon. Just be patient. The boys will get tired of getting their fingers smacked and learn to behave."

Having two older brothers and two younger brothers, I knew that the boys at school would never learn to behave. Kay and I grabbed our jackets and lunch boxes and ran out the door to join Cheryl, Bart and Keith at the bus stop.

At school, Mrs. Douglas, who seemed to grow taller every day, yelled at Matthew when he came in late. I desperately needed to go to the bathroom but didn't dare ask if I could go. I squirmed in my chair and twisted my hair and prayed that the boys would not upset her. When the bell rang, I grabbed my lunch and hurried to the bathroom. Then I met Keith and Kay outside at our usual lunch spot under the pine tree in back of the school. We pulled out our whole-wheat sandwiches.

"I hope Mother will give us a quarter so we can eat school lunch on Friday." Keith said. "The food is so yummy. You haven't had school lunch yet have you?" He looked over at me. "It's just like Thanksgiving Dinner every time. Mashed potatoes and gravy, dinner rolls as light as air." A mouth full of whole wheat bread and cheese muffled his voice.

"Yeah, that might make school a little better." I looked at my sandwich, appetite gone. "Mrs. Douglas was so grumpy today she made my stomach hurt and I can't even eat."

Keith swallowed. "Why don't you move into my room? We have first and second graders in my class. There are extra seats and Mrs. Cruiser is never mean."

"That's the best idea in the world. Keith you are so smart!"

"I wish you could come into my class, but all we have are second graders." Kay looked sad.

My appetite had magically returned. I snatched up my sandwich and gobbled it down. Back in my room, I gathered all the books and papers from my desk and balanced the crayon box and pencil on top. I walked out into the noisy hallway, side stepping a bunch of fifth grade girls headed for the door with a jump rope. A group of teachers stood in front of the principal's office talking. I looked to see if Mrs. Cruiser was with them. There she was, standing right next to Mrs. Douglas, her grey head barely reaching Mrs. Douglas's shoulder. I found an opening in the circle of teachers and bravely stood in front of Mrs. Cruiser.

"Mrs. Cruiser. Is it okay if I move into your room?"

She looked at me like she didn't quite understand what I was asking. She gave Mrs. Douglas a questioning look and they both shrugged their shoulders. "Sure, I guess that would be all right." She smiled down at me. I didn't wait a minute longer. I marched, grinning from ear to ear, into Mrs. Cruiser's room and found an empty desk. I pulled the chair out so I could arrange my books perfectly inside. I sat down and pulled the chair forward. I was home. Mrs. Cruiser wrote my name wrong all year, (Jolene) but I never corrected her. How could I correct her when I wrote my J's backward all year and besides, she took me in and loved me? And I stopped twisting my hair.

My first year of school, the bus carrying everyone from first graders to twelfth graders to school and home each day, was an hour-long ride of fun and adventure. Kay and I loved to sit behind Shelton and Jessica, the senior lovebirds. They talked and kissed and looked longingly into each other's eyes. We dreamed that someday we would be just like Jessica. The radio blasted out, *"Lollipop, Lollipop, Oh Lolli, Lollipop!"* or another one of our favorites, *"It was an Itsy, Bitsy, Teeny, Weeny, Yellow Polka Dot Bikini."*

"What's a bikini?" I asked Kay.

"I have no idea," Kay said.

"It's a teeny tiny swimming suit," Rosie Wallis spoke from the seat behind us. Rosie was a year older than Kay and knew all about the ways of the world. She wore store bought clothes and the prettiest pink fingernail polish.

"Mother probably wouldn't like this song, would she?" I asked. Kay shook her head.

We had the words memorized and sang along, knowing our parents would never approve of us singing these wicked songs and we would be leaving them on the bus when we stepped onto our graveled driveway.

One day on the ride home, Rosie waved Kay and I to the back of the bus to sit by her. "Look what I got in town yesterday." She pulled out a tiny curvy bottle of red fingernail polish. "Isn't it cute? Do you want me to paint your nails?"

"Oh, no." Kay put up her hand like she was stopping the

Devil. "We don't wear fingernail polish. Our father says it is wicked and worldly."

"I want to." I said, spreading my fingers like a fan.

"Father won't be happy." Bart said, craning his head around from the seat in front of us and raising his eyebrows.

"He won't care. I'll just tell him I forgot the rules. Nobody can remember all the rules all the time."

Bart shook his head as if to say, '*Okay. Don't say I didn't warn you.*'

I smiled at Rosie and nodded for her to start. She twisted the top off the bottle. The bus bumped and bounced and as much as Rosie tried to keep the polish on my fingernails, by the time she got done there was as much red polish on my fingers as on my nails. I was worried that there was so much red color coming from my fingers that I would never get past Father without the redness shouting out to him, "SIN ALERT!!!...SIN ALERT!!!"

On Sunday morning during our homemade Sunday school Father let me know that my errant ways had not gone unnoticed.

"Sweetie, come over here and sit on my lap." He reached into his pocket and brought out his pocketknife. I hid my hands behind my back. "Come on. Get over here. I'm not going to hurt you." My mind flashed to last night after our baths, Father shouting out orders like a drill sergeant as we stood before him, trying to do the exercises he learned in the Navy. I thought of the beating Bart and Keith got last week for building a fire in the pantry. I thought of the warmth of Father's arms when I sat on his lap and helped him turn the pages of the *Book of Mormon* while he read to us each night. A mixture of love and fear filled my heart and my head as I obediently walked over and sat on his lap. He flipped the knife blade out of the case with his thumbnail and took my hand gently in his. He began carefully scraping the red polish off my small nails with his knife. "Mother, read to us."

"Here in John it says: '*Love not the world, neither the things in the world. If any man love the world, the love of the Father is not in him.*' And in Peter," Mother's voice faded away as I thought about how much I loved that shiny red color. What was so wrong with a little fingernail polish? We'd always had rules, but since we left the Mormon Church and joined the Fundamentalist Polygamists, there were a whole bunch of new ones.

'But let your adornment be hidden in your heart.' Mother's sweet voice broke into my thoughts. I let out the breath that had been trapped in my chest and I relaxed into Father's arms. With each gentle scrape with the tip of his knife, I began to believe he was just trying to save my soul from the wicked world. I promised myself I would from this day forward learn and obey all the new rules, at least the really important ones like no bright red fingernail polish. Maybe I would ask Rosie to bring some clear polish next time.

The bus ride to and from school was a classroom all on its own. Jacob Stevens was eight and lived on the farm just up the road from us. He was always bragging that his father raised the best bulls in the county. I thought he was cute and found every excuse to sit near him on the bus. One day, Kay followed Keith to the back and I sat behind Jacob and his brother. We had just left the schoolyard when Jacob turned around and whispered, "I know how babies are made." He had my undivided attention. I leaned forward in my seat. His short, but graphic description of how the male and female anatomy fit together horrified me. For a moment I couldn't even speak. Then I stood up, towering over him.

"You are a biggest, fattest liar I have ever met! You're a very disgusting boy." I spit the words at him. "Don't ever talk to me again." I picked up my jacket and walked back to sit by Kay.

"What's the matter?" Kay asked.

I just shook my head. Even though Kay and I told each other everything, I couldn't tell her what I had just heard. I would never repeat anything so awful.

Over the next two years as more of our neighbors heard about us leaving the Mormon Church and joining the Polygamists, the long bus ride to and from school became anything but fun, especially for my twelve-year-old brother Bart. Being the oldest boy, he tried to protect us from the kids at school who made fun of us and called us names. Father wasn't making things any better by trying to convert everyone to the truthfulness of the gospel and the Principle of Plural Marriage. But after the brethren came from Colorado City to visit and word spread that we had chosen a new Prophet, life on the bus went downhill fast.

The high school boys who were three and four years older than Bart were the real problem. They were strong farm boys from good Mormon families across the valley who gathered every Sunday at church to learn about brotherly love. The other six days of the week they got up early, slopped the hogs, chucked heavy bales of hay to the cattle and ran the tractors, harvesters and swathers. In the spring they docked the sheep and cattle and in the fall they rounded them up for shearing and slaughter. The toughest, meanest one was Paul Stratton. He was tall and almost full-grown. His hair was curly and wild, like his eyes.

After school one day, as I climbed onto the bus, I heard Paul Stratton behind me say to his friend, "Have you heard there's a bunch of plygs out on the Pearson place? My Grandpa heard Bart's dad talking to Walter down at the feed store telling him that Adam was God and Joseph Smith had a ton of wives. What a weirdo."

I slid into the seat next to Kay and my brothers and did my best to ignore him. Suddenly, Paul looked over to where we were sitting and yelled across the bus, “Hey, plyg kids. Are you ready to go home to your plyg mommy and daddy?” All the boys roared with laughter and the girls turned their heads away from us like we were lepers.

When the bus arrived at Paul’s house, he walked down between the bus seats and stopped just long enough to take his gum out of his mouth and push it into my scalp. I reached up to feel the gooey mess, some of it sticking to my fingers. The more I tried to get it out the more my hair got stuck.

“I’m going to rip your eyes out!” Bart shouted out to Paul as he walked down the bus steps. We could hear Paul laughing as the bus driver closed the door. When we got home Mother showed Kay how to put butter on the gum in my hair and it took her an hour of pulling and yanking and me crying to get it all out.

After supper that night, Father reminded us we still had chores to do. I hated slopping the hogs. They always jumped up and tried to yank the bucket of sprouted wheat out of our hands with their slobbery snouts. Just that morning, the big sow had grabbed my coat sleeve and I thought I was going to go over the fence and into the pigpen.

“I hate those dang hogs,” I whispered to Kay, a little too loud as it turned out because Father turned his attention to me.

“But I bet you love the bacon.” Father chuckled. “Bart and I are going out to do a few more chores. You two come with us and feed that bacon.”

“Come on, son.”

Bart gulped the rest of his milk, slipped his coat on and followed Father out into the dark. Kay and I grabbed our coats and followed after them.

Father threw his arm around Bart’s shoulder when they got out the door. “Mother says the boys at school are picking on you. I guess it's time I taught you how to defend yourself. You're only twelve, but you're big for your age and I think you got it in you." Something in Father's voice made my stomach clench.

They walked over to the haystack. I wanted to stop and listen but reluctantly followed Kay to the pigpens. The glow from the barnyard light shone in a circle that covered the few cattle still standing at the stalls chomping on hay.

Kay and I grabbed the five-gallon bucket of soaked wheat we had prepared that morning. It took all the strength in our skinny arms to lift the handle and make the wheat hit the trough without losing the bucket and having to go in after it.

As I turned to watch the pigs dive into their food, Father's quick movement caught my eye. I saw his hands come toward Bart's head, slapping both sides of his face hard. Bart went down to his knees and grabbed his head. Father pulled him back up.

Horrified, I grabbed Kay's jacket sleeve and pulled her with me as I moved around the shed to watch.

"Why is Father doing that?" I whispered. My heart pounded with fear.

"I guess he is trying to teach Bart how to defend himself from the boys at school. You know how bad it has been on the bus lately," Kay whispered back.

"Okay, come on, that was nothing," Father was saying. "Stay with me. When you're fighting, boxing their ears will shock the hell out of them. The other thing you got to do is bite them." Father put his hand in front of Bart's face and said, "Now bite me." Bart bit down. Father said, "Oh, come on. I can't even feel that. He took Bart's little finger in his mouth and bit down.

Bart yelled out and tears glistened on his face. Father took the finger out of his mouth and bent it back as far as it would go, sending Bart to his knees again. "Now, that's how you do it. You bite. You break fingers. You kick."

Father took hold of Bart's arm and brought his boot up sideways against his knee. "You kick sideways on the knee and knock them to the ground. Knees are not made for sideways kicks. It brings them down every time. Don't ever stop fighting till they stop moving. If you let them up, they will come back and kill you."

"Okay. Okay. I'll try." Bart said. "Please stop. I'll do it. Just... stop." He grabbed his right knee and rubbed it.

Kay and I inched our way back toward the house as Father said to Bart, "My father and his brothers used to fight each other till they were bleeding. He taught my brothers and me to fight the same way. Your mother wouldn't approve of me passing these lessons onto you but it's my responsibility to teach you how to defend yourself." He threw his arm around Bart's shoulder but this time Bart kept his head down in silence.

A few days later we were almost to school when I felt something on my ear. I grabbed my ear, but didn't feel anything. Then Bart, who was sitting next to me, grabbed his ear. The boys behind us started laughing. We turned around. Paul had moved into the seat behind us with his buddies. When Bart realized that it was Paul flicking our ears, he jumped over the seat and right on top of Paul. He started pounding him. Paul pounded back and everyone started cheering. The bus came to a screeching stop. The bus driver, came back and grabbed both boys and dragged them up to the front of the bus.

"Now, you sit here and you sit there. And you both better stay sitting and shut up. No more fighting. The rest of y'all better settle down." He sat back down in his seat and turned up the radio.

As soon as the bus came to a stop at the school, Bart bolted out the door. Paul was right behind him. Paul reached out to grab Bart's collar. Bart swung around and grabbed Paul's belt buckle and slammed him up against the yellow School Zone sign, knocking the wind out of him. Paul fell to the ground and Bart was on top of him punching him in the face. It looked like Bart was really going to take his eyes out. He kept hitting and cursing, cursing and hitting. The principal saw the ruckus from his command post and ran over to break it up. He grabbed Bart's shirt and tried to pull him off Paul, but Bart kept pounding like a demon possessed.

The principal shouted, "Stop this nonsense!" He grabbed Bart around his chest and with some help from another teacher who had ran to help, they soon had my raging brother headed to detention and a two-week suspension.

Years later, Bart told me the rest to the story. The week after he came back to school after his suspension, Bart and his friends had a baseball game going during the long lunch recess. A few minutes before the bell rang he noticed Paul and one of his buddies leaning against the backstop.

'He's coming for revenge', Bart thought to himself. *'He's still sore about the pounding I gave him.'* He glanced around the ball field and saw three more of Paul's friends scattered around the field. *'Nope, I don't think they've come to watch me throw a perfect pitch.'*

The bell rang across the schoolyard and the kids ran back to class. Paul and his friends started walking toward Bart. Bart took off running toward the outfield, thinking, *'Maybe I can outrun them. I'm faster than they are.'* Then a second later, *'Damn, I should have run toward the school instead of clear out here in the sagebrush where no one can help me. God, I'm in trouble.'* He felt the ground vibrating underneath him. It felt like a pack of wolves were closing in on him. One of the boys grabbed his pants and yanked him off the ground.

"I got me a little plyg kid!" The boy yelled back to the others as he slammed Bart to the ground. They gathered around, breathing hard, gasping for breath.

"Pull his pants down. Let's do it," Paul said. Bart kicked and fought and screamed. Each boy grabbed a swinging leg or arm and held him fast to the ground.

Paul knelt down beside Bart and punched him in the face. "Shut your trap before someone hears you. You tell your big-mouthed dad that we want you plygs gone. We're going to teach you a lesson you ain't never gonna forget. You little bastard."

Paul ripped open the snap on Bart's pants and pulled them and his underwear down past his knees. Bart fought harder, blood squirting from his nose and tears from his eyes.

"Hold him tight boys." Paul took out his pocket knife and wiped the blade with his fingers. "I'm going to castrate you, so you can't have any little plyg babies." Bart stopped fighting.

"Wait, wait! Wait a minute! Listen to me!" he yelled. He looked Paul right in the eye.

"Why should I listen to a little plyg bastard like you?"

Bart tried to steady his voice, to sound strong. "If you castrate me, you need to slit my throat too. Because if you cut me and leave me alive, I will come for you and I will kill all of you. I will kill your fathers and mothers and your sisters and brothers. I will tie you up and I will kill them in front of you and then I will cut your balls off and then I'll kill you. Mark my word. Not one of you will live past twenty. You won't ever have a child of your own. If you take this away from me, I will take it away from you."

The boys looked at each other and then at Paul.

"I guess we've scared this little bastard enough." He snapped the blade back into place and stood up. The boys released their hold on Bart, turned and followed Paul back through the sagebrush to the school. Bart hurriedly pulled his pants up and rolled over into the cover of the sagebrush. Barely daring to breathe, he waited, praying they wouldn't return. He felt the bulge over his eye. It hurt every time he blinked. '*I bet it's already black and blue,*' he thought. Then he chuckled and muttered, "Boy, they really had me by the short hairs." After making sure it was safe, he got up, brushed off his pants and went back to class.

When Kay and I got on the bus after school, we went to the back where Bart and Keith were sitting.

"Why do you have your hand over your eye?" I asked Bart. He took his hand down and I saw his swollen black eye. "Oh, my gosh. What happened?" I said softly, trying not to raise attention.

"Paul and his buddies kinda pounded on me. But it'll be okay. Mother will fix me up when I get home." I didn't know what to say. I was scared and sad and confused. He was sitting there with a big black eye and a smile on his face.

That day on the ride home, I wished the bus was still the hour of fun it had been when I was six. Where I had learned the wicked songs I couldn't sing at home.

Where I had learned not to paint my fingernails with red nail polish.

Where I had learned how to kiss by watching Jessica and Sheldon.

Where I had learned how babies were made.

Where I believed everyone loved me no matter what.

But those days of sweet innocence were gone. That day on the bus ride home I looked at Bart's swollen black eye and reached up and got a tiny piece of hair at the nape of my neck and started twisting.

Losing Ground

The first two years of Father and Horace's partnership on the thousand-acre farm were good years. Father had successfully built a canal to bring the water to the farm from an artesian well five miles away. He had leveled the land so perfectly that he could flood irrigate it. But after a few years, Father found he was getting further and further into debt. Everywhere he went he ran into someone he owed money to. He couldn't buy a new Case tractor because he owed the dealership money for the last one he bought. After a while, the banks wouldn't loan him money so Father got a loan from the government in exchange for a granary full of wheat. But when the government agent came to collect the grain, he found the granary empty. Father had sold the grain to pay off another loan.

By the end of the third year Father realized he was going to have to file for bankruptcy. Horace had a large polygamist family in Salt Lake City to take care of and it had been months since he had sent money to Father to help with expenses.

Horace took Father to court to see if he could dissolve their partnership and get the land for himself. Father felt he deserved half of the land. Ending a partnership in the state of Idaho was worse than getting a divorce. Finally, after months of battling it out, the judge decided that because Horace had put up most of the money to finance the development of the farm, he received all the equity and Father and his investors got nothing.

In Mother's journal she wrote: "Mr. Knowlton became unhappy with us, so we left." There was nothing in her journal about filing for bankruptcy. No mention of the electricity being turned off or the fifteen lawsuits brought against Father.

Always the optimist, she was trying not to focus on the harsh realities of our situation. Her favorite saying was, "If you can't say anything nice, don't say anything at all," and despite her many heartaches, I never ever heard my mother say one bad word about my father. We weren't allowed to say anything bad about him either.

Father had to find work. After the last hay was baled in the fall of 1960, Father's brother, Lee, offered him a job in Farmington, New Mexico. Uncle Lee owned several gas stations and Father could drive the trucks that supplied the gas to the stations. Father and Mother held a family meeting at the breakfast table the morning he left for New Mexico.

"Okay, everyone listen. Listen!" Father spoke over the clatter of bowls and spoons and slurping children. We stopped eating and looked at him. "I am going to New Mexico to work for Uncle Lee. Mr. Knowlton is selling the farm, so your mother and I will be looking for a new place to live by the time school starts next year. Bart, you and Keith and the girls," he pointed to Kay and me, "all of you are going to have to help Mother do the chores and keep this farm running until we move. You know what to do. The most important thing I need you to do is obey your mother. Can I count on you to do that?"

"Yes," we said, nodding our heads in obedience.

"Good." Father reached for the last piece of toast in the

center of the table. "Everyone come over here and give me a hug. Bart, run into my bedroom and get my suitcase and I'll be off." He sounded more excited than sad. He was going someplace to have an adventure and I wanted to go with him.

"Can I come with you?" I blurted.

"No, you can't go, silly." Father found my head and ruffled my hair. "You all have to go to school and keep the farm running and love your mother while I'm gone. Everybody get busy with your chores now. Mother is going to walk me out." He picked up his suitcase and took Mother's hand and together they walked up the basement stairs out into the cool September morning.

When Mother came back in the house, her eyes were wet and I could tell that one blink would send the two tears waiting in her eyes tumbling down. She turned her head to the side and dabbed at her eyes with the cuff of her sleeve. Twelve-year-old Bart was still sitting at the table, stacking up the dishes and sliding them closer to the sink, where Kay and I were doing dishes. He looked like he might cry, too.

"Stop. You're going to break something, crashing the dishes together like that." Kay scolded.

Mother went over and sat across from him. "What's the matter, Bart?"

"I don't want to move. Why do we have to move? This is my farm. I love this place. I could run it myself." His voice trembled with emotion.

"Yes, I know you could. I don't know what we would do without you around here." Mother said, reassuringly.

"I've been driving the tractors for years. I've been feeding the cattle for years. If Father can just earn enough money to pay the bills, we can stay here and I can run it for him." His voice steadied with his last idea.

"I'm afraid it's not that simple, Love." Mother reached

across the table to take his hand. "You heard Father say that Mr. Knowlton has decided to sell this place. He owns it, so we don't have a say in the matter. We will find another place. A better place. Some place where you don't get ridiculed at school. Maybe we can find another farm somewhere. You would like that, wouldn't you?" The tears finally let loose and fell down Bart's freckled cheeks as he bit his quivering lip.

"I don't want another place. I want this one," he said, angrily.

"Bart, we just need to trust that God will take us where we need to go." Mother said, trying to console him. "He's taken care of us thus far. He'll take care of us in the days ahead." Bart pulled his hand from Mother's and ran down the hall and out the back door. I took a step closer to Kay, so that my shoulder touched hers. We did what we knew how to do, hold fast together and be quiet.

Mother went to the piano and began to play a hymn she had been teaching us. I heard a sigh from Kay and I knew everything would be okay as long as Mother was here. When she came to the chorus we heard her sweet voice begin to sing the words, begging God to give her strength to carry on without Father:

> *"Then sings my soul, My Savior God to thee,"*
> *" How great thou art, How great thou art."*
> *"Then sing my soul, my Savior God to thee,"*
> *" How great thou art, How great thou Art."*

Mother was our rock but Father was Mother's rock. Now he would be gone for weeks at a time. In the days ahead, I felt the cracks in her composure and heard the trembling in her voice. She did her best to hide her doubt and fear and we never heard her complain about the enormous difficulty of running things without him. They wrote letters back and forth and set up times for phone calls. Mother would drive or sometimes walk to the nearest neighbor just to hear Father's voice. It wasn't until Mother passed away that we found the letters.

My Dearest Husband,

How are you this lovely morning? I guess I should write to you in the mornings, because I am always in better spirits. The evenings are hard without you. I miss you so. Last night I really had to grab my feelings and tromp on them. I picked up the Bible and read this verse and it helped me. "Charity suffereth long and is kind. Charity beareth all things, believeth all things, hopeth all things and endureth all things. Charity is the pure love of Christ and endureth forever. Without Charity we are nothing.

Mother practiced charity in her daily life, moving through her long days without complaint. She made all our meals from fifty pound sacks of wheat, corn and potatoes. She milked cows. She made cheese and butter with the extra milk and cream. She mucked out chicken coops. She washed the poop off the eggs. And because Father came home often enough, she had a baby every fourteen to eighteen months. There wasn't time to mope around or feel sorry for herself. She always looked forward not backward and we followed her lead.

It was hard on her when she got the letter from her brother reminding her of the 'Annual Archibald Summer Fun Week at Yellowstone'. Every summer the Archibald clan packed up and went to Yellowstone Park to camp and fish. In years past we joined them and had a grand old time. Father loved to fish with the brother-in-laws while Mother spent time visiting with her sisters and sister-in-laws. But since we joined the fundamentalist group, tensions ran high and Mother felt like we should stay away from her family for a while. Besides we couldn't afford to go.

Mother's family wasn't the only one upset about us leaving the church. Father's family, with their deep Mormon roots, was just as unhappy as Mothers. It grieved Father that his family couldn't see that he was only trying to live the Gospel the way Joseph Smith and Brigham Young had. He wrote to Mother about his struggles:

> My Darling,
>
> I got back from Albuquerque at eleven this morning. I worked twenty-seven hours. I am now on my way to Shiprock with a load of gas. I got a wonderful letter from you today. It was written with love. I slept in the truck last night. It's sure unpleasant to sleep all cramped up.
>
> I sat down at the station and had a long talk with Lee about the true gospel. He just got angry with me. He said if he were to go out and talk with you, he's sure that you would leave me and cleave to the church. He said the church meant more to you than I did. He said he is ashamed of me for bringing duress and heartache to the Pearson Family. He said our mother will die and I will be to blame.
>
> We just have to have faith in the Lord. I am so thankful you and I see eye to eye. I am afraid I could not do this without you.

Father occasionally revealed some of the anxiety he felt about the challenges of leaving the church and family to live the fullness of the gospel.

The path looks rough. But I am as sure as I live and breathe that we are on the right road, the road that leads to eternal life. I would like to tell the whole world about this wonderful doctrine. I love it. It is part of my life and I hope and pray I may be strong enough to lead you and my family in the path of righteous. My love for you has grown so much since we've accepted the fullness. I didn't know love could grow as ours has. So full, so complete, so beautiful. I have tried to teach Lee about the true gospel, but he doesn't want to change his life. He couldn't stand to have his friends laugh at him as ours have at us. He is not willing to pay the price for eternal life, as we will have to pay before this thing is over.

Lovely Lady, I will write again tonight when I get home. May God bless You.

Love, Wayne.

Many times in years past when I tell my story to my friends, they ask me why my sweet mother stayed with my father and joined the polygamists. I believe my parents were asking themselves the same questions most people ask at some point in their lives. "*Why am I here and where am I going?* And, *how can I get back to The Father?*" They were earnestly seeking the answers to these questions and were willing to give up everything they had to accomplish their quest.

I believe Mother could have stopped Father from joining the Fundamentalists if she had refused but even she couldn't stand against the Prophet Joseph Smith, who said he saw God the Father and His Son, Jesus Christ in a vision. He restored the Gospel of Jesus Christ back to the Earth in these the latter days. Father and Mother figured that if you believed in the first vision, then you could not deny the rest. You didn't have the liberty to pick and choose which revelation you wanted to believe. If you believed one then you must believe them all; even the one the Mormon Church didn't want any more, the one about polygamy.

Through his letters, Father urged his children to be happy and rejoice in his newfound truth. He tried to teach us even from far away. One Sunday morning Mother gathered us together for Sunday school in the living room and took a letter from her apron pocket.

"Your father has sent you a letter." She waited for us to stop poking each other. "Roger, come over here and sit by me." She patted the tiny space next to her on the couch. "Okay, everyone listen."

> Dear Children,
>
> Each one of you please sometime today put your arms around your lovely Mother and kiss her for me. Do you know every time you do that you are doing it for me?

We looked at Mother. She blinked her eyes and took a deep breath.

> Be kind to each other. Don't push and shove each other. Let us always go the extra mile in the things we must do to get along and then we will receive extra blessings. Life is beautiful if you look for the beautiful things. Train yourselves to be happy and thankful for all you have. Do you know that you have more than anyone else in the world? Maybe not worldly things, but they don't count. It's the things like your lovely Mother that counts. She's the

best in the land.

The only thing we want is your one hundred percent love and devotion. You can always do as we tell you and you'll never go wrong. We are looking after you and trying to teach you all the right things. You can come to us with all your problems and we will hear you. If you trust us and we trust the Lord, then we will have a union that will last for time and all eternity.

God Bless you my children. Always remember these things.

Love Your Father

I never questioned my parent's love and devotion to us kids. I felt it as I watched my mother put food on the table three times a day and when she gathered us all around her to pray every night. I felt it with the lessons about the gospel she gave us everyday. I started to feel that we were Gods special children and I would have easily followed my parents to the ends of the earth if they asked me. I also worried about my mother and noticed the dark circles that began to grow under her eyes.

One of Mother's letters to Father was very honest and showed that she grew weary in his absence.

Dear Wayne,

You are a lucky man. I really have a grumpy bunch around here tonight. Janice threw up. Keith complains of a stomachache. He'll probably wait until the middle of the night and throw up all over everything. Bart hurt his thumb at school today. Some boy named Michael poked the sharp point of a pencil into it. It looks quite sore and he acts like he is going to die. I had him soak it in Epson salts. I hope it's better in the morning. I was ready to cry myself by the time I got the children all settled in their beds. I tried to go to town today. I got just to that old house, north of the post office and ran out of gas. So I ran up to Al's and he carried some gas back for me and we couldn't get the gas cap off. We tried and tried. Roger Williams came by and he pushed the car up to Al's and they had to beat that cap off and he bought a new one for me. He had to push me to get the car started again. See how I need you around. This is no country for a woman to live alone in.

I read my patriarchal blessing today to try to find some comfort. It says that I am to learn what my covenants are and live them. I surely have a lot to learn. I have really never read and studied the gospel as much as I have lately.

Well, my dear, I miss you so, especially in the evenings. I just hate to go to bed without you.

Sweet dreams my love.

Father and Mother were sealed together for eternity in the Mesa, Arizona temple on the second of March 1945; five months after their bishop married them. From the moment they repeated those sacred vows in the temple, they felt a deep commitment to each other. Even though they had left the Mormon Church for polygamy, their temple covenants still held them to one another, their children and their righteous ancestors for time and all eternity.

Father and Mother held tight to the polygamist beliefs adhered to by their ancestors.

My Dearest Wayne,

I just got through reading about Heber C. Kimball and his wife, Vilate. What torment Heber went through when Joseph Smith, the Prophet taught Heber about the Principle of plural marriage and commanded him to marry another lady without telling Vilate. He would walk the floor at night and weep as a child. But he never did tell her. She finally couldn't stand his suffering and went to the Lord and He showed her a vision. In the vision, the Lord showed her the blessings and glory of the Principle of Plural Marriage. Oh, I wonder if I am strong enough to stand by you through all that is apt to come, as Vilate stood by Heber.

As hard as she tried and wished he could be, I think Mother struggled to see Father, with all his imperfections, in the same light as the historic patriarchal heroes who introduced the practice of polygamy.

You know, as I read this book, Heber reminds me a lot of you. He was indeed a wonderful Missionary, as you are going to be, when you are called. You need to be careful about casting you pearls before swine. Because these things are indeed pearls. Oh, Wayne, be careful to be honest and true to your word. Sometimes, I feel you are a little slack about keeping you word. I just want you to be the finest man on earth. I love you so much. I wonder sometimes if my love is a selfish love. Maybe I expect too much from you and don't give enough. Oh, do write to me. Your letters cheer me so. Your little family prays constantly for you. They miss you. Jelene says, "I wish Daddy was here, so you wouldn't be so cross." But I am trying to be cheerful. I read the children a nice article on forgiveness today. Boy, we need it. I feel nearer to you while I am writing.

With all my love, Ilene.

Amid all the traveling for work, the scripture study and the doctrinal discussions, Mother and Father made time to fulfill the commandment to multiply and replenish the earth. One year and two months after our sweet little redheaded Helen was born, we welcomed Fara, a beautiful blonde, into our family. It was Mother's first home birth. The polygamist families who had come to work on the farm all had their babies at home. If they could do it, Mother told herself, surely she could. Two of the women from the polygamist families were midwives. Mother's experience with Fara's birth was a positive one and she felt good about the money she saved her family by staying at home.

By the next summer, Father had stopped working for Uncle Lee and found a job driving truck for a small oil refinery in Ogden, Utah, closer to home. Mother was pregnant again and tried to call Father to tell him she was very close to having her baby, but she couldn't reach him. The night Ruth was born, Mother woke up with contractions. She went to the couch and wrapped up in a blanket to count and time her contractions. She reached across the couch and grabbed the mass of soft, white cotton. She finally had time to fold the four dozen new flannel diapers she had just finished hemming the day before. It was the one thing she insisted on having every time she had a new baby. Four-dozen brand new, clean, fresh diapers, made from solid white flannel. By Mother's standards, old ones would never do. She had made sure to buy four new pair of plastic pants that went over the diaper to keep the babies' clothes dry.

She was just finishing the last fold, when she heard a knock on the door. She walked to the stairs where she saw Vera, peeking around the door at her, holding her own nine-month pregnant belly. A tall, broad-shouldered, two hundred and seventy-five-pound German woman, Vera was one of Horace's Knowlton's wives who lived upstairs in the farmhouse we shared. She whispered down to Mother.

"Ilene, can you go down to Viola's and get her? I am having contractions and I don't think it will be long now."

"Of course," Mother said. "I'll go right now." Mother quickly dressed and went to pick up Viola and the other midwife; because she now knew they were going to need both of them. Ruth arrived in the wee hours of the morning just ahead of Vera's ten-pound baby boy. Mother loved to tell the story about how she got up to use the bathroom the next morning and looked out the window and there was Vera, outside at the clothesline hanging out her wash. Mother would laugh and say, "I always figured I deserved a few days of rest after having a baby and I went back to bed."

Cheryl woke us earlier than usual that morning. We had to catch the bus but she knew we would all want to go into Mother's room and see the new baby. Mother was sitting up against her headboard, pillows behind her head. One-and-a-half year old Fara, was snuggled up next to her, sleeping.

"Yes. You can come in." With a wave of her hand, she motioned her tribe into the room. "Come in and see this cute one."

"Wow. Look at all that dark hair." We loved her instantly and were given just about that long to admire her before Cheryl shooed us out and up to the table for breakfast. "You can all take turns holding her tonight," She assured us.

"I get to hold her first," I said to Kay, as we walked to the table.

"I get to hold her second, then," Kay said, like second was okay with her. As long as she could get a bow in all that baby hair, she'd be happy.

I never understood or appreciated my mother fully until I became one myself. A mother spends hours fixing food so her babies can eat it in five minutes. She gathers everyone around the table so she can see that they are all safe and warm. It's where her children eat, laugh and argue. It's where I gagged on my peas, slyly taking them one by one, glad for all the commotion around me, then dropping them to the floor. I hated the rice pudding Mother made for dessert because sometimes it didn't get cooked all the way through and every other bite would bring up raw slimy egg whites. I wasn't allowed to leave the table until all my food was eaten. I waited until everyone else had finished eating and when Mother left the room I hurried and dumped it in the garbage. When she asked me if I finished my rice pudding, I always lied and said yes.

Regardless of whether we liked what she had fixed, Mother insisted we eat what was placed before us. No complaining. "Be grateful for what you have," she'd say. Sometimes it was, "Remember the starving pioneers." And sometimes it was, "There are hungry children in China." I never remember going hungry but I wasn't a boy. My brothers always seemed to be hungry. It's a good thing we lived in Idaho, because there were always potatoes. We had potatoes at least once, if not twice a day. I think we would have starved without potatoes. Mashed potatoes. Scalloped potatoes. Baked potatoes. When Father was home we had fried potatoes with onions because Father loved onions. I hated onions. It was tedious work pushing the potatoes around my plate to make sure I didn't accidently eat one of those ghastly onions.

Mother was up every morning bright and early. She loved

the morning hours, when the house held a stillness that would soon be replaced by the noise of her children. I was a light sleeper. I loved to wake up and follow the light into the kitchen, where I knew I would find Mother before she sat down to practice her scales. Without a word, she would smile and point to the long bench behind the table. There I would sit, my knees pulled up against my chest, nightgown tucked under my toes to keep warm while I watched her make bread, six loaves every morning. She sprinkled the yeast into the water, scooped some sugar with her fingers and tossed it into the yeast, stirring it in with her fingers. The large bowl in front of her held six cups of water. Six large eggs swam across the top. Mother added flour and stirred with a large spoon, mixing everything together. Salt, melted shortening and honey came next. When the yeast mixture was bubbly she added it in. More flour made the dough too stiff to stir. Sprinkling the table with flour, she eased the soft dough out of the pan with a plop. Pulling the dough into its center, she pushed and rolled, until it was a mass of soft, fragrant goodness. Before she oiled the bowl and put the dough back in to raise she tore off a small piece, the size of a doughnut hole and handed it to me. I put it up to my nose and smelled, the smell of heaven. I squished it in half and put some in my mouth. I could hardly wait until the bread came out of the oven. Mother would offer each of us each a warm slice spread with butter and honey. There wasn't anything that made us kids happier.

Despite my memories that everything was fine, some of Mother's letter's showed how she really felt during those long days without Father.

Dear Wayne,

Roger's been miserable with a fever all day. Bart and Keith helped me clean the chicken coop out today. I opened up the window and forked it out. We put clean straw in. I'll bet the chickens appreciate it. We are still getting six eggs a day.

What should I do about the license for the car? What if I get picked up? Where did you take the wringer for the washer to get fixed? Will you pick it up on your way home next time? I think I'll move to town and get me a job if you're going to be gone all the time. If I could work from about eight until twelve at night, it would work out pretty good. Cheryl could tend the children. I get so lonely at night I can hardly stand it. I didn't get up to the mailbox today. I hope I get a letter tomorrow.

Love, Ilene and all.

September came and school started but this year was different. Cheryl wouldn't be going to school with us. Years later, she told me the reason why Father made his decision to send her to school five-hundred miles away. She had a friend who talked her into staying after school to go to the basketball game one night. Cheryl couldn't get a hold of Mother to tell her where she was and she forgot to ask Bart to tell her when he got home. When she took the school bus home after the game, she found Mother sitting on the couch alone, waiting for her, looking very worried. She quietly told Cheryl how frightened she had been and that she hoped she would never do that again. Then she went to bed. When Father heard that Cheryl had stayed out late, he decided it was time to send her to the private Priesthood school in Colorado City, Arizona. She was fifteen and he felt she would be safer there, far away from the wicked boys at our school.

Marion Hammon, one of the brethren in the Priesthood Council, had rallied the Saints in the polygamist community of Colorado City, Arizona to build a new private high school called The Academy. Brother Hammon saw this as a way to bring up the standard of living for the people who had lived there for many generations. Previously the students had to travel twenty-five miles to Hurricane, Utah, if they wanted to attend high school. Tuition to attend the Academy was one hundred and fifty dollars a year. For most of the large families who lived in Colorado City, that was a lot of money. Father was determined to show his support to the brethren and he felt like Cheryl would get a better education there than in the public schools. Cheryl didn't want to leave her home and family but she wasn't given a choice in the matter.

Arrangements were made for her to stay with Fred Jessop and his family, along with some other girls from Salt Lake City, who came to attend the Academy. Fred had three wives but no children because he had had the mumps as a boy and was sterile.

Cheryl worked hard at her studies and tried to be happy, but she missed her family something awful. When Father realized how lonely Cheryl was he took our old horse, Dart, down and found a place to pasture him so she could ride him. He hoped this would alleviate some of her loneliness, but even her favorite horse couldn't keep Cheryl from being miserably homesick.

Dear Mother,

Mother, I want you to know along with the rest of the family that I love you more than anything else in the world.

The pictures I have that we took before I came down here turn me to tears every time I look at them and I look at them often. Mother, I miss and love you so much. The reason I didn't write is because I could not find the right things to say to such wonderful people. How is Ruth? Is she getting bigger? Can she remember me at all? Do Helen and Fara miss me very much? I hope so. I hope the other kids miss me like I do them. Please take care of yourself, Mother and don't stay up too late. I rode my horse last Friday. He keeps jumping the fence so I have to get Sharon to help me catch him. I like school. I have my blouse almost finished in sewing class. I better go. It's my turn to do the dishes. I love you so and will write to you more often. Please write to me too.

Love, Love, Love, Your Daughter, Cheryl.

Cheryl found a ride home every chance she got. One time she got a ride with Brother Rich Jessop, one of the Priesthood Council. He sat in the front with his arm around his new young wife, while Cheryl, who was only sixteen, drove them to Salt Lake City.

Another time she got a ride with someone and didn't realize until they were almost to Salt Lake City that they were being asphyxiated by the fumes coming from a broken muffler seeping into the back seat. Cheryl and her friend who sat beside her weren't as affected as the young man sitting against the window. He was so sick that by the time they got to Salt Lake City, he crawled up to the porch of his mother's home on his hands and knees.

Cheryl's absence was a particularly painful sacrifice for Mother. She was already struggling without Father, losing her oldest daughter and best helper to her new religion at the tender age of fifteen, made Mother sad. I know she missed her terribly even though I never heard her say she did.

Just when we didn't think we could stand another week without Father, he surprised us, coming home Halloween weekend with the washing machine from the repair shop in the back of his pick-up. Mother shooed us all outside to greet him. Before his feet touched the ground, he started barking orders.

"Bart and Keith, I need your help. Grab the legs on the other side of this washer and let's get it inside." Kay and I followed behind them, bursting with excitement.

"The kids at school are all dressing up and going trick or treating and filling bags of candy. Have you ever heard of anything so fantastic?" I said. I was trying to get Father's attention but he was only interested in getting the washer out of the truck and into the laundry room so he would have a happy wife.

"Yes, yes. You will have to ask your mother about that." He puffed, grunting under the weight of the washer. I dodged around him and into the house.

"Mother, can we go trick or treatin' up to the Bean's house tomorrow night? Father says it's up to you. The Beans are nice to us and they don't care if we're not Mormons anymore and its Halloween!"

Please!" I pleaded. "Bart will take us."

"I want to go too," Five-year-old Lee begged.

"Well, I guess you can all go, if you dress up warm and if Bart will take you. And you will have to go before it gets too dark"

The next evening, we hurried to finish our chores. We bundled the little boys in their coats and hats and wrapped a blanket around them in the red wagon. I slipped on my warm winter coat and wrapped my scarf up tight around my neck to keep my tender ears warm. The Bean's house was a half-mile up the graveled road. The full moon was already high in the cold October sky.

"They probably won't even have any candy." Bart grumbled as he picked up the wagon handle and began to pull.

"Wow, it is cold out here tonight. I'm freezing already," I said.

"Just be glad the damn wind isn't blowing," Bart swore. He loved to swear when Father and Mother weren't within earshot.

The stubble in the alfalfa field was black from the frost. Some yellow heads of wheat missed by the combine on harvest day, bobbed along the fence.

"Stop," I said suddenly, grabbing Kay's arm and pulling her to a stop. I ran over and broke off some full heads of grain. "Let's make farmer's gum!"

"Okay." She held out her hand. We rolled each of the wheat head in our hands and broke open the tiny pods at the end of each shaft. Carefully we blew away the chaff, then put each kernel of wheat in our mouths. Slowly we moved the wheat around in our mouths to soften it, then we bit into the kernels, breaking them up. The trick was to keep from swallowing any of it, because if you could keep it all together and chew it long enough for the gluten to congeal it felt like chewing gum. There was no wonderful sweetness like when you bit into a stick of Juicy Fruit. But it was farmer's gum, and it was always a challenge to see if we could even get it to work. Kay noticed that the boys pulling the wagon had moved far ahead of us. We ran to catch up, chewing and chewing, and not swallowing.

We were one hundred yards from the Bean's front door, when Bart sniffed. "What's that smell?"

"It smells like fresh bread," I said.

"No, it's cinnamon rolls!" he whispered.

Bart knocked loudly on the front door. We heard the footsteps of running children. Mrs. Bean opened the door with four young children peeking out around her.

"Well, look what we have here," Mrs. Bean said brushing flour off her apron. "Trick or Treaters! We don't have any candy but I just pulled some cinnamon rolls out of the oven. Would you like to have one? Come on in and take your coats off."

We gathered around the kitchen table and watched Mrs. Bean spread each cinnamon roll with creamy white frosting. With that first heavenly bite, I thought I heard angels singing.

"Wow! That was the best cinnamon roll in the whole world," Bart exclaimed, licking the frosting off his fingers. Mr. Bean had come into the doorway and stood watching the spectacle.

"Thank you so much for the delicious cinnamon rolls. Come on you guys, we better be heading back home." Bart said, sliding his chair back from the table.

"First, everyone come over here and wash up those sticky hands." Mrs. Bean lifted Roger and then Lee up to the sink and swished the water between their fingers. "Get those gloves back on so you can stay warm."

"Thanks again for the cinnamon rolls," we all chorused, leaving the warm kitchen. We walked into the cold night. Bart got Roger and Lee settled in the wagon and tucked the blanket all around and underneath them. The crisp night air nipped at our faces and crawled up our pant legs. About half way home we heard some coyotes howling far off in the hay field. The full moon gave off an eerie glow. The coyotes howled again. This time they were closer.

"Look over there," Bart whispered. "Can you see their eyes? Those four tiny shiny things right over there?" He pointed into the night. I pulled Kay in close to me to keep my heart from jumping out of my chest. There they were, four tiny lights moving in the hay field.

"Are they going to eat us?" Lee asked.

"No, there are too many of us. They are more scared of us than we are of them." Bart reassured him.

"I don't think they are more scared than me right now," I said, keeping Kay close.

Bart picked up the pace. We all matched his stride. "See that tiny light up there? That's our porch light. We're almost home."

As soon as we hit the long dirt driveway, we started running. Lee and Roger hung onto the sides of the wagon for dear life, letting out a loud, Ow! each time their butts hit the wagon bed. Our feet all hit the porch step at the same time, but Lee was the first one through the door and into Mother's arms. We threw our coats, hats and gloves onto the couch and started talking all at once.

"The Coyotes, Whoooo, Whoooo. The cinnamon rolls, angels singing and Yum! These babies were afraid of a little coyote. You've got to get her recipe, Mother. My bum hurts!"

"You all had quite the adventure," Mother laughed, and softly patted Lee's behind. "Father will be in soon with the milk. Everyone dress for bed and we'll have prayers."

Father came down the stairs, smelling of cow manure. He set the buckets of milk down on the kitchen floor. Mother followed him into the kitchen to strain the milk into the jugs and wash the buckets so they would be ready for morning milking. It felt so good to see Father coming down the stairs and Mother's face light up when he walked in.

We knelt in a circle on the hard linoleum floor and grabbed the hands of the ones beside us. Sometimes I hated holding the hand next to mine. A sweaty boy hand, who knew where that had been. I even hated grabbing Kay's hand if I was mad at her. But that was the rule. Father looked around the circle to make sure we were all connected. And we were. I knew deep down in my heart there was no one in the whole world I loved more than the people in this circle. Father prayed. I wasn't listening. I was thinking of Thanksgiving when I knew Father would be coming home again. Mother was happier when he was home.

The Last Christmas

In the middle of November, Mother helped us make a paper chain to count down the days until Father and Cheryl would be home for Thanksgiving. Kay and I lay in our bed the night before the feast.

"I can't wait till Father gets home tomorrow. That was a huge turkey Mother bought," I said.

"I know. I can't wait either. Do you think when we move we will still sleep together?" Kay asked.

"No. I think we are getting too big to sleep in the same bed. I think we should get our own beds when we get a new house." I plumped my pillow and drew the quilt up to my chin.

"Do you really? I like sleeping with you. Do you really want to move?"

"Sure, it might be fun. New people, new friends at school. Just imagine the adventures we will have."

When Kay and I woke up the next morning, we heard Father and Cheryl's voices coming down the hall. We ran into the kitchen and saw Father and Mother sitting in their usual places at the table, Mother's hand resting on Father's. Cheryl was sitting on the bench telling Mother about her friends at school. We ran to her and gave her a hug. It was so good to have her back home. She was wearing a dress with long-sleeves and a high collar and her hair was pulled back in a bun. She looked older than she did when she left.

"Well, good morning, sleepy heads." Father spread out his arm to take us both in, one on each knee. He gave us each a slobbery, garlicky kiss. We both said, "Ugh!" and wiped the kiss off with our hands. He pulled us in tighter and squeezed us harder.

"So you don't like my kisses? Well, here's another one then!" He proceeded to kiss us over and over while we laughed and twisted in his arms.

"You silly girls, go get dressed." Mother smiled. "We have a big dinner to get ready."

After breakfast, Mother divided up the chores to keep the work flowing so all the food would be hot and on the table at the same time.

"Jelene, you and your father are in charge of making the rolls for dinner. Cheryl, you get the cans of corn from the pantry. Oh, and get the cranberries and sugar started."

Father set the big flat baking pan on the cupboard and greased the bottom with butter. He broke a small piece of the soft roll dough Mother had made earlier away from the big mound in the bowl.

"You ready?" He smiled, winking at me. "Catch!" He tossed the small round ball into the air. I caught the ball and laughed.

"Now, you make a bun out of that and put it in the pan." I rolled the dough around and around under my hand, trying to make it look like the ones Mother made. How did she make it look so easy? I pulled and pinched the dough until I gave up. "It's never going to look like Mother's." I set the bun on the pan.

"It looks great. Couldn't have done it better myself." Father reassured me and I knew that was very true. Soon we had the whole pan full of crinkled buns in the oven. They tasted delicious with the hot mashed potatoes and gravy, cranberry sauce, dressing, and turkey we savored that afternoon.

"Now, I want to hear the Christmas Carols you have been practicing so we can go caroling when I come home for Christmas. We'll go down to Beans and up to Swivels and maybe into town to sing for Uncle Howard." Father shooed us all toward the piano. Mother sat on the piano bench and opened the Christmas book. Jingle Bells, Peace on Earth and Deck the Halls filled our basement home. Father's rich voice sang out with ours. Nothing thrilled him more than to hear his children sing.

After his nap, Father gathered us around for a family meeting. These family meetings had become common since we left the Mormon Church. We sat on the two couches that hugged the living room walls; Father grabbed a chair from the kitchen and sat facing us.

"In our new church," he started, "we believe that Christ was born on April 6th, not December 25th like everyone else in the world. We believe that we should celebrate Christ's real birthday, which just happens to also be the same day that Joseph Smith restored the church. Your mother and I have decided we will celebrate Christmas one last time. And you can tell us what you want this year, because it will be our last Christmas."

"What about Santa Claus?" Seven-year-old Roger asked, looking confused.

"I told you there ain't no Santa Claus," Bart said, looking very pleased that he had been the first to reveal the worlds best kept secret. Roger started to whimper.

"No Santa Claus? I love Santa Claus." Lee said, with a look of consternation. He hurried over to mother and climbed onto her lap, with Ruth, her baby. Mother wrapped her spare arm around him. After losing two baby boys, he would hold a special place in her heart the rest of her life.

"Santa is just make-believe, Love." She patted the couch beside her and motioned to Roger to come sit by her too. "Why don't you think about what you would like for Christmas this year?" Roger wiped his nose across his sleeve. "Maybe some Lincoln Logs like my friend James," he said, still trying to decide if he was finished crying.

"I want a miniature stove to cook things on." I interrupted, thinking I should hurry to make my request before the time limit was up or they changed their minds. "You know like the ones we saw at the store in Rexburg the other day. They look like so much fun." I clapped my hands. I was very excited. I couldn't believe I was lucky enough to pick my own Christmas present. This was the chance of a lifetime.

Mother wrote down everyone's wishes in her notebook: Lincoln logs for Roger, a big book with lots of stories in it for Kay, a bow and arrow set for Keith and bicycles for Bart and Cheryl. Janice wanted a new dress. Lee wanted a baseball and mitt and the three little girls wanted dolls. And of course, my stove.

On Christmas Eve, when Father pulled into the yard after driving from his job in Ogden, Utah, it was every bit as wonderful as if he were the real Santa Claus. Cheryl found a ride from Colorado City up to Salt Lake where Father picked her up so we could be together for Christmas. We ran outside when we heard the car roll across the gravel in the driveway and grabbed their coats, hands and legs, dragging them into the house.

Christmas morning was just as exciting as it had been when everything was a surprise. I ripped my big box open and brought out the smallest electric stove I had ever seen. The most adorable little frying pan, a saucepan, a tiny spoon and spatula came with the stove.

"Oh, Mother. Isn't this the best, cutest stove in the world?"

"It sure is! Why don't you make breakfast for us this morning? She chuckled. Have Cheryl help you read the instructions to your new stove." Cheryl and Bart were both sitting atop their new bikes, rolling around the living room.

"Cheryl, let's make scrambled eggs." I called to her. We went to the refrigerator and took out an egg. She got a bowl from the cupboard and broke the egg into it and handed me the fork.

"Stir it around like this. Get the yolks mixed in with the whites." She took the fork from me and showed me how and then handed the fork back to me. I stirred and stirred. We poured the egg into my new frying pan and plugged in my stove.

"Okay, it should be getting warm here in a minute." Cheryl said. She held her hand over the tiny round burner, painted on the stovetop. "I think it's ready." I placed the frying pan on the tiny burner and stirred with the miniature spatula. Soon the eggs began to cook.

"Oh, my gosh. I think it is actually working." Cheryl said.

"Yay! This is so great!" I squealed. The heat coming from the little stove cooked the eggs as I stirred and stirred. "I think they are done. Let's try them!" I said. Cheryl got some forks and Kay came over for a taste test. I took the first bite.

"They taste kind of funny. Not like Mother's." I said. Kay took a taste.

"Yeah, they taste bad. Maybe they need some salt and pepper."

"Oh, dang, we forgot salt and pepper." I said. It was Cheryl's turn to try some.

"I think maybe it's the pan. They taste like tin." She spit the eggs into her hand and headed for the trash.

"How are the eggs coming for breakfast?" asked Mother, a twinkle in her eye.

"Not so good," said Cheryl. "I think we better stick to the real stove for cooking."

I frowned and tossed my head. "Well, I like my eggs and this is what I'm having for breakfast."

I took another bite of eggs and swallowed them down. I smiled and took another bite. They were the worst eggs I had ever tasted.

Our love of Christmas didn't die when we entered the polygamist group even though we couldn't celebrate it. Every December Mother brought out the Christmas songs and we went Christmas Caroling to our friends and neighbors. We loved to look at the lights strung from the houses and trees in town. Then we went home, just happy that we got to enjoy everyone else's Christmas.

The next spring, Father was still driving truck for Mr. Crabtree, the owner of a small oil refinery, in Ogden, Utah, where they cleaned the oil from car repair shops and resold it at a cheaper price. Father drove all through Idaho, picking up old oil at the shops and selling them back the refined oil.

Father and Mother were trying to pay off all their outstanding debts and there was very little money left at the end to the month.

The phone had been turned off and debt collectors were showing up at our door. The gasman stopped delivering gas and suckers. The electricity was turned off in June. On one of his weekends home, Father rigged up an old cook stove out on a cement slab on the back porch so Mother could cook food and heat water for our baths and washing clothes. Thank goodness Cheryl was home for summer break. Mother needed all the help she could get.

Every Saturday we took turns taking a bath in the big metal tub. Kay and I were wrapped only in our towels behind the sheets Mother had hung between the kitchen and the living room. I was nine and becoming more self-conscious of my body.

"Cheryl, bring me some more hot water from the stove. The girls are ready to get in the tub," Mother shouted from the kitchen window to the back porch.

"As soon as she brings the water, you jump in there and get washed up quickly," Mother pointed to me. "Kay, you follow her. Bart and Keith will keep the fire going in the stove. We still have lots of baths to do and we will need more hot water." She went around the sheet barrier to keep things moving.

The Saturday night bathing ritual had started earlier that afternoon with the babies, Ruth, Fara and Helen. Then Roger and Lee. Now it was our turn. After that would come Keith and Bart, Janice and Cheryl and finally Mother. Hot water would be added each time to make it nice and cozy. Every time a new bather got into the tub, Mother would scoop the grey foam from the Castile soap we used off the top of the water and pour it down the kitchen sink.

"Oh, that feels good." I said sticking my toe in to test the water. Then I slowly slid my small body down into the warmth. I wanted to just scrunch up as tight as I could and enjoy the warm water surrounding me but I knew there was only one purpose to this bath. Wash up and get out.

"Hurry up, I'm cold." Kay said, shaking in her towel. I was out in two minutes. She handed me my towel and stepped into the water. I quickly dried and pulled my underwear up my legs and my long flannel nightgown over my head.

"Now come over here and let's get your hair washed." Mother had come back into the kitchen. She had a sink full of warm water waiting. I leaned over and tried to get my head as far down into the sink as I could so she could pour water on my head to shampoo it. She used the same Castile Soap we used to wash our bodies. It was cheap and did the job. She rubbed the bar of soap against my head, splashing some water up to mix with it and make it foam. This was the one thing I didn't mind about bath night. I loved the way Mother gently rubbed and scrubbed and scratched my scalp. It was a mixture of pleasure and pain, that satisfying sensation of scratching your itchy scalp, and the feeling that all your hair was being yanked from your head. When she was through shampooing, she moved me to the other sink and poured a mixture of water and apple cider vinegar over my hair to get the soap out. "Your hair is getting so long," Mother said. "I don't know how we will ever get all these snarls out."

After our supper of grilled cheese and bottled peaches, we knelt in a circle in the living room for family prayers. Mother prayed that Father would find us a place to live very soon and that it would be a place with electricity. Then I think she forgot she was still praying, because she began listing all the things she needed in her next house. "It will have a nice kitchen with an electric stove, and refrigerator. It will have two bathrooms and at least four bedrooms... and a fireplace would be nice." I opened my eyes to peek at her and she was smiling. "And God Bless these children that they will all grow big and strong and love each other. Amen."

Kay and I took the turban wrapped towels off our heads, hung them on the back of the kitchen chairs and ran to our bed.

"This mess of rats is never coming out of my hair." I said to her.

"We'll let it dry tonight and I'll brush it out for you in the morning. It's much easier to get the rats out when it's dry," she said.

We flopped onto our backs and spread our long matted locks over the pillow and down between the bed and the wall to dry.

"We forgot to blow the candle out." Kay said.

"Cheryl will blow it out when she comes to bed." I said.

"You're the closest. Go blow it out. Mother would not be happy if we disobeyed her. She says to always blow out the candles so we don't start a fire." Kay poked me in the side.

"Okay, okay." I hurried back to the tall candle stuck with wax to the bottom of a pork and bean can on top of the chest of drawers and blew it out. I ran back to bed and rearranged my hair over the pillow to dry and fell asleep.

The next night, I had a stomachache and Mother said I could sleep with her. I slid under the covers on Father's side of the bed and snuggled up to his pillow. I turned on my side and by candle light watched Mother slip her nightgown over her slender body and the long sacred garments that went from her neck to her ankles. She pulled her long hair through her fingers and braided it. It was finally quiet in the house. Not a child's cry or whisper or last request for "Mother" could be heard. Baby Ruth had finished her bottle and was wrapped up tight in her crib. I watched as Mother pulled a letter from her top drawer and brought the candle closer so she could read it. She read silently, and as she flipped the letter over to continue reading, a sweet, soft smile warmed her face and I saw the stress of the day disappear. She folded the letter and returned it to her drawer, blew out the candle and climbed into bed beside me.

"Who is that letter from?" I asked her.

"It's a letter from your father. I like to think of it as a love letter." In the dark I could feel the warmth of her smile. "When I get lonely, I love to pull it out and read it. It reminds me of how much I love him and with him so far away, sometimes I just need to be reminded."

I never doubted the love my parents shared. As a child, that love protected me from adult worries. Years later, when I found the letters they wrote to each other, I finally understood how hard it had been on them to be apart.

Father and Mother clung to each other for reassurance. They had stepped off a ledge into another world. The church they had relied on for their salvation was now gone. They had given their allegiance to another God. A God who says the one with the most wives wins; where the one with the most money and land has the most wives. Where daughters are traded like cattle to build up the kingdoms of men.

Staying in the Mormon Church would have been easy. It was a piece of cake compared to where Father and Mother were going. Paying tithing, leading the music, and giving a Sunday school lesson was easy. But father loved the mysteries and the intriguing world of Polygamy drew him in. Father and Mother had met the brethren and seen their many wives. They had read all the books that proved to them the Brethren were telling the truth. Joseph and Brigham said it was so, so it must be true. Maybe someday Father's new Prophet would give him another wife to build his kingdom. If he just paid enough tithing. If he could just prove to them he was good enough. They had to know how devoted he was, especially if he gave them his daughters.

On July 24th, Pioneer Day, Father drove into the yard in a big diesel truck, pulling a blue and white trailer with four-foot sideboards. Kay and I had helped Mother box up all our clothes, bathroom towels and everything from the kitchen cupboards. We had fun walking up and down the long ramp into the trailer with the small boxes we could carry. Father packed them up tight against each other. Then he tied a rope to the sideboard and started weaving it across the top to hold everything in place. Some neighbors were there to help him move the piano, refrigerator and stove. We were moving to Ogden, Utah. Father had found us a place to live....in an oil refinery.

Moving to Ogden

Father told us to think of moving into an oil refinery as a great adventure. I think Mother looked at it a little differently. She drove the car filled with children and followed Father in the diesel that carried our furniture. I noticed Mother's lips were so tight across her face it seemed she didn't have a mouth, as we slowed down and turned off the pavement, onto a dirt road that went behind some tall, old buildings. Abandoned cars, fifty gallon barrels and wooden pallets littered the yards of each building. Father stopped in front of a small building with a warehouse attached to it on the east.

We piled out of the car and began hauling sacks of clothes into our new home.

"Stop!" Mother hollered. "Nothing goes in there until it's swept and mopped. She reached into the back of the dusty station wagon and brought out her cleaning bucket, broom, and mop.

"Cheryl and Janice, you start in the kitchen and Kay and Jelene can wash the windows." Mother led the way and began washing off the small counter top. When all was clean, Mother instructed the boys to bring in her six-foot table and chairs and placed them in the center of the small kitchen. She said this would be the only furniture we needed for now. The piano and all the furniture from our old house would be stored upstairs in the oil refinery, covered with tarps, waiting until we found a decent home. Mother made it clear that we couldn't get too comfortable here; this was not a place for a piano.

Three cupboards and an industrial sink that stood on four metal legs were attached to the west wall. A double hot-plate sitting on the cupboard and a small refrigerator were plugged into the only electrical outlet in the room. There was a small half bath off the kitchen, but no tub. We would still get to use the number ten tub for baths every Saturday night. A fifteen-watt bulb swung from a white cord above the table. Someone had forgotten to sheetrock the ceiling. Later I wondered if Mother knew just how bad living in an oil refinery was going to be, when she agreed to move her family into what Father teasingly called 'the Knickerbocker Hotel'. At least there was electricity, something we had lived without for the last few months in Idaho.

The refinery was out in the county, west of Ogden, Utah, in an industrial park. We could see the tall white Farmers Grain Co-op Elevators just south of us through the fields. Our closest neighbor was the Del Monte tomato factory. Whenever we walked outside our noses took a break from the smell of oil, only to be hit with the pungent smell of tomato paste.

"Which smell do you like the best?" I asked Kay. "Oil or Tomato?"

"Tomato, I think." She sucked in a loud deep breath, and laughed.

The following morning, Father lined us kids up along the conveyer belt inside the oil refinery warehouse.

"Okay, guys, this is what I need you to do. You all know that I go out in the diesel truck to all the gas stations up and down the road in Idaho and Utah. I get all the old dirty oil the mechanics take out of the cars. I bring it back here and clean it with sulfur and filters. The clean oil is pumped into that tank up there." He pointed to a huge tank standing up on metal stilts at the end of the warehouse.

"Now, what I need you kids to do is can the clean oil, so I can take it back to the stations and sell it to them at a cheaper price." I looked at Kay and raised my eyebrows, as if to say, "What?" Father took twelve empty quart sized aluminum cans out of a box and placed them on the conveyer belt.

"Okay, Bart. Flip that switch."

The cans banged up against each other until they got to a certain spot. A small metal arm swung out to stop the cans just as the oil spigots opened. Six cans filled up with oil, moved on and the next six cans moved into place. Father stopped the belt and showed us how to place the lids on the cans just right so that when the cans went through the sealer it would make a good strong seal. He made it look easy.

"Okay, everyone in their places. Bart, you put the cans onto the belt. Kay and Jelene stand here and put the lids on the cans after they fill with oil." Father yanked ten-year-old Keith down to the end of the line. "You stand here and inspect each lid to make sure it sealed, or we'll have oil all over the place. Okay, let's have a run through. Bart, hit the switch."

When Bart flipped that little white switch, he also flipped the panic button in my stomach. I just knew this wasn't going to turn out well. The noise of the machine made me want to bolt but I moved closer to Kay until I could feel the warmth of her arm against mine. The cans clunked and banged together, stopping long enough to fill with oil. Then they were in front of us. Kay and I each had a hand full of lids. We each took a lid and placed it on the first two cans of oil. And then the next two cans. They were only in front of us for a second before they moved to the sealing machine. We didn't have time to wonder if we were doing it right because there were six more cans of oil in front of us again. We weren't left wondering very long.

"Stop the presses!" Father shouted from where he stood at the sealing machine. "Come down here, girls." Kay and I walked over to him. "Look at this. You girls have got to be more careful." He pointed to a lid that was flipped up, oil spilling over the side of the can. "This will never do. Every can and lid we waste is money wasted. Come back over here and let's try it again." We all walked back to our station and he took a lid from my hand. "If you take the lid like this, with your whole hand and place it on top like this, you can feel the edges of the can and then you will know it is centered," he said. "Okay, good. Let's try it one more time."

I looked at Kay and wanted to cry, but there wasn't time. The switch was flipped and I concentrated on the job at hand. I found it was easier to do it the way Father had shown us and soon Kay and I became professional oil can lid putter-oners. Everyday, we got better and soon we rarely had a bad seal. Whenever we made a mistake we had to stop the machine and pour the oil from the damaged can into a five-gallon bucket. When it was full, Bart carefully climbed up an old wooden ladder and dumped the oil back into the holding tank so we could try again. After the cans were sealed, we loaded twelve full cans into new cardboard boxes and folded it closed. Bart and Keith stacked them onto dollies as high as they could lift, then pushed and pulled and stacked them nice and tight in the diesel truck so they wouldn't shift on their trip up the road.

When we weren't working or sleeping we spent our time outside, building our tree house. On the north side of the driveway, there was a row of trees growing up out of a filthy canal fifty feet below, which looked and smelled like tomato soup with swirls of oil on the top. We were happy to discover a large pile of scrap lumber lying in a heap beside the refinery. We borrowed it. We pushed and pulled a two-by-ten over to the trees and slid it from the edge of the road over into the branches of the biggest, fattest tree. Bart stood in the middle of the tree and barked out orders.

"Bring me that board. No! Not that one. That one." He pointed. "Yes, that one will fit perfectly." Walking out onto the plank with our boards, we tried not to look down. We handed the board over to Bart, who began nailing down a floor and then side rails, to keep us from taking a fatal plunge. The boys spent hours each day in the tree house, shooting wild Indians with wooden guns and swinging from a rope over the soupy canal, yelling, Tarzan style, "Ah, Ahie, Ahie, Ahie!"

Kay and I had better things to do. "Let's have a tea party," I said.

"Aren't we too old for tea parties?" Kay was ten.

"No, of course not." I said. "I'm only nine."

"Okay then. Yes, let's!" Kay said. "I'll make the punch."

Kay climbed up into the middle of the large apricot tree that completely filled the west side yard. I handed her up two small glasses of cherry punch. When I got settled on my branch, she handed me my glass.

"Well, this is very nice." I said, instantly becoming an English Princess.

"Yes, it is very nice," she said.

We tipped our glasses and gazed at the three-story tower of the Del Monte factory.

"The Castle looks lovely today, don't you think?" I said.

"Indeed." Kay touched her lips with her pinky. "I do wonder

what the Prince is up to today and if he will stop by."

"That would be divine." I sipped my red wine.

"Let's talk about when school starts in two weeks," Kay frowned, suddenly losing her British accent. "I'm excited, but kind of scared. Do you think we will make friends?"

"Of course we will! We're so beautiful, who could resist us? They will flock around us, begging to be our friends," I was trying to keep my British accent going and disgusted that Kay was already done pretending.

"Do you think they will call us plygs?" Kay said in a whisper.

"They don't know anything about us and besides we aren't really plygs yet. Father only has Mother for a wife. The only reason they called us plygs in Idaho was because Mr. Horace and some of the other people who lived by us were plygs and we went to church with them. Besides, we're not going to tell anybody about our religion, so they will never know."

"That will be nice." Kay said. Her cute dimples spread like sunshine across her face and she sat up a little straighter and her British accent returned. "Let's have a toast! A toast to our new friends!"

We threw our glasses together with such gusto that they shattered. Glass and cherry punch flew everywhere. I looked at Kay and we burst out laughing. We laughed so hard we had to hug a tree branch to keep from falling.

We looked down at our dresses, splattered with red punch and wiped our hands on our skirts.

"Well, we might as well finish the punch. Don't you think?" I asked Kay.

I climbed down and handed the pitcher up to her. She waited until I was back up in the tree and then took a big gulp straight from the pitcher, wiping her mouth with the back of her hand.

"This is very fine wine," she said.

"Yes, it is," I said, taking a big drink. "When the Prince arrives, we shall serve this wine to him." I laughed. "If there's any left."

"And he shall ask me to marry him and I shall say yes!" Kay drank some more.

"Well, I hope you have a better dress to wear than the one you have on right now." I laughed, gulping down the last of the punch.

"Oh, yes, that reminds me. What are we going to wear to school?"

"We're just going to hope and pray that Uncle Don and Aunt Vera send us box of our cousin's hand-me-downs." I sighed.

"Maybe we'll get lucky and they will send some cute shoes too."

"Wouldn't that be great?" I glanced down at my scuffed loafers. "I'm getting out of these sticky clothes." We hopped down out of the tree and picked up all the pieces of glass we could find before we headed inside.

The dirt around the oil refinery was black with oil. Between our oil-canning job and playing outside all day, we came into supper every night covered in black dirt. First Mother took Roger and Lee and the little girls to the large industrial sink and ran some warm water. She scrubbed faces and hands and feet with Lava soap, until their skin was red. The rest of us had to scrub ourselves. After we were all clean, we sat down to supper. Mother had a big pot of hot pinto bean soup and grilled cheese sandwiches sitting in the middle of the table.

"When we get through with supper, I will read to you. Who remembers what happened in our story last night?" Mother said, scooping each of us a bowl full of beans. We all started talking at once. "Keith, why don't you tell us?"

"Well, the boy gets a boy dog and a girl dog and he is so happy and excited. He can't wait till they grow up big enough to go hunting with them." Keith eyes sparkled with excitement.

"Yes. That's right." Mother dished up the last of the beans in the pot and sat down to eat.

"Are there any more beans?" Bart asked.

"No. That's all there is. You had three bowls full already." Mother patted his stomach. "I think you're full. You can help clean off the table and Janice can start the dishes. " Soon we were gathered around her on the mattresses placed on the floor in the front office space to read another chapter of "Where the Red Fern Grows." Father and Mother slept on a big mattress under the big window in the office and the little girls on another one beside them. After reading, we six older kids went out into the refinery and pulled our sleeping bags up onto the stacks of cardboard boxes. We climbed into our bags and tried to get comfortable as we listened to the crickets chirp and the mice scurry across the cement floor hunting for their supper. I pulled the sleeping bag over my nose to filter the stench of oil and fell asleep, exhausted.

We were excited for school to start in September. The night before the first day, Mother had us take turns scrubbing our dirty, oily shoes with Lava soap. We lined them up along the wall to dry. We hadn't been blessed with a box of hand-me-downs from our cousins yet, but Mother had washed and ironed the boy's jeans and shirts and Kay and I wore our Sunday dresses. We went off to our first day of school feeling loved and very excited. We walked down the dirt road beside a tomato field to the bus stop. When we stepped up the bus steps the bus driver, who wore a kind smile, shouted, "Welcome Aboard". The six of us found two back seats and huddled together. I smiled at the kids looking back at us and felt my braids pulling against my scalp. Mother had braided my hair so tight I wondered if they would think I was part Chinese.

"See. I told you they don't know we're plygs." I whispered to

Kay. "They don't know anything about us." I felt an unfamiliar freedom and took a deep breath. I felt Kay do the same thing beside me. I looked over at Bart who was frowning, his guard up, ready to defend us.

"They don't know who we are here. This is going to be so great." I whispered. I punched his arm hoping to make him laugh. But he wore his frown into the second week when he realized that all he had to do now was be a boy.

Our new schoolhouse was almost an exact replica of the schoolhouse we left in Idaho: a giant granite structure, with a wide staircase going up to classrooms and another staircase going down to more classrooms. There was a gymnasium built at the back of the school where we played cat-and-mouse almost every day in the winter months. When it was warm outside we played kick ball, and I wasn't all that bad, unlike baseball, which I stunk at.

My fourth grade teacher, Mrs. Neilson, was a good teacher. Her only problem was that her son, Kyle was in her class and he was such a discipline problem that he made her cry almost every day, which made my nervous stomach hurt. But then I started paying more attention to the cute boy in the desk next to mine and suddenly my stomachaches were gone. Oh, Brent, my first love. He was blond, round-faced, and had a smile I couldn't resist. We bumped into each other as often as we could when we played cat-and-mouse. If he was on my team I stood next to him. If he was the mouse I ran a little faster to catch and tag him. The best thing about him was that he never asked nosy questions about my family when we sat next to each other at lunch. I made plans to marry him.

One day at school I got an invitation to a birthday party for a girl in my class. I told Mother about it and asked her if there was a present I could take. I knew we didn't have money for presents. Mother said she would pick up a pretty coloring book to give her. I was so excited to go to my very first party. The hand-me-down box of clothes from Aunt Vera and Uncle Don's family had arrived the Friday before the party so I knew I would find something spectacular to wear. As Kay and I riffled though the box, we found a pair of pants that looked like they were sewn together like a patchwork quilt, but it was really just fabric that had been printed to look that way. They fit my legs tight all the way to my ankle and I found a pink button up blouse to match. Now if only there were some cute shoes. We dug deeper and there at the very bottom of the box was a pair of black patent leather slip-ons. A tiny black bow graced the arch over the top. Kay slipped them on. A perfect fit. *Dang!* I knew if they fit her they would be too small for me because I wore a size bigger than Kay. She handed them to me. "Just try them on. They're just perfect with your cute clothes. You have to wear them to the party. You can stand them being tight for an hour or so." I tried them on. They were so tight my toes hurt but I agreed with her that I just had to wear them anyway.

Ten noisy nine-year-old girls stood around my friend as she opened presents. I was having so much fun feeling accepted and normal I hardly remembered my shoes were killing me. When my friend ripped the wrapping paper off the coloring book I had brought, she exclaimed her delight over my gift. Then she open the coloring book to look at it and to my horror, the first two pages had already been colored on. She shook her head and looked up at me in surprise. My hand was covering my mouth and I said, "I'm so sorry. My little sisters must have gotten a hold of your coloring book before it was wrapped." I felt every eye in the room on me. Everything had been going so well. But I was never going to be a normal girl like all these cute girls surrounding me. Why did I think I could even try?

"That's ok, I have a little sister, too, and I know how they are." She smiled and reached down for another gift to unwrap. The redness in my face made me feel hot and my stomach felt like it was going to send something up and out. The beautiful cake sitting on the table in the corner of the room didn't look so pretty anymore. I just wanted to go home, take off my shoes and cry.

Lee was in first grade when we started school in Ogden. He struggled to understand why he had to go to school at all, when he just wanted to stay home and play baseball. One morning he came running back into the house from the bus stop. "Where's my mitt? I need my mitt. I can't go to school without it."

"You're going to miss the bus." Mother said. "Why do you need your mitt?"

"Because there is no reason to go to school if I can't have my mitt to play with at recess."

Mother found his mitt under a pair of jeans and hurried him out to the bus, waving to the bus driver who was not leaving without his little guy.

"Every day I think that more of your toes show up to say hi." The bus driver laughed, looking down at Lee's shoes, where two toes on each foot showed through the canvas.

"Yea, these here are my farming shoes." Lee said, punching his mitt with his fist.

"Well, come a couple months, those are going to be snow shoes." The bus driver laughed.

Miss Wilson, Lee's teacher must have been worried about the snow too, because one day Lee came home with a brand new pair of shoes on his feet and a note in his hand. He handed the note to mother and she read it out loud. *"I hope you don't mind. I noticed Lee's shoes were a little worn."* Mother sat down on the closest chair and pulled Lee up onto her lap. "What a sweet thing for your teacher to do." She hugged Lee up tight against her. "Now, you make sure you tell your teacher how much you appreciate these new shoes. You must whisper in her ear like this." She cupped her hands around his ear and whispered. "I love my new shoes. Thank you." Lee wiggled and giggled from the air in his ear.

"Now you show me how you will do it." Mother said.

Lee smiled and wrapped his small hands around Mother's ear and whispered back to her. "I love my new shoes. Like that?"

"Yes, just like that." Mother squeezed him one more time and set him down on the floor. She looked at his new shoes and then brushed her apron with her hands and went to the sink, her back facing us. She didn't do the dishes or anything. She just stood there and looked out the window.

The dirt road we walked to and from the bus each day was lined with milkweed bushes and we discovered that the plants were crawling with caterpillars. Bart told us that if we would catch some of the caterpillars and put them in a bottle, we could watch them turn into butterflies. After school we each got a quart jar out of the cupboard and ran back to the field, tore off a branch of the milkweed plant and filled the jar with leaves. We each gently picked off a caterpillar and placed it in the jar. There were six-quart jars sitting on the windowsill. Each day we carefully inspected the progress of each cocoon.

"I bet mine is going to beat yours." Lee poked at Roger.

"I bet not," Roger said.

We brought so many caterpillars home over the next few weeks that one morning at breakfast we looked up to see a cocoon hanging from the wooden rafters.

"Fara and me named her Maria." Four-year-old Helen announced, as we all looked up at the cocoon.

"Why do girls have to name everything?" Lee muttered.

"Because, girls are cute and sweet. That's why," Mother said, smiling.

We watched the cocoon over the next week, hoping not to miss the big event. And sure enough Maria slowly broke out of her cocoon, unfolding one wing and then the other, while we were all gathered around the table eating our bowls of pinto beans, like she had planned the whole show. Mother cleared the center of the table and lifted Helen and Fara up onto the table so they could get a better look. Swinging from her cocoon, Maria's black and yellow wings moved back and forth together. Then her body emerged.

"Wow, she is so beautiful," whispered Helen. "Is she going to fly away, Mother?"

"Yes, honey. She will fly away any minute now. Just watch," Mother said.

Maria broke away from the cocoon and fluttered above the table for a few minutes then headed toward the big window in the office. Helen and Fara ran after her squealing and laughing.

"Look, Mother. She knows how to fly!" Helen laughed.

"Open the door and let her out," said Mother.

Helen opened the door and we watched Maria fly away.

"I wish I could fly. Do you wish you could fly away sometimes, Mother? Helen asked.

"Yes, sometimes I think that would be lovely." Mother said, almost in a whisper.

We were only in school two weeks when Roger, who was in second grade, came home with exciting news. "My friend is moving. His house is going to be empty. Mother, don't you think we should move into his house?" Mother couldn't have agreed more.

"What's his name? I will call his mother tomorrow. We

really need that house." Mother said, grabbing a pen.

Mother called on the house the next day and rented it. It cost $75 a month and in her journal she confessed that she often didn't know where the rent money was going to come from. We moved out of the refinery the next weekend. Mother was so happy to finally have a home again.

The Red Brick House

It was a beautiful red brick house that sat on ten acres of neglected land just far enough from the street to make a great baseball field for us kids. Out behind the house was an old pond, full of frogs and pollywogs, hedged in by willow and sage-brush, a perfect place for boys to roam or do battle with the local Vikings. The house had a large living room with a big picture window facing the street. The three kids' bedrooms and a bathroom were on the east side of the living room. Mother and Father's bedroom, a bathroom, laundry and kitchen were west of the large living room, which became our gathering place. It's where we helped Mother set up the quilting frames and took our first big stitches. It's where Kay and I sat close to Mother while she taught us to crochet around the pillowcases we had embroidered. As a family we played hide the thimble, started the family band, put our arms around Mother as she taught us each how to waltz, and stayed up until midnight every New Year's Eve. One of the neighbors gave us their old TV and we lay on our stomachs every afternoon watching *The Mickey Mouse Club* with Annette Funicello, *Bonanza* and *The Lone Ranger*.

Mother's piano took its place of importance again on the east wall of the living room and we each started taking turns practicing everyday. Mother sat on a chair next to us, with a baby in her lap, counting, *one two three four, one two three four.* It was very important to Mother that we all learn to play the piano. Even the boys had to learn. It would teach us all about notes and scales so that when we learned to play an instrument we would already have the basics down. I soon learned that if I was at the piano practicing I could get out of a lot of work.

"What about Jelene?" Kay said, complaining. "Can't she help?" I began playing louder and faster.

"She's practicing." Mother called from the kitchen. "Go ahead. You can make the beds without her this time." I just smiled and kept right on playing.

Over summer vacation, Mother decided the living room floor needed to be stripped and re-varnished. Cheryl was home from school in Colorado City. We loved having her home because she always came home with new delicious casserole recipes to make for us. Now we begged Mother to let her make us some Honey Taffy as soon as we got the floors done. Bart took hold of the electric sander Mother rented and started sanding back and forth across the huge floor. After sweeping up as much dust and dirt as we could, Kay and I got down on our hands and knees and wiped the floor with a damp cloth. The next day Cheryl and Bart began to varnish. They varnished the north half of the floor, let it dry and added two more coats. When it was completely dry, we moved all the furniture to the newly varnished side and started on the other side. By the end of the week, we had a new shiny floor. Aunt Vera had been blessed with new drapes, which meant we received her old ones. Mother and Cheryl took turns standing on the step stool hanging our newly inherited drapes, black with very large red and yellow flowers. Standing in the kitchen doorway, Mother smiled. "Wow, now doesn't that look beautiful," she said.

The big front yard was the perfect size for a baseball diamond. Every Saturday afternoon after every sheet was changed and every floor was swept and mopped, we headed out for a nine-inning baseball game. The boys put pieces of wood around the yard where first, second and third bases should be. My brothers were huge Dodger fans and during baseball season, their baseball mitts were attached like body parts. They constantly oiled and rubbed their mitts, slamming their fists into the mitt to get them ready for that hard fastball. Kay and I were sent to the outfield. We couldn't hit the ball and we couldn't throw either, so we scrambled after the balls and threw as hard as we could to keep the game going. Our balls usually didn't even make it to second base.

"Geez, you throw like a girl."

I hollered back. "I am a girl, Stupid!" I loved calling boys stupid.

After the supper dishes were done, thirteen-year-old Bart grabbed the keys to our 1960 Rambler Station wagon and jingled them in the air at Mother. With a nod of her head, the rest of us followed him outside and into the car, three to a seat. Bart turned the dial on the radio and found the game. The Dodgers were playing the Yankees in the World Series. We just knew the Dodgers were going to win. Leaning over the front seat, we listened to the announcer's voice rise and fall with every play. We felt like we were there in the Yankee Stadium that night. The boys shouted out their approval for everything good and groaned with every defeat. When the last ball sounded against the bat, the Dodgers were victorious and six kids in Ogden, Utah, flew from the car, screaming and cheering.

In our bed that night, Kay and I could hear the boys in their room talking about the game, reciting it word for word, play-by-play, until their sentences grew further and further apart. The last one to speak was eight-year-old Roger, who finished with his best New York accent, "And the ball's outta hea!" I felt Kay smile.

One of our favorite things to do during the summers when we lived in Ogden was ride our bikes into the city and go to the library and a movie.

Roger started begging early in the morning, "Mother, can we go to the library today? Please!"

"Could we maybe go to the movie too, while we're there?" I added.

"I'll have to check and see if I have enough dimes for each of you." Mother said. Kay and I hurried to pack sandwiches and apples for our lunch in the park. We ran outside to check on the bike tires and make sure we each had a bike to ride. Bart and Keith were constantly sticking patches over patches to keep them all inflated.

Mother came outside and handed Bart seven dimes. "Keep them deep in your pocket." she told him. "The seventh dime is so you can stop at the market on the way back home and each get a piece of penny candy." She turned to the rest of us. "Please watch Lee and make sure you all use your manners." The library books we got two weeks ago were in the wire baskets that hung in front of my bike and Kay's bike.

"We're off!" Shouted Keith, the boys all trying to spit rocks off their back tires.

We had only gone four blocks east and we could already smell the huge puffs of putrid steam shooting out of the tall stacks at the Swift Meat Packing Plant that sat down in the railroad yard.

"Wow! That stinks." Kay shouted behind me and I nodded in agreement. Four more blocks and we were standing at the west end of the viaduct that crossed over fifteen sets of railroad tracks and then curved down, flowing into downtown Ogden. The Wasatch Mountains towered over the city like guardians, each peak crowned with sparkling white snow. We could see the tiny American flag blowing in the wind atop the Ben Lomond Hotel in downtown Ogden. Suddenly the earth began to vibrate as two yellow Union Pacific engines pulling hundreds of cars behind them came underneath the bridge. As I took in the expanse of the scene ahead of me, I couldn't believe how different this was from the farm in Idaho. Before moving here I had never smelled anything as bad as the Swift Meat Packing Factory. I had never seen a lady with a tattoo, like the one who worked at the grocery store near our house and I had never tasted anything as delicious as the pudding filled donuts Father brought home after his latest trip.

Bart, our big brother, protector and leader, got our attention by raising his arm up high and shouted over the cars whizzing by us on the street. "Everyone ready? Follow Me!" He didn't seem to have any misgivings about seven-year-old Lee's ability to keep up.

We sped down the wooden sidewalk that hung out over the train cars listening to the noisy wood planks clap together as we rolled over them. When we came to the end of the sidewalk, Bart waited for a big enough space between cars so that we could all make it down the hill together.

"Let's go!" Bart shouted. All six of us rode onto the street and down the hill with cars coming at us from the opposite direction. When we made it down the hill and onto the sidewalk we just kept right on pedaling. We sped down 14th Street to the grey stone library in City Square and parked our bikes. Bart led us to a table next to the fountain that sprayed water out of a fish's mouth. Kay brought the lunch from her basket and spread it out on the table. The boys each grabbed a sandwich and ate like they were starving. We shared a drink of water from the water jug Kay had hung on her handlebars.

"Even these dry old whole wheat sandwiches taste better in the city." I said. "Anybody for an apple?"

Bart sprawled out on the grass and bit into his apple with a satisfied sigh.

"When I grow up I'm going to have a ranch up in the mountains with lots of beautiful horses and cattle. I'll have a log cabin and a beautiful wife. What do you want to be when you grow up, Keith?"

"I want to be a famous baseball player and hit lots of home runs. Everyone will cheer and clap every time I hit a home run and the other players will hoist me up on their shoulders when we win. I'll be the MVP of the year. Roger how about you?"

"You stole mine. I'm going to be a famous baseball player," Roger said, irritated.

"No. You both stole mine," Lee sulked.

"Oh, you're all being silly," I said. "None of you know what you will be when you grow up. Only God knows that. But I think I'll be an actress. Someday I'm going to be on TV!"

"Like Queen Athena in the Hercules Movie?" Kay asked.

"Or maybe like Annette Funicello." I added.

"Now that's silly!" Bart repeated my words.

"Let's go get our books from the library," Kay said eagerly. "I can't wait to see if I can find the next *Nancy Drew Mystery*. Last time she found the map to the treasure in a cave. I can't wait to see what happens next. I think I'll take home four books this week."

We entered the huge open foyer of the library and fanned

out, each heading to our favorite sections. I followed Kay around until I found a book that looked interesting. She had a dreamy smile on her face, touching each book with her finger as she walked down the row of books. When she picked out the four she wanted, we went to find the boys. Bart was helping Lee find an easy book to read. Bart had two thick ones in the crook of his arm.

"Go get the boys so we can get checked out," Bart whispered.

"They're already up front," I said.

"Okay, let's go."

When we were outside, we looked up at the big clock built into the thick granite walls high above the library doors. "It's almost time for the movie. Let's leave our bikes here and walk the two blocks to the movie. We'll get there just in time," Bart said. Kay and I picked up the two bags full of books and followed the boys.

"I'm so excited," Keith said. "I love it when Hercules starts knocking things over with his big muscles."

"It's kind of scary to me sometimes," Lee said.

"You can hide your eyes if you need to," I told him. "That's what I do sometimes. I'll sit by you. Okay?"

The words, *Mighty Hercules* were printed on the movie marquee. We paid our ten cents each and walked into royal surrounding of the theater. I loved going to the movies, which was a rare treat, and losing myself in the story on the screen. My heart beat a little faster when I saw the way Hercules looked longingly into Athena's eyes. I knew that Hercules would keep her safe and conquer the world too. I was not disappointed. Lee and I only had to cover our eyes three times.

"I wasn't too scared this time, was I?" Lee said, proudly.

"No, you did good. Wasn't that the scariest when that three-headed monster came out of no-where? Did you see me jump?" I laughed. "Wow! That was great!"

We got our bikes and headed for home. This time Bart and Keith helped us pull and push and tug our bikes up the long flight of stairs because we couldn't ride up the hill on the street. We sped across the bridge toward home. We stopped at the market and stood in front of the boxes of candy next to the cash register. The same lady who was there last time stared down at us. She never smiled. I don't think she liked us. It might have been because we took too long picking a different piece each time so we could see what they tasted like. We paid our six cents and walked outside.

"Do you want to taste mine?" I asked Kay.

"Sure. Here, taste mine," She said. "Wow. That is delicious."

In two weeks we would return our library books. I was lucky if my book was read. But every book Kay brought home was read from cover to cover at least twice.

Sometimes I wonder how Mother dared let us go downtown all by ourselves. Sometimes I think she sent us because she knew kids needed adventure. Other times I think she was just happy to get rid of six rambunctious kids for a Saturday afternoon. Either way, I'm glad she let us go. Those are trips to the city I will always remember.

Mother's Cow

One morning, right after we got out of school for the summer, Father came to breakfast and said he was tired of buying ten gallons of milk every week and had a grand idea of how to fix that problem. He had talked to Mr. Fielding, the dairyman who sold us milk and also raised beets on his farm, and they had agreed that we, meaning us kids, would hoe beets all summer in exchange for a cow.

"You need a cow, Mother. There's plenty of free feed right out there." Father said, pointing out the window to the green grass surrounding the house. "We would never have to buy milk again."

I wondered if this grand plan to get a cow was all my fault because the week before, when Father was teaching me how to drive the stick shift in the station wagon, I popped the clutch so hard that the four glass gallon jugs all sitting together nicely in the back on the floor had banged together with such a clap that two of them broke, sending milk everywhere and filling up the back floor board. I had the privilege of cleaning it all up. From that day forward it smelled like sour milk whenever we went anywhere in the car. Maybe eleven is too young to drive.

Hoeing beets was nothing new for my Mother. She always said she was born with a hoe in her hand. She had six older brothers, all with hair as dark as the rich black soil they farmed in the Snake River Valley in Salem, Idaho.

Every summer from the time she was six, Mother picked bucket after bucket of raspberries and kept the weeds out of the garden with that hoe she was born with. She scrubbed the floors, washed all those boys' overalls along with stacks of dishes.

When she wasn't pricking her fingers on the raspberry bushes, Mother had them pressed down on the keyboard of the piano in the big front room of the old farmhouse. The two younger boys and two little girls born after Mother crowded around her on the piano bench and sang as she played *Cowboy Jack* and *Home on the Range*. Every evening after all the milking and chores were done, the big boys would join in with their trombones, trumpets, and clarinets. Music was a big part of their lives and so it became a big part of our lives too. Mother and Father made sure of that.

On the first day of our beet hoeing adventure, Mother left sixteen-year-old Cheryl and Janice, who was fifteen, home to watch the four littlest girls. And because she never asked us to do anything she wasn't willing to do herself, Mother piled us six middle kids and our hoes into the car and every hot day from June 1 to August 30, drove us five miles to the beet fields. We grabbed our hoes, waved to the hired Mexicans already at work, and started up the rows.

Bart and Mother each took a row with six-year-old Lee crawling behind Mother to get the weeds she missed. Kay and I took a row together, one of us hoed, the other weeded and then we switched on the next row. Keith and Roger worked together the same way. Back and forth, up and down the rows we weeded. Soon the boys got tired and grumpy and started throwing dirt clods at each other. That was when Mother said, "Okay, let's sing." We waited to hear her beautiful voice ring across the field.

"Lazy bones, sleepin' in the sun, how ya speck to get your day's work done? Never get your days work done, sleepin' in the noon day sun," she sang.

The Mexicans pointed at us and laughed. We went on singing because Mother went on singing.

By the end of the first week the blisters on our hands turned to tough, hard, calluses. The boys' noses blistered and peeled all summer long.

With sweat dripping into my eyes, I took Kay with me, far away into my daydreams. I dreamed of being with Father on the diesel truck. We would go to faraway places and see tall buildings in famous cities. We would stay on the tenth floor of fancy hotels and eat all the food we wanted. Everyone would treat us like royal princesses. Father would buy us our very own soda to drink. I could almost taste it, hearing the loud slurping noises we would make with our straws, sipping up every last drop.

"Keep movin', slow poke," Kay said, interrupting my daydream.

"Mother, can't we stop and have a drink?" I moaned.

"Sure. Everybody come," she gestured with a sweep of her arm. "It's time for lunch." We sat on the ground and ate Mother's homemade bread with a slice of cheese in the middle. We passed the water jug around to help wash it down.

Later in the afternoon, my arms hurt and my back ached and I hated my sister Cheryl. Why did she get to stay home with the little girls? I was eleven now and I could watch them as good as she could. She should be out here hoeing beets. She was stronger than I was. She was probably this very minute leaning back on the couch, sipping ice-cold lemonade from a tall, clear glass. I could imagine her slowly, meticulously painting her fingernails with the ruby-red fingernail polish Father forbade us to wear. She probably had the radio tuned to the station that played those bad songs Mother said had words in them that kids ears shouldn't hear. The babies were probably in the kitchen drinking Drano, but she didn't care. Each sweet delicious gulp of lemonade swished around in her mouth, the fan, propped up on the piano bench, blowing her long black hair away from her face. Life was really unfair, that's all. Truth be told, those were all things I wanted to do, but knew Cheryl would never do. She had been going to school in Colorado City, at the Academy, where she was learning to be a righteous Saint of Zion.

"Okay, girls, you start right here on this next row. I'm right here next to you." Mother called.

"Is it really going to take us all summer to get a cow?" I complained.

"Of course it is, miss Lazy Lu. Do you think we can have one for free?" Bart said.

"Now Bart," Mother said, "If you can't say something nice, don't say anything at all."

I could hardly wait for Saturday to come so we could have two days away from the beets.

Maybe this Saturday Mother would let Kay, Roger, Lee, and I take the big Red Flyer wagon over to the tall white Farmers Grain Co-op, just through the field from our house, to get wheat to feed the chickens. The farmers brought their wheat to the granary from the huge farms in the west valley. All the way over to "The Castle" we used our dustpans to fight off dragons and vicious knights of wicked King Henry. We were safe when we finally scurried under the barbed-wire fence and crossed the two-lane highway next to the railroad tracks.

We pulled our wagon as close to the railroad tracks as we could. Then we climbed under the railroad cars and scooped up the wheat kernels that had fallen out of the bottom of the train cars lying in perfect cone-shaped piles. We used our hands to brush every precious kernel into our dustpans before moving on to the next pile.

With our wagon full, we crossed the highway and back under the barbed-wire fence and became pioneers all the way home. Our imaginary children, all sick and in desperate need of a doctor, would be supper for the wolves that surrounded us and were being fought off by our brave and fearless men.

Saturday was the day the house had to be cleaned and polished to be ready for the Sabbath. The girls cleaned their rooms and the rest of the house. The boys cleaned their room, did the outside chores and played ball.

Mother sprinkled what seemed like a half a teaspoon of Ajax into the bathtub, the thick layer of soap scum daring me to scrub it off.

"How do I get this clean with a dot of Ajax?" I asked.

"Elbow grease, use some elbow grease," she said.

"What's elbow grease?" I asked.

"It's the grease in your elbow that makes it move back and forth."

"Why are the boys already outside playing?"

"Because boys are boys. And they are using their elbow grease to play ball." Mother laughed.

The next Saturday I got out of cleaning the tub. The week before, when Father had come to pick me up from playing at my friend, Kathy Minigs house, he began talking to Kathy's dad.

Before I knew it, Father told him, "We would be happy to

come and weed and thin your five acres of sugar beets. My kids are professional beet hoers. They do it all day, all summer long. They're paying for a cow."

Kathy was my best friend in fifth grade and even though she stole my boyfriend Brent, away from me, I still loved her. I was sick of hoeing beets and was not happy that I was going to have to spend my Saturday hoeing beets at my best friend's house instead of playing with her. Saturday morning, Cheryl drove Bart, Keith, Kay and I over to the Minigs field and we started down the rows.

The day was hot and muggy. Kay was crawling behind me, pulling out the smallest weeds I missed with my hoe.

"Don't get so close to me. I don't want to hit you. Give me some room." I scolded.

I moved on down the row, Kay following close behind. The next thing I knew, the hoe came down right on top of her head, cutting a three-inch gash. The sound of the hoe hitting her skull made me sick. Kay looked up at me with a bewildered expression, as if to say, "What just happened?"

"Oh, my gosh! I'm so sorry." I knelt down beside her, grabbed her and held her close to me.

"Cheryl, come over here quick! Kay's been hurt." I screamed.

Blood was pouring out of her head and running into her eyes. Cheryl and I helped Kay up and rushed to Minig's house and into the bathroom. Kathy's mom and Cheryl started cutting Kay's long hair away from the bleeding hole so they could see how bad it was. When Mrs. Minig saw how big the gash was, she said, "We're going to the hospital. Cheryl, take her to my car." Bart and Keith gathered up our hoes and we drove home to tell Mother and Father what I had done.

"I am so sorry, I didn't mean to." I sobbed, telling Mother about the accident.

"I know, love. Do you know which hospital they were going to?" Mother asked, looking worried.

"No, they didn't say."

"Well, all we can do now is put it in God's hands and pray that Kay will get the best care possible and be home soon." Mother put her arms around me again.

I tried to keep from crying as I set the plates around the long wooden table. I was sure I would die if anything happened to my sister. Kay was my very best friend in the whole world. Kathy was my friend at school but nobody could take the place of my sister. We shared our bed. We shared our clothes. We shared our secrets. To have a sister like Kay was the best gift God could have ever given me. She just had to be okay. I said a silent prayer to God and promised Him that when she came walking through that kitchen door, I would throw my arms around her and hug her tighter than I ever had before. I would never, ever be mean to her again. I would always give her first choice of the good underwear. I would always brush her hair for her without pulling on the rat's nests. I would let her wear my white blouse with the ruffles at the wrists and I would not yell at her when she got it dirty, which she always did.

I heard the car pull up in the driveway. "They're home," I yelled, running to the door. Cheryl and Kay got out of the car and waved good-bye to Mrs. Minig. Kay had a white bandage wrapped all the way around her head like a mummy. There was dried blood on her collar and all the way down the front of her blouse. I felt sick to my stomach. But the minute she saw me, she smiled and I felt better.

"How are you feeling?" Mother hugged Kay tight, like she'd never let her go.

"Are you okay, sis?" asked Father.

"Yeah," Kay said. "The doctor had to put twelve stitches in

my head. It will be a long time before this hair grows as long as my other hair." She pointed to where the stitches were.

"He had to give her a tetanus shot." Cheryl said. "Mrs. Minig paid the doctor bill. I told her you would pay her back next week." She handed Father a copy of the bill.

"Sixty-five dollars!" He yelled. "Why, that's outrageous! You should have just tied her hair together around that cut and saved me sixty-five dollars! It's not like you're ever going to see the scar. Sixty-five dollars!" He shook his head and walked into the house.

I wrapped my arms around Kay and gave her a tight squeeze. "I'm so glad you're okay. I'm so sorry."

"I know." Kay squeezed me back.

What was Father so upset about, I wondered? I'm sure he spent at least sixty-five-dollars on the twenty-five plain white lampshades, fuchsia pleated satin fabric, bags of black beads and bright pink fringe he brought home; the latest of his genius business ventures. He showed Kay and I how to glue the pink fringe and black beads on the top and bottom of each shade, after making sure the bright fuchsia satin that went around the middle was smooth and even. How about the time he went to the Smith and Wesson Surplus Store and bought seven Army gas masks so that when the Russians dropped the bomb on us, we would be the only survivors. At least, seven of us would be. I bet they cost him at least sixty-five dollars. And how was he going to choose which one of us was going to get to wear the gas masks? Maybe that's what he meant when he said, "Many are called, but few are chosen." I decided I had better start being nice like Kay.

One Saturday afternoon in late July, the boys decided they wanted to see how big the frogs were getting in the pond out behind our house. They took the arrows from their bow-and -arrow sets and waded out into the water. Kay and I sat on the bank, waiting for the show to begin. Spreading out into the willows that surrounded the edge of the large pond, the boys held their arrows high above their heads. Soon we heard war hoops coming from all directions.

"I got me a big one!"

"I got me a bigger one!" They sloshed their wet bodies up onto the bank and spread their catches out lengthwise to see who had caught the prize frog. Of course, Bart's frog was the biggest. He always won at everything because he was the oldest and the biggest. And even if it hadn't been the biggest, he would have somehow talked us little kids into thinking his was the biggest.

"You know how Mother says you can't waste things and you can't kill anything unless you eat it?" Bart asked. "Well, now you know, we have to eat these frogs."

"Yuck!" We chorused in unison.

"Heck no!" Keith frowned, "You ain't getting me to eat no frog!"

"Oh, come on," Bart said. "It'll be good. I read in school where they eat frog legs in all the fancy French restaurants. They say it tastes just like chicken."

Taking out his pocketknife, he spread the frogs out on the wooden raft at the edge of the pond and chopped the legs off all four of them. Then four soggy wet boys, eight frog legs, and Kay and I went to the back porch and called for Mother to come out. She stepped out onto the porch and surveyed the sight before her.

"Oh, mercy. What do we have here?" She said.

"Mother, look what we brought you," Bart announced proudly. "We were all wondering if we could fry up these delicious frog legs for supper. We want to see if the French people have good taste."

"Oh, I suppose, if we must." The corner of her mouth quivered to keep the smile in.

She placed the big black caste-iron skillet on the stove, and while the boys stripped off their wet clothes and had a bath, Mother showed Kay and I how to wash, coat with flour, and fry in butter, eight frog legs. By the time our French cuisine was cooked, the boys were spit and polished and sitting in their places at the table. Mother placed one crispy brown frog leg on each of our plates. Lee looked like he might throw up.

"Okay, you big sissies, I'll go first," Bart said. He lifted a frog leg to his lips and took a teeny, tiny bit. "Yum!" he exclaimed. "It's delicious! Now you try yours." He encouraged, with an elbow jab to Keith's side. All eyes turned to Keith, knowing the real truth was about to be revealed. Keith took a bite of the frog leg and chewed, slowly. His eyebrows lifted with the corners of his mouth and he smiled.

"Yep! You were right. It does taste like chicken!" The color returned to Lee's face and we all reached for our frog legs and ate a tiny bit of meat off a tiny little bone.

The long-awaited day when Mother's cow was to arrive had finally come. Mr. Fielding pulled his horse trailer into the yard behind his new Ford pick-up. Twelve brown calloused hands reached out to touch and caress the beautiful taffy-colored Guernsey cow as she walked down the plank and onto our dirt driveway. Mr. Fielding helped the boys tie the rope around her neck and the whole family paraded behind them as they led her down to the green grass spreading over the field, fed by the small stream running away from the pond.

"Can we call her Taffy, Mother?" I begged, stroking the cow's soft, rich reddish-brown-and-white spotted coat.

"She is beautiful, isn't she?" Mother glowed.

The boys anchored the rope to the fence and the cow bent

her head to eat the tall grass and drink from the stream. All the hot days of summer hoeing beets had been worth it after all. Now, we would have all the milk and cream we wanted from our own beautiful cow. That evening the boys took turns milking. The foam rose higher and higher, each stream of milk making a swishing sound into the bucket. Kay and I had the babies dressed for bed when the boys brought the milk in for Mother to strain into the pans.

"We'll probably get a whole quart of cream off this pan in the morning," Mother said proudly. "Maybe we'll even have enough to churn some butter. Okay, everyone up to the table to eat supper. Let's pray." Mother's prayer was extra-long that night. She prayed that Father would get home safe. She prayed for Grandpa and Grandma and all her brothers and sisters. She thanked God for her children and for the joy that each one of us brought into her life. She thanked God for the bean soup and the wheat bread set before us on the table. And, she thanked God for our cow.

Morning came and Kay and I dressed quickly so we could run down and watch the boys milk the cow. Mother was staring out the window in the kitchen, tears streaming down her face. Racing to the kitchen door, we looked out to see the four boys standing over our cow. We ran towards them, knowing something was terribly wrong.

"Taffy is dead," Bart said sadly.

"No, she can't be dead!" I proclaimed. "Have you checked her heart?" I threw my body down across the cow's middle, listening and searching for where I thought her heart might be. Not a sound came from her cold body.

"She got twisted up in her rope and fell into the stream and drowned." Keith's voice quivered, big tears fell over the freckles on his cheeks.

Mother came down the walk, dragging two shovels behind her. "It's going to be okay, sweet boy." She pulled Lees arms from around the cows neck where he had buried his face, sobbing.

"Is there any way we can save the meat?" Bart asked Mother, almost in a whisper.

"No, she's been down too long," Mother said, patting him on the shoulder.

Bart and Keith picked up the shovels and began digging a hole next to the cow. It took them most of the day to dig the hole big enough. We buried our cow.

On June 1st, the next summer, we found ourselves, with Mother, standing in Mr. Fielding's beet field, next to the same Mexicans, singing the same songs, working for a new cow. Her name was Jan. She gave our family many gallons of milk and delicious cream for years to come.

Those two summers, hoeing beets with Mother taught us more than how to work hard. She taught us how to laugh, how to cry, how to love, and how to sing.

Number Fifteen

"Sunday School is at ten sharp." Mother announced from her place at the head of the table. Each Sunday Mother gave us a poem or a scripture to memorize from her notebook full of poems and scriptures she loved.

The scripture she had chosen for me was Luke 11, verse 2, *The Lord's Prayer*. I copied it from the Bible onto a page from Mother's stationary notebook so I could keep it with me all week and get it memorized. It had been three weeks since she had assigned it to me and I still didn't have it memorized. I tried to remember where I had left it last. I went to my room and pulled out my treasure box from under my bed. I had claimed the old wooden apple-crate when we moved into the red house and no one seemed to belong to it. My most treasured possessions were in this box: The little five inch rubber doll Father had given me; who still had all her hair braided in long braids that fell clear to her feet. I took her out of her box quite often to comb her hair and braid it back nice and neat. I also had some beautiful rocks; some had veins of sparkling gold running through them, which I imagined were worth millions. I also had the insides to a music box my favorite cousin Peggy had given me. It still had the winder on it so I could wind it up and watch the metal parts bang together to make the song, *It's A Small World After All.* It always amazed me. How did they make it do that? There, in my box of treasures was the paper with my scripture written on it. I sat down cross-legged on the floor and read it through. I said the first sentence without looking at the paper, then the second, then the third. I thought I might be able to recite it without the paper this week.

The sun was shining hot through the south window when we all grabbed a chair from the kitchen and set them in a circle in the living room.

"Jelene, since you have the 'Lord's Prayer' as your scripture, why don't you open our meeting? We all need to have it memorized so we can say it by heart. Everyone close your eyes and fold your arms. Jelene, you say one line and we will all repeat after you."

"Our Father which art in heaven," I said.

"Our Father which art in heaven," they all repeated.

"Hallowed be Thy Name."

"Hallowed be Thy Name."

Bart was memorizing *Invictus* by William Ernest Henley.

Out of the night that covers me.
Black as the pit from pole to pole.
I thank whatever Gods may be, for my unconquerable soul.

Bart put feeling into his words and was good at memorizing because he went with Father on the truck sometimes and they would recite poems to each other to stay awake. Father loved to recite *Doctrine and Covenants*, verse 34-40, beginning with, *many are called, but few are chosen.* Then Bart would recite, *The Arrow and the Song.* by Henry Wadsworth Longfellow.

I shot an arrow into the air.
It fell to Earth, I knew not where.
For so swiftly it flew, the sight could not follow it in its flight.

"Keith, it's your turn," Mother said, interrupting my thoughts. Keith stood in front of the fireplace and without looking at his paper, he began.

"You Mustn't Quit. Author Unknown."

When things go wrong, as they sometimes will,
"When the road your trudging, seems all-uphill"
"When the funds are low and the debts are high,"
"Rest if you must but never quit."

Kay, who always had a book in her face, memorized easier than the rest of us. She had learned a beautiful poem by John Burton.

"I often say my prayers. But do I really pray."
"And do the wishes of my heart go with the words I say."
"I might as well kneel down and worship Gods of stone."
"As offer to the living God a Prayer of words alone."

Roger and Lee had both learned, *Be the Best of Whatever You Are*, by Douglas Malloch. "Okay, stand up straight and tall, boys." Mother reached over to straighten Roger's shirt.

"If you can't be a pine on the top of the hill,

"Be a scrub in the valley but be,
"The best little scrub by the side of the rill,
"Be a bush if you can't be a tree."

The little girls were next. Helen, Fara and Ruth stood up and Mother helped them. Two-year-old Ruth was just learning to talk. She looked up at Helen and copied her.

"Whoever you are, be noble; Whatever you do, do well.
"Whenever you speak, speak kindly. Give joy wherever you dwell."

"Very good. You cuties have that all learned." Mother closed our Sunday school with a prayer, blessing Father wherever he was today, that he would be protected and come home safely very soon. We loved Father and missed him but knew that when he came home, we would be blessed with another money making scheme and the peace that Mother was able to maintain in our lives would vanish the minute he stepped in the door.

There was never a time when Father wasn't making a deal or coming up with a new invention or idea. This included new ways to improve his children and give them a better chance for survival. One of the biggest influences on his ideas about child rearing was Harold Blackmore.

Father's friend, Roger Williams introduced him to Harold Blackmore on one of Harold's trips to the lower forty eight to visit with the Priesthood Brethren. Harold was a polygamist from Canada who married two of Roger's sisters, Gwen and Florence. He was a well-read college graduate who challenged Father to read and study the scriptures and to question every belief he ever had. Harold loved to talk about the Gospel, how to get to the Celestial Kingdom, and how to raise obedient children. He also shared how to save money by going through the dumpsters at Safeway, buying your clothes and shoes at thrift stores. He basically made a living out of being poor.

We met the Blackmore family early on in our polygamy adventure. I was only seven the summer we took a trip to Canada to visit them. They had a beautiful ranch carved out of the tall pines and ancient evergreens that shaded their lovely home. When we arrived, Kay and I quickly made friends with their girls, Brenda, Wendy and Marla and ran off to play house. There were chickens and goats roaming free everywhere and a tall fence to keep them out of the garden. They were self-sufficient; they planted it, they grew it, they ate it. Mother was enjoying her visit with Aunt Gwen and Aunt Florence. They were teaching Mother about the herbs they used for every kind of aliment. Mother had her trusty notebook and was writing it all down for future use.

The thing I remember most about the trip was the food. It was atrocious. The goat milk tasted like weeds. It was so bad I couldn't swallow it and my brothers and sisters were having as much trouble as I was.

Mother leaned across the table where she was sitting and whispered, "Just swallow it and I mean now!" Her lips were pursed into her, *'I mean it'* lips. So, we swallowed. The mush every morning was some kind of mixture of oats, barley and rye, with that horrid goat milk added in for extra flavor. The bread was two inches high and hard as a rock. I guess they didn't believe in buying yeast. It made Mother's one hundred percent whole wheat bread taste like Wonder Bread. And no butter. No butter? The vegetable soup we had for lunch and dinner had a strange spice in it that I didn't like but at least it didn't have goat milk in it. I would have given anything for a bowl of Mother's rice pudding that I hated because the egg whites were runny sometimes.

Not too far from their house there was a large pond, where they caught fish and baptized their children in the summer and ice-skated on in the winter. Kay and Keith were turning eight in August. It was July. Close enough. Father would baptize the twins and Harold would baptize his daughter on Sunday. But Father went on a motorcycle ride with Cheryl on the back, hit a hole and crashed the bike, injuring and scraping up Fathers knee so bad he could hardly walk. Cheryl wasn't hurt, just humiliated, because Harold's handsome sons her age were watching the whole thing take place. So, Harold baptized all three of the newest members of our polygamist clan.

The four days we were there we gathered every evening to listen to Harold recite the scriptures, church history and teachings of the Prophets word-for-word. Whenever he preached he could stir your soul to repentance. He was a strict disciplinarian and his own children feared him. He believed that when a father asked his children to do something, they should obey completely and immediately because their lives would depend on it when the wars and pestilence came in the last days. He believed that in a crisis, children must be completely quiet. Harold challenged Father to go home and teach his children to obey. Father took his teachings to heart. Little did we know that Harold would become Father's mentor and he would follow him the rest of his life.

When we got home from Canada, Father took his challenge seriously and the obedience lessons began. Every time two-year-old Ruth cried, it was teaching time. Time to teach her, and all of us, that when your father says, be quiet, we better obey. Two-year-olds cry a lot. They get frustrated. Crying is their way of communicating. And this two-year-old had a stubborn streak a mile long. Whenever Ruth began to cry, Father would ask her to be quiet and stop crying and when she wouldn't, he would hold her on his lap and press his big hand over her mouth and nose so she couldn't make any noise. She felt like she was being suffocated. She kicked and screamed, afraid for her life. He would let his hand off and ask her if she was going to be still and of course she was so scared she kept on crying. Then he would put his hand over her mouth and nose again. This went on until Father grew tired of it and let her go, warning her that this would happen again until she learned to obey.

Fear had never ruled our lives like it did the day the lessons began. Mother was always able to make us feel safe. Sure, we had times when we thought Father was crazy, but a harmless kind of crazy. This was something different. We feared that he might actually to do harm to one of us, a member of our tribe.

It was usually around the table at mealtime that we got to experience this torture and learn the lesson of obedience. I wanted to cry out and rush and take Ruth from Father but I didn't dare defy his authority. The acid came up from my stomach and sat in my throat and I swallowed it back down. Kay took my hand and I could tell that she was holding her breath just like I was. My heart pounded in my chest and I had to look away. The song came to my mind, *'There is Beauty All Around. When there's Love at Home.'* And then I thought, *Didn't we just sing that in Sunday School? You talk to us about loving each other and being kind to each other. This is not love. But I will be silent for now and soon you will be gone and peace will return to our home. Mother will reign again. There will be laughter and joy again. 'Just be patient'*, I hear Mother say in my head.

We endured this torment a few more times when Father came home from his truck trips and then it was over because Ruth stopped crying when Father was home. She cried when he was gone but not when he was home. Smart girl. That stubborn spirit inside of her helped her grow strong. But that time of torture, took a heavy toll on the love we had for our father.

There was one more reason we didn't want to pray too hard for Father to come home and that was because he would most likely bring home another job for us kids to do. One day he brought home twelve boxes of ceramic Japanese lady cigarette lighters. Each box held twelve ladies, each four inches tall, wrapped up carefully in a piece of white tissue paper. She stood in a beautifully painted kimono on top of a ceramic box that held a small holding tank where unpaid child labor, my siblings and I, could insert lighter fluid and then attach the fire starter that was hidden under the folds of her skirt. Father took us all downstairs and started setting out the ladies onto the tables set up for our work stations. He showed us how to carefully and gently take each lady and fill her with lighter fluid, insert the lighter mechanism. Then he showed us how to carefully repackage her in tissue paper and back into the boxes.

"As soon as you have these filled I can bring you more. We will make lots of money and maybe we will have enough to buy Mother a new washing machine. You know, like one of those automatic things so she doesn't have to wring them out anymore," Father said, encouragingly. I would have been happy to work for a washing machine for Mother, but somehow I knew that she would be using the old wringer washer for quite some time and I would be filling up Japanese ladies with smelly lighter fluid.

"Don't light a match down here whatever you do," Father instructed as he walked up the stairs.

On a hot Sunday in June of 1962, Father was home from one of his truck trips and he was anxious to go to church in Salt Lake City to mingle with the Saints and hear the Prophet's words of counsel. Mother was eight-and-a-half months pregnant and felt that she would probably go full term. She left Janice and Kay home to watch the little ones, the boys home to play ball and Cheryl and I got to go with them to church.

In the summer months, saints from all over the Salt Lake Area gathered at Brother Charles Zitting's home on 20th East and Cottonwood Creek Road. I loved going to the Cottonwood home because it was down in a nice cool ravine, surrounded by Cottonwood trees. The adults' spread their chairs out under the trees to listen to the Brethren speak while all the kids gathered to play hide-and-seek all afternoon.

In the winter months we met at the home of another one of Charles Zitting's wives near the Cottonwood home. They pushed the furniture up against the walls of every room in the house and set up chairs in every square inch of each room. There were speakers hanging from the ceiling so we could hear the sermons. Brother Marion Hammon would bang the pulpit while shouting the horrors of the coming great calamities, the end of the world and the Second Coming of Christ. Brother Holms would extol the virtues of Plural Marriage, encouraging the husbands to be better to their wives and the wives to be kinder to their sister-wives. Brother Jessop emphasized how important it was to teach your children strict obedience.

For some reason we didn't go to the summer place; instead, we were in the winter house that day in June. Mother sat next to me fanning herself with a piece of paper. They had just announced the closing song when I looked over at Mother and I could see her face was glistening with perspiration. Mother stood up to sing and then suddenly reached around me to grab Father's arm. Mother's eyes grew wide and I followed their eyes to the small puddle that was growing at Mother's feet.

"Let's go," Father whispered to Mother, taking her gently by the arm and helping her maneuver around the chairs. Cheryl and I followed, hustling to our car. Father was always a fast driver; most times when you were with him you would just say a prayer and tell God that if he wanted you to live, then he was going to have to make it happen, because you were now in the hands of a mad man. But that day he drove so fast I called on God and all the angels in all the heavens everywhere.

There were no freeways in Utah in 1962. Highway 91 went down Main Street in Salt Lake City, around the mountain by the gravel pit and then up through Farmington and Centerville, all the way to Ogden. We made it to Kaysville before we heard the siren behind us. Father said a few carefully chosen words, because Mother was present and then pulled over. The policeman walked up to Father's already open window.

"You know you were driving over the speed limit, don't you Sir?"

"Yes, officer, but as you can see, we are about to have a baby," Father said, pointing to Mother's belly. The officer took one look at Mother who had her hands pressed up against her big belly and said, "You folks just follow me and I'll take you right up to McKay Dee Hospital. Yes, you just follow me." We heard him say as he ran back to his car. The cop pulled out ahead of us and we followed him until he turned up toward the hospital, where Father stepped on the gas and kept going straight. I don't know what the poor cop did when he saw we weren't following him but he probably just shook his head and said, "Crazy people." We made it home and got Mother safely in her bed just in time for Beth, her fifteenth baby, to make her entrance into our amazingly crazy family.

Kay, Keith and I stood huddled against the door, listening for the baby's first cry. "Come on, Keith. Let's go out and hit some balls. This baby stuff is boring," thirteen-year-old Bart coaxed.

"No. I want to see him when he comes. It's gonna be a boy

this time. I just know it. Then we can play," Keith whispered, shushing Bart so he could hear.

Years later, I asked Cheryl what happened in Mother's bedroom after our wild ride. She said Mother wasn't nervous or anxious. She just let the baby come on her own. It was Mother's third home birth, but she had had a midwife with Fara's and Ruth's births.

"I think Mother thought I knew more than I did." Cheryl told me. "I had been living with Uncle Fred and Aunt Lydia, the town midwife, in Colorado City while I went to school but I was just a sixteen-year-old girl and didn't know anything. Mother never asked me to do anything. Father sat on the edge of the bed encouraging her and I just stood by watching. We were there if she needed us. Soon the baby just came out on her own." Mother went through each contraction without a sound. She knew that we were huddled at her bedroom door waiting the baby's arrival and she didn't want to scare us.

"Father and I tied the baby's cord with some dental floss and I helped Mother clean up the baby. Father took the placenta out and buried it in the back yard." Cheryl remembered.

Cheryl opened the door at Mother's request. "Okay, come in and see this new little one." We all burst through the door at once, noisy and loud.

"You are going to have to try to be quiet because our new baby in not used to so much noise," Mother said with her right hand up like she wanted to push us back out of the room. Cheryl shushed us with her finger over her lips and we stopped at the foot of Mother's bed, suddenly still. Mother had the baby snuggled in the crook of her arm and turned her so we could see her. She opened her blanket and took the baby's hand and pushed up the long sleeve of her nightgown. "Look here at her tiny fingers." Four-year-old Helen stood at the end of the bed.

Cheryl lifted two-year-old Fara and one-year-old Ruth up onto the end of the bed so they could meet their new sister. "Look at her cute toes. She has very long legs, doesn't she?" Mother chuckled. "Maybe she will be tall and beautiful like Cheryl." She winked at Cheryl. "Oh, yes and let's not forget this red hair." She turned the baby around and ran her fingers over her still wet head. "We haven't had a red head since we had Helen." Mother smiled down at Helen and Helen giggled. I looked over at Keith and I guess the red hair on the new baby's head that matched his own perfectly had won him over. The smile on his face let me know he suddenly didn't care that we had another sister.

"Everyone, let's give Mother some time to rest." Father said, from behind us. I didn't want to leave. I wanted to whisper in our new baby's ear and tell her she was very brave to come here and be with us.

Mother wrapped the baby up tight in her blanket and leaned back to rest against her pillow.

"Cheryl, can you fix the baby a bottle of milk? She's acting like she is hungry. Kay and Jelene, get the potatoes peeled for the potato soup?" Kay tugged at my arm and we turned to leave.

For the first four weeks of Beth's life, she thrived and grew strong. But then she began to throw up; a kind of projectile vomiting that would cover any near-by surface or bystander. Mother wasn't worried at first but then she realized Beth was throwing up every time she fed her. What could be wrong? Mother tried every formula at the store. She even found a goat farmer and bought goat milk to try. Nothing helped.

Mother made an appointment and took Beth to the doctor. After Mother explained to the doctor that Beth had been throwing everything up for a week he checked her out and told Mother that her baby had a telescoped intestine, or intussusceptions. A simple operation would make her as good as new. He would go in and open up the valve between the stomach and small intestine, that for some reason closes at four to six weeks of age in some babies. Mother was never as relieved as when she heard that her baby would be okay.

After the operation, Beth started gaining weight. She learned to smile and then laugh. Mother was back to her happy self. The rest of the summer would be spent singing. She had a stack of music on the piano she was excited to teach us. And every day we stood beside her as she plunked out our parts. *God Bless America, Heaven is in Your Back Yard*, and *When Irish Eyes are Smiling* and about one hundred more. Father had plans. He said fame and fortune were ours. We would be famous. He was already lining up shows for us to do at Christmas time. So we learned *'White Christmas'*, *'Silver Bells'* and *'Silent Night'*. It was Mother's job to get us ready. The show must go on.

ALL 14 OF US

for the Best in Entertainment

contact the

PEARSON FAMILY

1½ hour Show - Barber Shop Songs

Family Band - Trio - Group

Phone 393-5905

Holy Stockings

One Saturday, Kay and I were standing at the kitchen cupboard ready and excited to make a batch of oatmeal raisin cookies. "Read your recipe, and gather all the ingredients here on the cupboard and then we will start," Mother said, as she finished wiping down the cupboard around us with a wet rag.

I went to the five-gallon bucket that was supposed to be full of flour and found it empty. "Well, it looks like you haven't done your Saturday work yet. Is it your turn to grind the flour for the week?"

"Yes," I admitted.

"When you get your work done, we will make cookies." I looked at Kay and shrugged.

I walked into the pantry where the heavy wheat grinder sat bolted to the cupboard and reached into the hundred pound bag of wheat and found the tin can we used to scoop the wheat into the grinder. I flipped the switch to the grinder and began loading the hopper. The motor went from a high-pitched whine to a steady roar as I added more wheat. The dust billowed from under the small drawer that was filling with flour and filled the room, dancing with the light shining through the windows. The hundred pound gunnysacks of wheat, corn, potatoes, and pinto beans leaned up against each other in front of the cupboard. Every Saturday we took turns standing vigil over the faithful stone grinder, emptying the small drawer of finely ground flour into five gallon buckets so Mother could make bread. Then we would change the setting on top of the grinder and fill the hopper with dried kernels of corn for cornmeal mush.

Mother made nine loaves of dry, heavy one- hundred percent hard red wheat bread every day. Bread was our main source of subsistence. Wheat was certainly our staff of life. It was good if you toasted it and covered it with enough butter and jam or honey. We rarely had meat to add to the soup made of pinto beans, some carrots, celery and tomatoes. If we could get the chickens to squeeze out an egg or two, Mother would surprise us with the most delicious vanilla pudding, topped with a dollop of any kind of jam she had bottled during the summer fruit season. We loved her baked chocolate pudding, the rich chocolate sauce scooped up and over the baked cakey part. We also loved Grandma's Boiled Raisin cake with a thin layer of frosting.

I emerged from the laundry room looking like a ghost, dust covering my hair, my eyelashes and clothes. I carried the five-gallon bucket of flour to the cupboard. Now I was ready to make my oatmeal raisin cookies. I yelled for Kay to come to the kitchen and join me. We spread out the ingredients all over the cupboard and began measuring, sifting, and stirring. Mother brought the bag of raisins from her secret hiding place. Raisins were such a special treat that Mother had to keep them hidden from us kids or there would never be any for salads, cookies or cakes. I filled a cup with raisins, helping myself to some of those sweet nuggets, before dumping them into the batter. By the time the cookies were baked, half of the dough was in our bellies.

"What kind of treat do you think they will have for us when we sing at the Lions Club Christmas Party tonight?" Kay asked.

"We'll be lucky if we get candy canes or hot chocolate. They're not going to be serving a whole meal like they do when we sing at the LDS Churches."

Father had made appointments for us to sing every Saturday night through the Christmas season. Mother had been preparing for the show at the Lions Club, all week, pressing the boy's shirts and vests, making sure their dress pants were clean. She told us all to get our shoes scrubbed. Kay and I were sent to check our clothes and then to the little girl's closet to pick out their nicest dresses and make sure they were ready for the show. Our songs were perfect. We needed to look perfect, too.

That evening, Mother ran through the house calling out orders. "No, Roger. Keith help him find his red tie. It's Christmas, for Pete's sake."

Kay was struggling to get her garter belt on without it twisting in the back.

"Take it off and I'll help you," I said. I shook the twist out of the straps and held it up for her to put on. She turned so her back was to me, then reached her arms through each strap that went over her shoulders. She pulled the waistband strap around her middle and snapped it closed. We both hurried to put on our long white stockings, clipping them at the top of our legs with the garters that hung from the waistband. Next, we added cotton slips and then our best white blouses. "My skirt is getting a little short. It's up above my knees," I said to Kay. "Mine, too," she said, tugging down on the red pleated skirt she wore.

"Jelene, go help Fara find her black shoes," Mother yelled from the living room. "Kay, come and help me get these little girls dressed. Hurry up, we haven't got all day."

"I'm warming up the car," Father yelled across the house. "Everybody get out here."

Mother grabbed her music off the piano and all thirteen of us piled into the station wagon and headed into the foggy night.

"Looks like we have lots of moisture coming in off the lake tonight." Father chuckled. "Should be an exciting ride."

I hated how fast Father drove anyway, but the fog made it worse. He acted like there was no fog, and drove as fast as he always did. I had a bad stomachache when we finally pulled into the parking lot at the Lions Club.

Mother took her place at the piano and Father got us lined up on stage, tallest to smallest. I looked over at Mother and she looked right at me. She looked agitated, tugging at her skirt and mouthing something. I couldn't understand what she was saying.

The man with the microphone was announcing us. The curtain parted and there were one hundred people sitting around tables with red tablecloths and pinecone centerpieces, clapping and cheering. Mother started playing the introduction to *White Christmas* and we sang as though we had practiced it one hundred times, which we had. Bart sang the bass part. Keith sang tenor. Kay and Lee sang lead and Roger and I sang alto. The little girls joined in at the end of the line, singing and getting all the attention. People in the audience were laughing and pointing at them, amazed that they could sing, and stand there and behave.

The boys sang *Santa Claus Is Coming to Town* in four-part harmony. The audience laughed as Lee, who was seven, struggled to remember his actions.

Next on the program, Father brought out Helen, who was four, Fara three, and Ruth two. Father introduced them as the youngest trio in the world. They sang, *I Love Her and She Loves*

Me. The people cheered so loud, Ruth ran into Mother's arms ready to cry.

We finished the show with, *I'll Be Home for Christmas.* As the curtain closed, we bowed and the crowd clapped and cheered. I felt a surge of pride for my family and even though I got tired of practicing, when I was on stage playing my part in the show, hearing my brothers and sisters sing with me, there was a certain kind of sweet satisfaction. "That was fun," I whispered to Kay.

As soon as we got in the car, Mother said, "I don't suppose you girls could have found some stocking that didn't have holes the size of the Grand Canyon?" Her voice rose an octave higher in a single sentence, looking straight at Kay and I. We both looked down at our knees. Sure enough. Big holes. The size of the Grand Canyon.

"I was mortified. You looked like a couple of orphans, standing up there with holes in your stockings. I wanted to climb under the piano I was so embarrassed," she said.

"We're sorry, Mother. But these are the best ones we have," I said.

"Well, I'm sorry too, then. Next time we'll have new stockings," Mother said.

Father drove us home through the fog. I hated the way Father drove in the fog.

In Ogden we were known as a singing family, not a polygamist family. I'm sure Father passed us off as faithful, upstanding Mormons so he could get us gigs at the LDS Ward Christmas parties.

We looked like a good Mormon family. We didn't think we were anything special but it was quite a sight to see nine kids, one right after the other, from the age of fifteen to two. We loved singing at the LDS Church programs, because they always had a delicious meal for us when we were done. It was hard to focus on singing with the delicious smells of roast beef and country fried chicken, mashed potatoes and rich brown gravy wafting up onto the stage and making our mouths water. We could hardly wait until the final *I'll Be Home for Christmas* was sung so we could to go into the kitchen and fill our bellies with delicious Mormon food.

The night before our show was always bath night. Mother sent Kay and I into the bathroom to run the tub half full of water, strip the little girls down and get them all bathed. We let them play for a few minutes and then we started scrubbing. Laying their heads back carefully in the water, we lathered their hair with a bar of Castile soap and scrubbed their heads until they cried. Trying to get all the soap out of their hair was now impossible because they were screaming and rubbing their eyes. But we tried. We gave them a good rub down with a scratchy towel, squeezing every last drop of water out of their hair and then we combed and brushed and tugged at the matted mess until there were no more snarls to be found. The little girls were screaming again by the time we were through.

I dreaded washing my waist long hair too, because we couldn't afford to buy hair conditioner. Instead, we rinsed our hair in a sink full of water with a little apple cider vinegar added to it. It took the soap out but it didn't help the snarls. The snarls came out easier if I let my long hair dry first. Then I brushed and brushed until all the snarls were gone and it was silky smooth.

Mother insisted on putting our hair up in rag curls every Friday night, so we would look well cared for when we performed on Saturday. We brought the bag of rags Mother had cut into long strips of cloth and sat in front of her on a short stool. She took a small section of hair and combed through it to make it smooth. We held the rag up on top of our heads as she twisted the hair close together around the rag until she finished that strand of hair. Then she twisted the rag back up covering the hair and tied a knot. In the morning, when we unwrapped the rags, we had two-dozen springy, bouncy curls all around our heads. On Monday, the boys on the bus loved to pull on them and watch them bounce back.

I was eleven and way too old to have ringlets in my hair, like the little girls. I was the last one to sit down before Mother on the little stool.

"You were supposed to have all the snarls combed out of your hair already. Look at this mess," Mother said.

"I tried. But there are just too many," I said.

She tried to part my hair down the middle of my head, but there was a large rat's nest. She pulled and tugged. I twisted and squirmed.

"Go get me the scissors." She said, exasperated.

I couldn't believe my ears. Was Mother suggesting that she would cut off my beautiful hair? I didn't know what to say. I didn't stop to beg for forgiveness. I didn't ask her about the part where a woman's hair is her crowning glory and aren't we going to wipe our husbands feet with our glorious locks someday in Heaven? No way. She would never do it.

"Go on, get me the scissors." She pointed toward her bedroom door.

I walked into her bedroom, opened the top dresser drawer and found the long pointy hair scissors she used to cut the boy's hair. I walked back into the living room and sat down in front of her. She took a piece of hair in her hand. I heard the scissors slice through the hair by my neck and watched it fall to the floor. I felt tears well up in my eyes and tried to think how great it was going to be to not have those snarls to brush through any more. The mounds of hair grew bigger on the floor. My head felt lighter. Mother swished her hand through my hair and I shook my head back and forth.

"Okay, you're beautiful. Go look in the mirror and see what you think." Mother said.

I ran to the bathroom and looked in the mirror over the sink. I smiled. I frowned. Then I cried. Mother came into the bathroom. "You are going to love it when we get it all curled up cute." She wrapped her arms around me and squeezed me tight. "Come on, let's put some pink sponge curlers in right now and in the morning you will love it."

I did love it. Monday morning I went to school no longer the girl with the ringlets and braids, but the girl with the new modern hairstyle. I felt like the prettiest girl in the world.

Meeting The Osmonds

When Mother told Kay, who was eighteen months older than me about menstruation she decided to include me in the conversation, so she wouldn't have to repeat herself the following year. She also knew that Kay and I never kept secrets from each other and that Kay would spill the beans and tell me everything anyway. Mother began by saying that this information was for our ears only. She said we shouldn't talk to our friends at school about this, because their mothers would want to be the ones to tell their own girls. She proceeded to tell us that we were old enough to have our period and that our bodies would start to mature.

I was feeling pretty smug the day all the fifth grade girls were sent to watch the 'Maturation Movie'. I believed that I was the only one in the whole class who knew all about 'IT'. Looking into my friend's nervous, questioning eyes, I said, "Oh, yeah, my mother already told me all about it. It's no big deal."

Riding home on the bus after school, we were all leaning over our seats whispering to each other about the 'movie'. My friend, Kathy said, "I can't believe this. I'm so mad. We have to have a period every month until we're forty five years old!"

I couldn't breathe. "Forty Five Years!" I yelled. "You have got to be kidding me. I thought we only had to do it once, not once a month for FORTY-FIVE YEARS!"

The boys on the bus looked over at us and I stuck out my tongue.

How could I have gotten my information so mixed up? How could I have been so excited about something that was not going to be fun at all? I guess I had heard "once" and stopped listening. I certainly hadn't heard, "once a month" for the rest of my life! Now I knew why all my friends were so bummed out about the whole growing-up thing.

Kay slid across the bus seat to sit close to me. She put her arm around my shoulder. "Oh, come on. It won't be that bad," she smiled.

I frowned back at her. "I don't want to talk about it."

For years after I realized I was going to have to have a period every month for the rest of my life, I thought it was only fair that boys must have to suffer something of equally horrific proportions as blood coming out of you every month or God was not a just and fair God. I kept my eyes open, knowing someday I would discover what it was and that I'd be horrified and pleased at the same time. When I found that boys suffered from no such curse I felt betrayed.

I loved being a girl because girls could make other people, but boys seemed to be Gods favorite. The world was theirs to conquer. They could throw farther and run faster and eat more than girls. Parents were proud and pleased when they had sons. The more boys they had, the bigger their kingdom would be. Girls were ok, but girls just went off and got married and built someone else's kingdom.

Father was proud of his four sons and it was a good thing because all he seemed to be making lately was a bunch of girls.

He loved to take the boys with him on the truck and make them sing for everyone they met.

Father had a love for the wonderful, rich harmonies of barbershop music. He was attending a barbershop convention in downtown Ogden when he overheard the man next to him say to his friend, "Hey, did you hear that the Osmonds are moving to L.A.?"

"No."

"Yeah, they just signed with the Andy Williams Show."

Father butted in and asked. "Who are the Osmonds?"

"They are the young boys who opened the show here tonight."

Father left his seat and went back stage and asked around until he found Mr. George Osmond. George was a kind, gracious man and listened as Father went on and on about his herd of kids and how great they could sing and how he would love it if they could learn to sing barbershop. "Well, why don't you bring your family over to our home next Friday evening and we will sing for you and you can sing for us. That sounds like fun."

"Yes, that sounds swell," Father agreed. He could hardly believe his luck.

When the day came for our visit to the Osmonds, I hunted through the mess of shoes in the bottom of our closet and found the red high-heels and slipped them on my feet. They matched the red-and-white-stripped dress I wore. I didn't know anything about the Osmonds, but Father had mentioned something about boys. I ran my fingers through my short new haircut and smiled at myself in the mirror. *'Not too bad'*, I thought. I was already full-grown at twelve and I forgot that the red high heels would make me almost six feet of graceful beauty. Cat-eyed glasses included.

The first thing we noticed when we pulled up to their house

was how nice it was. The lawn was lush and green. We didn't have a lawn, not even a scrubby piece of one. The shrubs were manicured. I didn't think the lilac bush that banged up against my window, when the wind blew at night, was related to any of these shrubs. The big front porch was painted white and there was even a porch swing. The inside was equally lovely. Everything was immaculate, everything in its place.

Mr. Osmond welcomed us with a cheerful smile and Mrs. Osmond was just as kind. The kids were a little shy and reserved, but so were we. I was trying to stay up right and walk gracefully in my high-heels as I eyed their boys my age. When we all got settled in chairs around the room, Mr. Osmond went around the circle and introduced us to his family and Father did the same with all of us.

"Boys, why don't you sing a song for the Pearsons?"

The boys got up quickly and lined up without a word. The oldest boy played a note on the pitch pipe and they hummed their note and began singing. They smiled while they sang. They looked like they were having fun. I wondered if they were really having a good time or just putting on a show.

We all stood up and sang, *Heaven Is In Your Back Yard.* With my high-heels I stood a foot taller than my older brother Keith, standing next to me. I felt like the tallest tree in the forest. But we sounded pretty good and that was all that mattered.

"So, what should we do to get these four boys of mine singing barbershop?" Father asked Mr. Osmond.

"Well, Olive can get you some of our music and I'll asked my friend, Mr. Dean, who is our music coach, if he can come to your house and help you with the right sound and you'll be on your way."

Mrs. Osmond motioned to Mother to join her at her filing cabinet and she began pulling out pieces of sheet music. She told mother a little about each piece as she added it to the growing pile. We went home with a box of music and encouragement. After that, every time we saw the Osmonds singing on the Andy Williams show we fought to see who would be the first to say, "We know them. We went to their house and sang for them!"

The boys picked up the style of barbershop singing quickly. They were already used to singing hymns in four parts and trios with the family show. Mother spent hours helping each one of them by pounding out each part on the piano, and Mr. Dean came to help with the arm gestures and holding the notes out at the right times. Soon the boys were opening for the same shows the Osmonds had. At a Barbershop Competition in Sun Valley, Idaho, the boys were up on stage singing when Lee sneezed. His straw hat flipped off his head and he reached around his back and retrieved it and brought it back and put it on his head. The audience went crazy. They thought it was part of the show. Father spent any extra time he had promoting his family. We sang our show for high school programs, church and community events throughout the year and every weekend at Christmas time.

Sometimes Father's truck trips took him as far away as Chicago and he would be gone for weeks at a time. Whenever he took a load of potatoes down to California he took the four boys with him so they could sing for anyone who might advance their singing careers. They packed a few clothes in a suitcase and off they went. They could catch up on schoolwork when they got home. When they got to Los Angeles Father dropped the trailer at the warehouse and he and the boys drove off into the traffic. Father had the address of the building where he thought Andy Williams had his office.

"You boys stay here and I'll go in and see if we can get an appointment to sing," Father said as he parked the truck. The boys saw that they had been blessed with a huge parking lot next to where they were parked. They got out their mitts and began throwing the ball back and forth to each other. There weren't too many cars parked out there; no way would they ever hit any of them. Then they heard the crash as their ball went through a windshield.

"Dang, what are we going to do now? Father is going to kill us," Keith said.

"Father is never going to know anything about this," Bart said. "We are going to go find the person the car belongs to and tell him that we will pay for the window ourselves. I have some money saved from my candy machines." The boys memorized the license plate number and walked over to the other side of the parking lot to where there was a little building with a man in it and ask him if there was any way he could he help them find the man who owned the car that the number went to. They told him they were playing ball and had accidentally broken his windshield. The parking attendant looked nervously through a card file and called a number on the card.

"He'll be down shortly." The boys walked back to the car and waited to be yelled at. The man appeared and silently examined the damage.

Bart stepped forward. "We are very sorry we broke your windshield and we want to pay you for it. We promise that we will go home and work and send you the money until we have it paid off," Bart began his explanation. The man looked at the boys and the mitts still on their hands. He smiled. "Where are you boys from? I don't think I've met any boys like you before. Most boys around here would have just run off. They would never have stayed and then offered to pay for the damages. I like you boys. You have good parents. Let's just call it a learning experience."

"Well, at least let us sing you a song," Bart said.

"Yeah, we are going to sing for Andy Williams up there," Lee pointed up to the top of the building next to them. The boys sang *Yes Sir, That's My Baby* for the man and he shook each of their hands and walked back to work.

Soon after, Father came hurrying out of the building.

"We met the nicest man," Lee spoke up. Bart picked him up and squished all the air out of his lungs so he couldn't say another word.

"Are you ready to sing? Keith, grab your vests and shirts out of the truck. We will use the bathroom up there to comb your hair. Come on, follow me."

Andy William's brother, Danny, welcomed them into his large office. The north window filled the whole wall and they could see the Hollywood sign far away up on the hill. There was a metal heater under the window and Mr. Williams motioned with his arm for the boys to stand there as he sat behind his desk. Bart blew a B on his pitch pipe and they began to sing, *Hello My Baby*. In the middle of the song, Keith felt so at ease that he leaned back and set his elbow on the heater. When they got through singing the gentleman said, "Well, that was pretty good. At least you were relaxed." Father waited until they were inside the elevator and then he started yelling, "Relaxed? Is that the best you could do? Relaxed?" And the scowl didn't leave his face until the next day when they pulled into the driveway at home.

The Christmas Box

I was really looking forward to playing the clarinet when I got into junior high. Kay was playing the saxophone; Keith was playing the trombone and Bart the trumpet. Father had a beautiful black clarinet he played and I just assumed that I would get to take it to school with me to play in the band.

"Okay, Jelene," Father said, walking into the living room. "I got you a clarinet to take to school. Come here and I'll show you how it works. I love these old clarinets. I remember watching Benny Goodman play one just like this in his band."

"Who's Benny Goodman?" I asked.

"Just the most famous clarinet player in the world." Father exclaimed. He opened the long narrow case that was lying across his lap and pulled out the ugliest clarinet in the world. It was a tarnished silver color, with rust around each of the keys. It didn't come apart at the center, like his black one. It was all in one piece.

"Thank you?" I said, stiffly. But I was thinking to myself, *'Why do you always make life harder than it needs to be?'*

Father gently took a reed out of the side pocket of the case, licked it and tightened it into the mouthpiece. He took the clarinet into his expert hands and began to trill up and down the scale. He could make anything sound good. *'Okay, alright. At least it sounds good.'* I thought, wiping the frown off my face.

"You take this one to school and when you learn how to play well enough, then you can take mine." Father said. I knew there was no need to say anything and kept my mouth shut and trudged off to school with my ugly clarinet under my arm on Monday. When I got to band class, I sat down in a chair and pulled out my one-piece relic. The other kids opened their cases and began putting together their beautiful black clarinets. One girl looked over at me and made a face.

"What is that?" She said so loud, even the teacher turned to look at me.

"It's the very clarinet Benny Goodman used to play," I lied.

"Who's Benny Goodman?" The boy next to me asked.

I just rolled my eyes and shook my head. I picked up my clarinet and played the scale I had been practicing all weekend, my fingers tapping each key lightly and expertly. They were impressed. I was in the club.

In November, as soon as it got cold enough to freeze the hairs in our nostrils we started working on the ice pond in the front yard. We got as many shovels as we could find and took turns building a six-inch dike around a large circle, trying to make the ground as level as possible. Then we turned on the hose. It took hours to fill up our pond. The next day Bart turned on the water again to give the top of our ice-skating rink a glassy topcoat. We already had our skates dug out of the box in the basement, hoping that we could wear the same pair we wore the year before. Thank goodness Father was always bringing home used pairs from the thrift store, knowing that when winter came again it would be necessary for each of us to have pair of skates to wear. The boys set up the goals, which were three boards from the woodpile, set into the shape of rectangle without one side. Bart and Keith went through the woodpile and found us each a long narrow stick that would work for a hockey stick and threw a piece of two-by-four six inches long to use as the puck, out into the center of the rink and the game was on. Kay and I had finally found a sport where we could keep up with the boys. We pushed and shoved and elbowed with the best of them. Soon, we were shedding our warm coats and sweating like pigs. The neighbors could hear our cheers clear up the street when one of us managed to get the 'puck' in the goal.

When Father was home, he showed us how to skate backwards and do jumps. He learned to skate when he was a boy, having spent hours with his cousins on their skating rink. "You have to practice to become good at anything," he reminded us. When the snow fell on the pond, we scraped it off and built up huge walls of snow around it. We loved our time on the ice and were glad to have an empty Saturday afternoon when we didn't have a Christmas Show to perform.

One early Sunday morning I snuck out of the house to practice skating backward and I fell and busted my chin open. Father patched me up with a piece of white medical tape and told me it served me right for skating on Sunday and not keeping the Sabbath Day holy.

We hadn't celebrated Christmas since I was nine when we joined the polygamist group. Our prophet had told us that we shouldn't celebrate the world's pagan holiday anymore. But just because we didn't celebrate it didn't mean we could escape it. In fact we were totally immersed in it with all the Christmas shows we performed, the Christmas carols we sang and watching the neighbors put up their beautiful Christmas lights. Mother still read the story of Jesus' Birth to us on Christmas Eve, because she said the "words are beautiful."

"And suddenly there was with the angel a multitude of heavenly hosts, praising God and saying, "Glory to God in the highest and on earth peace, good will toward men." Mother held the Bible in her lap. We sat around her on the floor in our pajamas, ready for bed. It was nice to be out of school for Christmas break.

Ding, Dong, sounded the doorbell to the back porch door. We all jumped up and ran to the door. The porch light above the icy cold porch shone brightly over a six foot Christmas tree, nailed to a wooden stand and a huge box over-flowing with toys.

"Wow! Mother, it's a box full of Christmas gifts and a Christmas tree!" I shouted.

"We don't believe in Christmas," Keith said, softly.

"How did it get here? There's nobody out here." Kay said, looking out over the yard.

"Bring in the box, Bart. Kay and Jelene, you bring the tree. It's freezing out there," Mother said from behind us. Bart and Keith picked up the box and brought it into the center of the living room. Kay and I laughed at each other as we struggled to bring the tree through the door. We were so excited we could hardly stand it. Christmas at our house!

"Look, Mother. They even sent a box of ornaments for the tree." Kay said, setting another box from the porch down beside the tree. Mother, who was pregnant again, brought a chair from the table and sat down close to the box. "Okay, let's see what our kind neighbors have brought us." We sat in a circle around the box, breathless with anticipation. Mother leaned over her belly into the box and brought out two brand new dolls. She gave one doll to Helen and one to Fara. "Now, you share these dolls with your little sisters, okay?" They both squealed with delight. "Oh, look Janice. A pretty bottle of lotion and perfume for you and Cheryl." Next, she brought out a long package of cars and trucks. Roger and Lee divided them up quickly. There were bags of candy and colored popcorn, a brand new ball and bat, and four new baseball mitts. With each one the boys got more excited. Finally, mother pulled out two coats from the bottom of the box.

"I think these coats will fit you girls perfectly," Mother said, smiling. I had been wearing a hand-me-down from Cheryl that looked like it had been in a war and that new pink coat with white fur around the hood, meant the world to a prideful twelve-year-old girl. Kay tried on the blue one with black fur around the hood. Someone must have known our exact sizes.

"Wow, they are so nice and warm," I said. Kay and I grabbed each other by the hands and spun around together.

We spent the next hour stringing lights, carefully placing an ornament on every branch and hanging silver icicles on the tips of the branches. When the last sparkly red ball was hung and the electric angel crowned the top, Mother said, "Okay, everyone ready? Roger, why don't you plug it in?"

"Wow!" We all exclaimed in unison. A Christmas tree just for us.

That night I lay under the covers and listened as Mother played *Christmas Fantasia* and *Oh Holy Night* on the piano. Snuggled up next to Kay, I told myself if I ever doubted whether God could love a bunch of rag-a-muffins like us, I just had to remember the night He made Christmas show up on our back porch.

A Very Special Knot

"Wake up girls. I need your help." Mother's gentle shaking brought Kay and I out of a deep sleep. We sat up on the edge of the bed we shared, rubbing our eyes. Mother stood over us, her hand on her big pregnant belly.

"The baby's coming and I need your help," she whispered, turning back toward the door. I suddenly thought of how quiet Mother had been the night before. When we had ask her if we could play hide and seek she had told us all to "Go to bed!" because she didn't feel like having a bunch of noisy kids running around the house.

Kay and I tip-toped quietly down the hall, following Mother to her bedroom.

Mother got to the foot of her bed and suddenly stopped. She gripped the footboard with both hands and slowly lowered herself to her knees. She let out a slow, long moan. Then reaching under her nightgown, she brought out a wet naked baby girl and laid her on a blanket set out beside her on the floor. The baby flailed her arms and let out a little cry.

Kay and I stood frozen, staring wide-eyed at the baby and

then at Mother. '*Oh my. How I wish Father were here*,' I thought.

"She's breathing. She's perfect," Mother said, taking a deep breath. "Now, bring that bowl of warm water over here. You can wash her up a bit." Very gently Mother ran her fingers softly across the baby's chin, down her arms and over her stomach, where a bluish purple cord was attached to her belly button and ran under Mother's nightgown. The baby's eyelids blinked up and down, adjusting to the bright light above her.

Still speechless, Kay and I found the bowl of water Mother had prepared earlier. We knelt down beside the baby. Kay dipped the washrag into the water and wrung it out. Gently she began washing the white paste off the baby's shoulders and chest. The baby let out a wail.

"Oh, I'm sorry. Did I hurt her?" Kay looked up at Mother.

"She's fine. You are doing great. She needs to try out those lungs. But she might be getting cold. Jelene, bring me that little blanket." Mother covered the baby with the blanket and tucked it under each tiny shoulder.

"Now, hand me that big bowl," Mother said to me, pointing to the bowl behind her. She placed the bowl next to her and reached under her nightgown again. She brought out a large, bloody object and placed it in the bowl. Covering it with a towel, she said, "That is the placenta. It's where the baby grows and gets its food. We will bury that in the morning. She shivered and closed her eyes for a minute. Then she took a pair of underwear off the end of the bed and slipped them on over her legs. She sat down on the floor beside us.

"Now, do either of you know how to tie a square knot?" Mother asked.

"No." We shook our heads in unison.

"We have to tie the cord with a square knot so it can't come undone.

"Keith knows how to tie a square knot." I blurted.

"Go wake him up and tell him to come and help us." Mother waved me toward the door. Stepping from Mother's room, I felt I had stepped back into the real world. A world where I was a twelve-year-old girl, who went to school every day and talked about boys one minute and played with dolls the next. I didn't want to go back to Mother's room, where babies were made and born and laid out naked and crying on the floor. But I knew I had to do what Mother asked of me.

I tiptoed to the boys' room and knelt beside Keith sleeping on the bottom bunk. I shook him. "Keith, we need you," I whispered.

He squinted at me, frowned and closed his eyes. I could hear the other boys breathing in rhythm with each other.

"Keith," I shook him again. "Wake up, Mother needs you." Hearing the urgency in my voice, he quickly slid out of bed and followed me to Mother's bedroom. At the door, he stopped, frozen at the sight before him. Mother had the baby snuggled up against her.

"Keith, we need to you to tie a square knot around the baby's cord. Come on over here and I will show you where," Mother said. She laid the baby on the floor in front of her and opened the blanket. Placing a string around the baby's cord, up close to her belly, she said, "There, I think that will be perfect."

Without a word, Keith knelt down close to the baby, tied once, then slowly twisted his fingers just so, to make sure he had a perfect square knot. This wasn't just any square knot. It was a special one.

"Thank you, Love," Mother said. "You can go back to bed now." He didn't waste a minute getting out the door.

Mother took a pair of scissors and cut the cord an inch away from the square knot. She wrapped the baby up tight in her blanket, scooped her up and placed her in my arms.

"She's heavier than she looks," I said. I couldn't take my eyes off this amazing little creature.

"Yes, she must be at least eight pounds. Kay, fold up that blanket and put it in the washroom. I need to lie down." Mother climbed into bed. Kay took the baby and I propped Mother's pillows up behind her.

"We all better get some sleep now." Mother held out her arms and Kay placed the baby in them. She laid the baby on her breast and let out an exhausted sigh. She closed her eyes.

I looked over at Kay, worried that something was wrong.

I knelt down at Mother's bedside. "Are you okay, Mother?" I whispered.

"I'm fine, Honey. Everything is fine now. Thank you for your help. I don't know what I would have done without you girls. Now, you both go back to bed and get some sleep." She closed her eyes again and began to hum a song we had heard her sing many times before, *"When Whippoorwills call, and evening in nigh, I'll hurry to my Blue Heaven."* I stood in the doorway and didn't want to leave. I had just witnessed a miracle that was as messy as it was magical, and I didn't want to break the spell.

Kay took my hand and led me through the dark living room and hall, back to our room. We climbed into our bed and lay side-by-side, wide-awake, not saying a word.

The Chicken Coop

In her journal, in 1964, Mother wrote: "Wayne left the final decision up to me when we talked of moving to Colorado City. I finally decided we should go." Harold Blackmore, Father's friend and mentor had moved to Colorado City in 1963. I think it was more Father's choice than Mother's because it always seemed that whatever Harold did, we did. The Priesthood Brethren warned us from the pulpit that the evils of the world would befall anyone who was not prepared for the second coming of the Lord. Brother Marion Hammon, of the Priesthood Council, got up in church in Salt Lake City and told the faithful saints that they should sell their homes and move to Colorado City to help build up the Kingdom of God. Each family would be given an acre lot where they could build a home and plant a garden. It was a place of refuge from the wicked world. A place they could practice polygamy, free from persecution. Father and Mother felt that the Priesthood Brethren were honorable men and they were ready to show their faith by moving to Colorado City.

Bart was just starting high school, and Kay and Keith and I were attending Walquist Junior High School with fifteen hundred kids from the Ogden Valley. The 1960s were tumultuous times. In 1963, President Kennedy was killed. In 1964, the Beatles came to America with, what Mother called "horrid rock and roll music." The girls at school were wearing shorter and shorter skirts, which Mother considered absolutely scandalous and Bart thought they were just the right length. Protecting their children from the wicked world was uppermost on Father and Mother's minds. I think the mini skirt was the straw that broke the camels back.

Mother woke us early. We could barely see the new morning light out our bedroom window.

"Time to get up, girls. Finish getting all of your clothes into these boxes. We still have your beds to tear down and get into the truck." Mother said, starting back down the hallway.

Looking around our tiny bedroom, I wondered if Kay and I would ever have our own room again. "I'm really going to miss this house," I told Kay as we pulled the last of our underwear from drawers and threw them into a box.

Every step across the varnished oak floor of the big living room brought me closer to saying goodbye to our beautiful red brick house we loved so much. It's funny what a house can do. It gives you more than shelter. It gives you a sense of pride. It gives you belonging. It calms you in a storm and gives you a sense of security and safety that somehow blankets every part of your life, not just the stormy parts. It's home base. It's where your belly is filled. We could always find Mother there.

After living in an oil refinery and coming from the persecution in Idaho, this house had been like a warm hug. It had taken us in and loved us despite who we were: "Weirdos," "plygs," "apostates". And even though we tried to burn it down, blow it up and infest it with bed bugs, it didn't seem to matter to the red brick house.

Bart reminded me recently about the summer in the red brick house, when the June grass was a foot high and dry as a bone. It surrounded the house and covered the ten acres of undeveloped land behind it. The boys decided it would be a good idea if they just burned a small section in the front yard so they could make a better bike trail.

The fire trucks came, sirens a-blaze. Bart and Cheryl were able to keep the water hoses running full blast, wetting down the house and keeping it safe as the rest of the ten acres went up in flames.

We were lucky we didn't blow the place up filling the Japanese lady cigarette lighters with highly flammable lighter fluid that Father hauled down the stairs to our work stations.

We laughed about the used mattresses Father brought home from the thrift store. Soon after we got them set on the bed frames and fitted with clean sheets, Cheryl woke up scratching her skin off and decided to see where the bugs were coming from. She turned on a flashlight and followed a band of bedbugs from her bed to the doorframe; out the door and along the wall to the room Kay and I shared. The mattresses were burned, the bedrooms repainted and that was the end of the bedbugs.

We were about to leave these adventures behind, moving from a place that felt like home to the desert town of Colorado City, Arizona.

Everything was packed by one o'clock and we each grabbed a tuna sandwich Mother had set out on the counter. Eating as we walked out the door Kay and I fought with Janice for the front seat of the car. Mother was driving the girls in the car and the boys and Father would drive in the diesel truck. This was going to be a good trip, with room to spare and no boys fighting and jabbing each other all the way.

I looked straight ahead as we pulled out of the driveway, hoping that no one would say anything to make me cry. From the back seat Helen said, "Good-bye nice house. We love you."

"Yes. That was a lovely home. We'll have a lovely home again someday." Mother said.

Mother didn't seem sad. She even sounded excited. *'I guess if she can be excited, I can be excited too,'* I thought. We drove down the highway past the blue Wasatch Mountain Range, following the diesel truck that carried our belongings. We felt relief when Father finally pulled off the highway in Fillmore, as we had been complaining to Mother for miles about our full bladders. After the quick break, we climbed back into the car and got comfortable. The next thing I knew I woke up with my head on Janice's shoulder and Fara sleeping across our laps. When we pulled up the switchbacks east of Hurricane, Utah, we saw desert and cactus and tall red bluffs all around us.

"Only about thirty minutes." Mother said to the little girls who had just asked how much longer. We had been to Colorado City a few times to visit Cheryl who had been attending the 'The Academy' the last four years. We had stayed with Bill Cook, his two wives, and their families. Their girls, Janice, Jeanie and Myrna, were the same ages as Kay and I.

When we saw the beautiful orange Vermillion Cliffs jutting out of the sand to the east of us, we knew we had finally made it. Father pulled the truck off the highway onto the poorly paved road and we followed him into town. Mother zigzagged the car to miss the potholes that littered the thin pavement. I looked around at the huge unfinished houses, some looking like they had been added onto two or three times. "Why are the houses so big?" I asked Mother.

"A wing for every wife, I suppose," Mother laughed. Kay and I laughed with her even though we didn't understand why it was funny. Some of the big yards were filled with weeds and others well manicured. We drove all the way to the end of the street and then onto a dirt road that was lined with scraggly cottonwoods. The red mountains before us would be our new back yard. We were home.

Father backed the truck up to the front door of our new home, barely missing the outhouse that graced the front yard. Before us sat a tiny wooden house, which was actually more of a lean-to. There were four walls and a slanted roof that made it look more like a chicken coop than a house. '*Maybe someone started building a house and forgot to build the other side*?' I thought. This half house was the dwelling the Priesthood Brethren had assigned us. We would live here, crammed together, until we could build a house of our own.

I jumped from the car and ran into the house to inspect it. '*It might be better on the inside,*' I thought. It wasn't. There was an industrial sink and a stove against the south wall of the first small room: a big window in the east wall for Mother, who loved the morning sun. There was no door attached to the doorframe leading to the only other room in the house; a large room that would serve as the bedroom we would all share. A metal shower stall occupied the north corner, a ripped curtain hanging from one hook.

"Everyone grab something and help me get unloaded," Father yelled from behind the truck. He lifted the latch that locked the trailer doors on the diesel truck holding everything we owned. "Bart and Keith, find some tools and get the bunk beds put together first. Girls, get over here and get these mattresses hauled inside."

I grunted out loud, as I struggled with Kay's help to keep from dropping the floppy mattress we were carrying. "Mother, we want the very back corner for our room." I said.

"That's fine. Just start stacking your things over in the corner, then we will know it's your space." She had six-month-old Lillith draped over her hip and two year old Beth by the hand, to keep them from under our feet.

Cheryl was trying to stay ahead of us with her broom, sweeping the cement floor. Light from the only window in the big room caught the dust and made it sparkle. Kay and I left room in the far corner for our mattress and started stacking everything in rows in front of it. As soon as the beds were set up, Cheryl and Janice began nailing sheets from the wooden rafters to separate the space into bedrooms. Kay and I had our bedroom again, our own little spot. The boys had a room. Father and Mother had a room and Cheryl and Janice shared a room with the little girls. Life was grand. I sat on our bed with Kay and looked around. "This is not so bad after all."

"Yeah. Good idea, getting us our own space." She said, poking me in the side.

"Well, it's not as nice as our room in the red house, but it will do."

Soon we had the kitchen table and chairs and bench set up and sat down to take a break.

"Aren't we going to bring in the piano?" I asked Mother.

"No. This is no place for a piano. It will stay in the storage trailer until we get our new house built. Hopefully that won't be too long." She looked around her. "Girls, why don't you get the bread and cheese out of the box over there and make some sandwiches."

I was sick of sandwiches.

As a teenager, and a newcomer, I accepted Colorado City and the people who lived there, for what it was: a place where the people were dedicated to their polygamist way of life, where everyone was called Aunt and Uncle or Brother and Sister. They were just people who wanted to live their religion in peace. They became my friends and were like family to me. Over the seven years we lived there, I learned about the early history of this strange polygamist town.

In the early 1930's there were only a handful of families living and practicing polygamy in Short Creek, which would eventually become Colorado City. Early settlers like Fred Jessop, and his brothers, some of John Y. Barlow's plural wives, Brother Leroy Johnson, (who was the Prophet when we lived there), and his two brothers were barely surviving and had to travel elsewhere to find work. Leroy Johnson and his brothers went to Salt Lake City and offered their land in Short Creek to their Priesthood Leaders, John Y. Barlow and Joseph Musser, as a gathering place for the Saints.

In the early 1950's the U.S. Marshalls in both Utah and Arizona were prosecuting polygamists for breaking the law against 'Unlawful Cohabitation', sending the men to jail, and leaving their wives and children destitute. According to Benjamin Bistline, author of *"The Polygamists, A History of Colorado City, Arizona"*, on the morning of July 26th, 1953, the governor of Arizona sent an army of law enforcement officers into Short Creek... "to rid the state of the abomination of polygamy and law breakers who live it."

The Brethren were warned that the U.S. Marshalls were coming, but decided not to run. Instead they gathered the whole community to the church and began singing praises to the Lord. They believed that the Lord would save them from persecution. But the Marshalls had their orders. The men were gathered up and taken to Kingman, Arizona. The mothers and their children were taken to Phoenix and some of the children were put into foster homes. The people of Arizona turned against their governor when they saw what they were doing to the families and after state appeals and court decisions, the children were returned to their parents and they were all free to go home. But the fear that another raid could happen again was always present. And the next generations were taught to fear and despise the Government and those in authority.

Bistline writes that, "When Brother Hammon moved to Short Creek in 1958, he envisioned a beautiful, prosperous place for the Saints to thrive." As one of the younger members of Priesthood Council, Hammon had the authority and respect of the people, the enthusiasm and energy to take on this huge challenge, but he had a lot to do. In 1958, there was no running water in any of the homes, no electricity and no plumbing. Schools only went to the eighth grade, so the girls married very young. The dirt road from Hurricane, Utah, to Short Creek twisted up switchbacks on the side of cliffs and dipped through gullies full of red blowing sand. It wasn't until 1962 that the road was improved and paved.

Brother Hammon started a missionary program that required all the boys to serve a two-year mission. He put Edson Jessop in charge of the missionary building projects. If the boys were willing to work for two years for the Kingdom, they would be given a wife and a lot to build a home on. While on their missions they would donate all their time and money to Brother Hammon for improvements in the community. Brother Hammon knew he would not succeed without this free work force and often acknowledged them and their hard work when he was preaching on Sundays. The missionaries laid the pipeline that would bring water down the canyon and into every home. They were the force behind the establishment of Garkane Power Company. Brother Hammon was constantly asking the workingmen and fathers to give more money to complete these new projects. They could see that their lives were being improved for the better but it was a strain on their families. The next project was to build a Priesthood-run high school, 'The Academy'. The whole community came out to help make the red sand adobe bricks used to build the school.

Brother Hammon invited other polygamists from far and wide to help his community be successful. He asked Parley Harker, who owned a prosperous farm in Beryl, Utah, and was married to two of Hammon's daughters, to come and turn the sandy soil surrounding the town into a fertile community garden. Harold Blackmore, Father's friend, a prosperous home builder from the FLDS polygamist followers in Canada, moved down to help each family build a home they could be proud of.

Fred Jessop, who had lived in Short Creek from the early days, had been the community's organizer, coordinating work projects, town parades and picnics, and dance socials. He came to resent Marion's influence and the changes he was making to his beloved town. Uncle Fred decided to make a new town on the Utah side of Short Creek where he lived. He named it Hildale, elected a mayor and made himself the town clerk. Marion Hammon decided it would be good if the Arizona side had a new name too, so it would no longer be associated with the raid of 1953. He named his new town Colorado City.

The town was changing for the better, but when we moved there in 1964, it was still like stepping back in time to the 1940s or even the 1930s, when kids walked, rode a horse or a bike everywhere they went. Back to a simpler time when girls wore dresses and boys wore pants. Where television and radio were forbidden because they were worldly. A time when no one ever said, "There's nothing to do." There was always something to do.

Mother walked to school with us the first day to make sure we found our classes. Bart headed up the street to the Academy. Keith, Kay and I followed Mother as she took Roger and

Lee by the hand through the double door of the large adobe grade school.

"The seventh and eighth graders will need to head over to the white building on the north side of the school yard," the second grade teacher told us when she saw all six of us standing at her door.

Keith and Kay and I had come from a school of fifteen hundred students in Ogden. We were surprised when we walked up the six steps and opened the door to only thirty kids that comprised both the seventh and eighth grades. All the girls looked alike, their long hair braided neat and tight against their heads. Their homemade dresses of gingham cotton fell to the middle of their calves. The boys wore long sleeved shirts and pants; their hair cut short and neat. I was still growing my hair out so it only came to my shoulder. I had pulled it into two pigtails that covered my ears. My dress barely came to my knees and I pulled at my skirt to make it longer, but the kids didn't seem to notice and were all very friendly and interested in "the new family." Kay and I recognized our friends, the Cook girls. Janice, Jeanie, and Myrna waved with excitement when they saw us come in the door and waved us over to sit by them. Mr. Petty, the teacher, stopped his lesson, and asked us to introduce ourselves.

It didn't take me long for me to notice Norman. At recess I kept checking to see where he was. We were busy playing foursquare when suddenly there he was in the square across from me. I blushed. '*Wow. He is cute.*' I couldn't even concentrate enough to catch the ball, which flew right by me and I was out. I went to stand by Janice Cook and the girl next to her said, "Hi, my name is Alice May. I'm Norman's sister. We don't have the same mothers, but we live in the same house."

"Who's Norman?" I asked her.

"The cute boy you've been staring at since you got here," she said, pointing to Norman, who was still intensely involved in winning at foursquare. I blushed again. "Where do you guys live?" she asked me. I pointed south. "That way, a few blocks."

"Maybe Norman and I can walk you home after school, so we will know where you live and we can be friends."

"I would love that. It's nice to meet you, Alice May? Is it?"

"Yes. Meet you here after school."

There was nothing I didn't love about Norman. He smelled good. He looked good. He dressed nice. He had nice hair. I admired him all the way to my house and I didn't have to talk because I had collected my brothers and Kay for the walk home. Keith asked Norman if he had any horses and he said he did so there went the conversation. Boy talk. But I didn't care. I wouldn't have known what to say anyway.

I was a little apprehensive about showing them our house but there were a lot of houses along the route home that didn't look any better than ours. Everyone here seemed poor. But when we opened the door and Mother turned and smiled, it made everything okay.

"New friends, already?" She smiled and reached out her hand to shake theirs.

"Mother, this is Alice May Hammon and her brother Norman," I said, shyly. "They are in my grade at school."

"It's nice to meet you. How was your first day of school?" she asked, looking at each of us.

"It was great," Lee shouted above everyone. "We played flag football and there is not one of those kids who could get past me to grab my flag. I am the fastest kid in town."

Mother laughed. "Well, I am not surprised at all." She patted his head. "I made some cookies, they're on the table. Everyone have one and then get your clothes changed. We still have some boxes to unpack."

I handed Norman and Alice May a cookie. "It looks like you are busy. We better head home. We live on the other side of the creek, so we have a long walk," Alice May said.

"Well, thanks for walking us home. It was fun." "See you tomorrow." They waved as they walked out the door.

Over the next two weeks, I made friends with every girl in my class. I loved learning about their families, how many mothers and brothers and sisters they had. Sometimes they would even tell me which mothers they liked and which ones they didn't, and why. I loved learning about all the family drama. They invited Kay and me to come to their homes. It seemed strange to walk into their kitchens and see three or four mothers cooking and cleaning and picking up babies off the floor.

Church on Sundays was a new experience too. Men walked proudly into church with a wife on each arm, a bunch of kids toddling behind them. Some men had four wives, some seven. The Priesthood Brethren had as many as twelve. I tried to remember names and faces and who belonged to whom, but there were so many new and fascinating stories, so many people to remember.

I had only been in school two weeks when Janice Cook came up to me during recess.

"Go get the bell right now and ring it as hard as you can. It's your turn and it's time to come in from recess. Go now."

"Are you sure? Did Mr. Petty tell you it was my turn?"

"Yes!" She grabbed my hand and pulled me toward the classroom. She put the bell in my hand and pushed me to the door. I stood at the open door that looked out over the playground and began to ring the bell as hard as I could. Mr. Petty came from around the corner of the building and stomped up the stairs and into the room waving his hands for me to stop.

"Who told you to ring the bell? Did I tell you to ring that bell?"

"No. Janice told me to ring it."

"Janice is not the teacher of this class, is she? I am the only one who can tell you to ring the bell. You get your things and go home. You are expelled from class." He pointed toward my desk. "Right now! Get your things and go home."

I looked at Janice hoping she would be clever enough to come up with something to save my life or at least come to my defense since she was the one who had sent me over the cliff in the first place, but she was somehow speechless. A bunch of the kids had gathered at the bottom of the stairs, curious to see who Mr. Petty was yelling at. I was humiliated. I grabbed my jacket off the hook on the wall and ran out the door, passing my new friends. Alice May's face told me she was sorry and I loved her for that. I cried all the way home, where I threw myself onto my bed and sobbed. Mother followed after me and sat down beside me. "What on earth is going on?" she asked. Through my sobs I told her the whole story. She rubbed my back and told me everything would be okay. "All you have to do is apologize to Mr. Petty and I'm sure he will be more than happy to have you back in class." She helped me write an apology letter and the next morning I walked back into class and handed him the note. My hands were shaking. He read the letter and said. "Yes, you can come back to school. I think you have probably learned your lesson." I looked over to where Janice sat at her desk and the smirk on her face said it all. I wanted to say. '*Yes, I think I learned more than one lesson. Thank you very much.*'

Looking back, I think Janice was a little jealous of the new girl. I was getting too much attention and maybe she wanted to do something to put me in my place. In a world where there is never enough of anything you sometimes find yourself fighting the very people you are supposed to love. And it's not just about being poor and lacking the basic necessities of life. My family was poor but we were a different poor. We weren't emotionally poor. Mother didn't have to compete for Father's attention and love. She was happy, so her children were happy. So many of the mothers in our polygamous community were unhappy, so their children were unhappy. You can't help but be sad when you see your mother sad.

As I watched and learned over the years, I realized that in polygamy there is competition for everything. Competition for attention from your parents: too many kids. Wives competing for the attention of their husbands: too many wives. Not enough food. Not enough room. Not enough time. There is even competition between the men in the community to see who can have the most wives: between wives, to see who can have the most kids. Not enough love to go around. Not enough of anything, but jealousy, sadness and broken hearts.

A Night on the Mountain

Keith's new best friend was Evan Johnson, but everybody called him "Kabeezer".

He fit right in with my brothers with his red hair and freckles. When he was walking home from school with us one warm February day, Evan asked Keith if he wanted to go with him to look for arrowheads and Indian writings up on the mountain behind our house.

"I want to go too," Roger piped in.

"I've got to tell Mother where we're goin," Keith said as he ran into the house. "Do you want to come in for a drink before we take off?" Keith asked, sticking his head back out of the front door.

"Sure. I could use some water."

"We'll be home before supper," Keith called back to Mother as he walked out with Roger and Evan at his heels.

They hiked through the sagebrush and the sand to where the mountain jutted out and looked like a panhandle. They sifted through the sand for arrowheads and walked along the cliffs looking for Indians petroglyphs, but came up empty handed.

"Look at this big crack in the cliff," Keith said, pointing up to the red rocks. "We could climb all the way to the top pretty easily, don't you think? We'll climb up and then come right back down." The crags in the sandstone opened just enough for them to squeeze through.

"It will be faster than going all the way over to 'The Fish', where we usually go up." Evan agreed. Everyone in town knew what you were talking about when you referred to 'The Fish'. Mr. Barlow, our principal, took the grade school kids on the popular hike every year. A large chunk of rock had fallen out of the front face of the mountain in the shape of a fish, making it a well-known landmark.

The boys each found a foot hold in the sandstone rocks where a piece of the mountain had fallen away and before they knew it they were standing on top of the mountain overlooking the whole expansive desert plains. Red sand as far as the eye could see. Roger pointed to our house and Evan found his where it was surrounded by some trees.

"You know, that was pretty steep coming up at that spot, but I don't really want to try to go back down that way. Do you think we can find another way down?" Keith asked Evan. They walked east along the edge of the mountain before coming to a small sand hill. It looked like a sand dune that was sliding down the mountain but the closer the boys got they realized that beyond the slide was a sheer cliff. By the time they walked all the way along one edge and then turned and walked back along the other edge of the panhandle to where they'd climbed up, hours had passed and it was getting dark. "There's no other way down." Evan said.

"Well, I definitely don't want to climb down in the dark. Looks like we're going to have to spend the night up here. Do you think there are any mountain lions up here?" Keith asked.

"I have some matches and my pocket knife," Evan said,

reaching in his pocket. "If we build a big enough fire it will keep the mountain lions and the Gadianton Robbers away."

"What robbers?" Keith turned around to look at Evan.

"You know. The Gadianton Robbers in the *Book of Mormon*. Their ghosts live up here in these very mountains."

"H-H-How do you know?" Roger looked worried.

"My dad said so. In the *Book of Mormon* the Gadianton Robbers were a band of killers who fought against the Nephites. My dad said that their ghosts are holed up in these hills, still trying to fight against the righteous Saints today. And we're the righteous Saints."

"Ok." Keith looked over at Roger wondering if he believed Evan's tall tale. "Looks like we'll have more than mountain lions to worry about. Let's build our fire close to the edge, over here, so Mother can see the fire and know we are okay."

They gathered some small pieces of wood and then began stacking whole branches on top. Evan used his hand to protect the match flame from any breeze and the dry leaves they had laid in a small pile burst into flame. A large flat rock sat right in front of their fire like a bed; the boys lay down and looked up at the stars.

"I bet Mother's not too happy, about right now," Keith said.

"Yea, she's probably pretty worried about us," Roger agreed.

"My mom ain't worried about me. She knows I can take care of myself," Evan said.

Earlier that afternoon, Father had called Mother from California, which he very rarely did, just to check on her and the kids to see if everyone was okay. She told him that Keith and Roger had gone with their friend on a hike but she expected them back soon. Father told her he was bored and stuck in L.A. waiting for his truck to load and would call later to make sure the boys got back home safe. When he called a few hours later it was dark. Cheryl answered and Father could hear the sheriff talking to Mother. "Look up there." She pointed toward the mountain. "You see that fire. I think that's my boys."

"Okay, Ma'am. We'll go up to the bottom of the mountain and see if we can communicate with the boys and see if they are okay."

Cheryl handed the phone to Mother. On the other end, Father was in a panic. "What's goin' on? Do I need to get on a plane and fly home?"

"No, no. The boys are still on the mountain, but they have built a fire to stay warm. They'll be fine. And besides it would take you all night and tomorrow to get home. You'd have to fly into Las Vegas and try and find a ride all the way out here. They'll be fine. You know kids. They survive all sorts of things."

The sheriff, followed by five other trucks, drove through the bushes as far as they could go and then hiked up to the base of the mountain. The sheriff took out his bullhorn, "You boys okay up there?"

The boys had been watching all the lights and trucks coming through the desert toward them.

Keith cupped his hands around his mouth. "Yes, we're okay."

"We have some climbing experts here. You boys just sit tight and we'll have you down in a jiffy." The rescue team was already headed up the crack in the cliff where the boys had climbed up. But when they got to a certain point, they didn't have enough light to see how to get up safely.

Pretty soon the boys heard the sheriff on the bullhorn again.

"Boys, we are not going to be able to get to you tonight. Keep the fire going and we'll come up to you in the morning."

"Okay." Keith shouted back. He wondered if anyone could hear him.

"Let's go collect some more wood for the fire and try to get some sleep," Keith said. When they had a large pile stacked up beside their sleeping rock, the boys settled down on the large red flagstone and leaned toward the fire so they could stay warm. There was no moon, but the Milky Way seemed to fill the whole sky.

"Let's look for flying saucers," Roger said, pointing to a star that was blinking off and on. "Maybe that one over there is a flying saucer. What does Father's friend, Paul Soulam say? It's a flying saucer if it blinks red, then blue, then green?"

"Yea, I think that's what he says, but I think he's a little nuts myself."

"Well, Father believes him," Roger said, "so it must be true."

"Well, he does have a point. Do you really believe that we're the only ones in the whole universe? Look at all those stars. There's got to be other planets with aliens on them out there somewhere." Keith said.

Just then they heard a branch break in the distance and they practically jumped on top of each other. They sat perfectly still for a long time and then Keith got up to put some more wood on the fire.

He didn't think he had fallen asleep, but a few hours later Keith woke and shook Roger and Evan. "Guys, we need more wood. The fire is almost out." Evan rolled over and mumbled something about being too tired. "Come on, Roger. I'm not going out there by myself." They walked through the dark until they found a small tree that had fallen over. They pulled and heaved until they got it on top of the hot coals. The dry wood leapt into flames and Roger and Keith backed off to the back of the rock. Evan was sleeping with his feet facing the fire. Suddenly he jumped up and began dancing like a wild Indian. "Oh, my feet!" He screamed. He hopped and danced around the rock.

"Hurry!" Keith grabbed him and set him on the rock. "Let's get your shoes off."

Roger started unlacing his right boot and Keith worked on his left. As soon as they got the shoes off, Evan stuck his feet into the cold sand. "Oh, that's better." Evan sighed, relieved.

"You looked pretty funny dancin' just then." Keith winked at Roger. He held it in as long as he could and then Roger sat down beside Keith on the rock and they enjoyed a good laugh.

"I've seen you two dance with your family before and you dance like girls," Evan said, trying to even the score.

"Yeah, you're probably right. But we sing while we dance."

"You don't call what I was doing, singing?"

"No, I don't. But it sure was entertaining." They all laughed.

At the first sign of light in the sky, Keith woke the other boys. "Guys, I think we can make it down the way we came up. We'll just go slow and help each other and we can make it." They started for the edge and Keith began the descent. He talked Roger over the edge and Evan followed. They surprised the rescue team who were just starting up from the bottom.

"You boys alright?" The sheriff asked them. "You know, you need to be more prepared next time."

"Yes, sir." The boys chorused.

"Well, y'all get home now. Your parents have been up all night worrying about you."

About half way across the field, Evan's soles fell off his shoes. Just fell off. He sat down on the ground and held the soles in one hand and the shoes in the other. "What am I going to do?" He cried. "These are the only shoes I have."

"Come home with us and we'll see if we have an old pair you can have."

Mother was putting the oatmeal mush on the table when the three hikers walked through the door. "Oh, I'm so glad you made it," She said, throwing her arms around her boys. "Now, get up here and eat your breakfast. You can't be late for school."

"Mother, Evan kind of ruined his shoes and the soles fell off. Do we have an extra pair that might fit him?" Keith looked down at Evan's feet.

"Bart, go look through that box of old shoes under my bed and see if you can find that old pair of gym shoes. Hopefully they won't be too big for Evan." Bart left the room and came back a moment later.

"See if these will work," Bart said, tossing the shoes at Evan.

"Oh, good. They fit." Mother said, as she shooed us all out the door to school.

"Okay, tell us everything." I said to Keith excitedly, as we walked down the path to school. "That was a huge fire you guys had going. I think everyone in the valley could see it."

The oatmeal must have given all three of the boys a second wind because they all started talking at once, telling us the story of how they survived like mountain men. It was the first telling of the adventure on the mountain but certainly not the last. They must have told it a hundred times over the next week. Everyone wanted to hear the story of the night on the mountain. It got bigger and better each time they told it. Even to this day, Keith loves telling that story to his grandkids.

Our New House

The whole family was counting pennies so we could build our new house. Father had a good job with Hatchco trucking. Cheryl drove to St. George every day with a carload of women to sew tents at Hawthorn, an outdoor sporting goods factory. Bart and Keith hauled hay, cut cedar posts, and cleaned out barns to make money. The brethren had assigned us a two-acre lot on the Arizona side of town. We knew we didn't own the land. It was understood that if we ever moved away, we would have to leave the house we built and not expect to receive any money for it. It belonged to the United Effort Plan.

Finally, our new house began to take shape. Brother Edson Jessop, who was in charge of the missionaries had them there working hard every Saturday. It was two years before Bart would graduate from school and serve his two-year mission. But he and Keith were there beside Uncle Edson, pounding nails to build our walls and roof.

Father had decided we would build a Harold Blackmore-style home. Basically, it was a square box with a flat roof, and no hallways. According to Harold, hallways were a waste of space and lumber. In his home across town, every room, even the bathrooms, came off the great room, where the kitchen and living room were one large room. We did have one small hallway at the north end of the house that had doors to a girl's bedroom, a boy's bedroom, Mother and Father's bedroom and a bathroom. The large front door facing south onto the street, opened into a large living room that could be closed off from the kitchen and family room. The door on the east side of the house entered the laundry room and a smaller bathroom, and then into the kitchen.

Father found a heavy five-foot round oak table and built a Lazy-Susan in the middle. We put our food on the Lazy-Susan and turned it around to get our food. He also found some swivel chairs with turquoise vinyl seats that he attached to the underside of the table. It was like a very short carnival ride every time you sat down. It was a one of a kind table, kind of like Father. He brought home a huge black army stove from the salvage yard in Ogden and hooked a water heater up to it. Every time we built a fire in the stove (which was every day, even in the summer) we were also heating water for dishes, laundry and baths.

When we moved in, almost six months to the day we arrived in town, we still had to sheetrock some of the rooms, paint, and carpet the living room.

Harold Blackmore was a frequent visitor to our home, bringing food to help with the budget. He brought us bones from a butcher shop in town, covered in sawdust. Butchers spread sawdust on the cement floor to soak up the blood from the bones. Mother washed the bones up good and boiled them for hours to make broth. Then she added potatoes, carrots, celery and if we were lucky, maybe a couple of bottles of tomatoes. No matter how thoroughly she washed the bones we could still taste the pine sawdust. We called it turpentine soup and we ate it almost every day.

One day, Mother asked Kay to make a batch of noodles for the turpentine soup. Bart had just mixed up a batch of mud to do some taping on the sheetrock wall, and left a bag of powder on the counter. Kay got out a big bowl and cracked six eggs into it. She began stirring and adding her ingredients: flour, salt, a little more flour, just enough to make them easy to roll out on the counter, cut them into thin strips and let them dry a little before putting them into the soup. When we sat down to eat, we each took our first bite, looked over to Mother and waited. "These noodles taste a little different," she said, looking around the table at our expressions. "What flour did you use?" She asked Kay.

"That flour right there," Kay said, pointing to the bag of perfatape powder.

"Oh dear," Mother said, smiling. "That's perfatape powder. No wonder the noodles taste funny. Jelene and Roger, go get four quarts of peaches from the cellar and we'll make some grilled cheese sandwiches." We all silently thanked Kay for saving us from one more bowl of turpentine soup.

I never thought about it at the time but I wonder now what would have happened if we had eaten those perfatape noodles.

California Here We Come

As soon as the piano found its special place against the wall in the new family room, Father started finding places for us to sing. He still dreamed about us being a rich and famous singing family like the Osmonds, and he was not ready to give that up yet. Now that we lived in the country, we had to travel farther to do our shows. Father had a poster made with our family picture on it so he could pull it out and show everyone his talented family. When he was driving truck and he came to a town that had a theatre or a high school, he would stop and ask if he could bring his family to their town to do a show for them.

Father was willing to take us just about anywhere to impress the right person. We performed one weekend in Milford, Utah, on Friday night and in Delta, Utah on Saturday night. During the program I was telling my joke about the Priest, the Rabbi and the Mormon Missionary and when I finished no one laughed. '*Did I mess up the punch line or something*?' I wondered. Then someone booed me. I was humiliated and couldn't imagine how anyone could be so rude. It was funny the last time I told it. What was wrong with these people? I went right on and introduced the next act in the show, which was the family band and then I stomped off the stage.

After the show in Delta, an elderly gentleman came up to us and introduced himself. Father heard his name and they embraced. He had been Father's first band teacher in Rexburg, Idaho.

"Wow. To think that I might have had a tiny part of something this great, makes my heart happy," He said, looking around at our family and grabbing Father's hand again.

Among Mother's papers and letters, I found a newspaper article and a large picture of us in the "Glendale Independent" after we put on a show in Glendale, California. It read:

Singing Family Comes to Glendale...

"James Wayne Pearson, a trucker from St. George, Utah, called Nathan Hale of the theater last week, saying, "Our singing family wants to come to Glendale and sing for you."

"Come along," was Hale's genial answer.

Wednesday the 15 Pearsons arrived in a Pontiac Station Wagon and settled themselves with sleeping bags in the Doran Street Playhouse of Centre Theatre as guests of the Hales and the Allan Dietleins. Wednesday night, the family sang during intermission at the Orange Street Playhouse and made a big hit with the Hales and the audience. They usually sing with piano accompaniment by Mrs. Pearson, but with no piano in the theater, they sang acappella. In addition to their ensemble performance they featured a quartet of boys and a trio of tiny girls, and they also have a band. The red haired, freckled faced youngsters are personable, friendly and well groomed." Says Mrs. Hale, "And we enjoyed all 15 of them." After a trip to the beach with the Hales on Thursday, they headed for home."

1964 was an election year and Governor Barry Goldwater announced that he was stopping by Colorado City on his campaign tour. Brother Hammon quickly put together a program to impress the governor and his entourage. He asked our family to sing a song. Father was home that day and he was so proud and pleased that we were going to be singing for some very important people. We put on our best Sunday clothes and gathered with the elite of the town at the Academy auditorium. When our performance was announced, we all marched onto the stage and sang '*Too Many Chiefs and Not Enough Indians.*' We had actions and harmonies and the little girls were adorable. When we finished singing, Governor Goldwater could hardly speak, he was laughing and enjoying himself so much. When everyone stopped clapping, he stood up and said, "I don't think I've ever seen anything quite as wonderful as that." Then, looking at Mother still sitting at the piano, he said. "Can you just do it one more time for me?" Mother smiled and nodded. Then, turning back to the piano she began the introduction and we all stepped right into place and sang it one more time.

One day, driving down the road in his diesel, Father was listening to the radio and heard someone talking about the Arizona State Fair Talent Show. The winners of the State Fair Talent Show got to be on the Ted Mack Amateur Hour and this would give us national exposure. Father and Mother went over a stack of music before picking the song, *Give My Regards to Broadway*, hoping it would be a showstopper. We practiced hard every day. On the days Father was home, he stood us in front of him after school for what seemed like hours. "No. That wasn't good enough. Start again." Over and over we sang until the little girls were crying and needed to go to bed. Every note and every action had to be perfect.

We had to go to the first tryouts in Kingman, Arizona.

If we won there, then we would go to Phoenix for the State Fair Competition. We sang in Kingman on September 25, just wearing our regular singing outfits. We won! We were so excited about going to the State Fair. After watching the other contestants in Kingman, Cheryl and Mother decided we definitely needed new costumes. The State Fair was November 13, less than two months away. Mother went with Cheryl to St. George and picked out some nice blue fabric and a matching stripe for the girl's blouses. The boys would each have a blue jacket with matching pants, a white shirt and a tie. The girls had matching blue jumpers with pleated skirts and a blue-and-white striped blouse with a bow at the neck. This also included Janice, who never sang with us because she couldn't talk or dance, but she was in every picture and newspaper article as if she was just as important as the rest of us, all dressed up and smiling.

Cheryl soon realized that even if she and Mother sewed day and night, they were not going to have time to make all the costumes themselves, so she asked some of her friends in the community to help her. Uncle Grover and Aunt Cora, Father's sister, owned a shoe store in Rexburg. They were excited to help us on our way to stardom and told Father that they would outfit the whole family with black patent leather shoes. The costumes were perfect. Now we had to sound as good as we looked.

Every day when Helen got home from first grade, Mother gathered the little girls around her at the piano.

"Okay girls. You have a very important part in the show. You already know your parts really well but we need to practice a little every day, just to make sure it's perfect. Okay? Yes?" Mother asked. Helen (six), Fara (five), Ruth (four) and Beth (three), nodded their heads in agreement.

"Okay, go line up in the laundry room and as soon as you

hear the music, Helen will start marching in and you follow her and do exactly what she does. We won't be too long. Just five times through and then you can go play." Mother instructed. Kay took Lillith by the hand and helped her follow along.

"I don't know how we are going to keep her up there on stage with us but it sure would be cute if we could get her to do it," Mother said. She started playing the piano right before the key change they had heard a hundred times and right on cue they marched into the family room, left hand held high just like the big kids. "*Give My Regards to Broadway. Remember me to Harold Square.*" They marched and did their actions just like little professionals.

"Good, good. Okay, only four more times." Mother was gentle and never overworked the little ones, but they got so used to hearing Father say, "One More Time," that at one of our shows, in Cortez, Colorado, the little girls finished singing their trio and Fara called out, "One More Time!" The audience thought it was hilarious, but we knew better.

Some days it was dark before the boys finished their chores outside and could come in to practice with us. They were building a garage east of the house and putting up the fence posts for the corrals out back for the horses and cows. Father had just bought some baby pigs and Bart was helping him get the wire fencing strung around the posts to keep the pigs in.

"Keith. Take the diesel over to Fredonia and pick up that load of wood that's waiting for me." Father said, one morning at breakfast. "Bart and I will finish this pen, because tomorrow I have a load of spuds to take to California."

"I'm only fifteen. I don't have a driver's license," Keith said. "What if I get pulled over?"

"It's only twenty miles. What's the chance that there'll be a cop out there?"

Roger and Lee jumped in the diesel with Keith, ready for an adventure. They made it safely to Fredonia, backed up to the waiting trailer already loaded down with lumber and headed back home. Just five miles from the turn off to home, they saw the lights of the Highway Patrolman behind them. Keith pulled the truck off the road, saying, "Dang! We almost made it. Now I'm in deep crap."

"License and registration please," the Patrolman ordered.

Keith reached over to get the registration out of the jockey box and there was nothing there. Father must have taken it out of the truck for some reason.

"I'm sorry sir, but it looks like there's nothing in there," Keith said, a little panicked.

"Well, how about your driver's license? Maybe you have one of those."

"Ah, I don't have my driver's license quite yet, sir. My dad just told me to go over to Fredonia and pick up this here load of wood for him and you know we are almost home. We just live right over there." Keith pointed toward the red mountain cliffs. "Could, just maybe, could you let us just go home?" Keith didn't mind begging at this point.

"I don't think I can do that." The officer began to write on his tablet. "We're going to have to call someone to come and drive you home." Keith got out of the truck and followed the officer back to his car and radioed into the gas station in Colorado City. Keith knew one of the Jessop boys who lived across the street from us and worked at the station. He brought another licensed driver with him and came out to drive the boys and the truck back home. The officer handed Keith five tickets. No registration on the truck. No registration on the trailer. No driver's license. No back lights and no insurance.

"Wow. That's a lot of tickets," Keith said, biting his lip.

"Yes it is. I suggest you give them to your dad and I don't expect to see you boys out here anytime soon. Is that understood?"

"Yes, sir." Keith tried to imagine if there was any way to possibly soften the blow when he handed Father the five tickets in his hand.

All Father said was, "Damn." Five times. He called over to the courthouse in Kingman, two weeks later to see if he could get the judge to be sympathetic to his situation and drop some of the charges. When he got the judge on the line, he explained to him that he had a large family to support and a truck to keep running to provide for them. The judge pulled the case out of his stack of papers on his desk. He looked it over as they talked. "You aren't the Pearson's who were singing at the talent show here two weeks ago, are you?"

"Yes, Yes. That was us!" Father said, enthusiastically.

"Well, I just happened to be at that show and I watched your family sing. What a beautiful family you have. You know I think that someone who has a family that can sing like that can't be all-bad. I'm going to drop all the charges and let you go take care of your family. Try to get your registration caught up and all legal like. Will you do that, Mr. Pearson?"

Yes, there are good people in the world. One of them was Father's Aunt Birdie, who said yes, when Father called her to ask if all fifteen of us could stay at her house in Phoenix when we came to sing at the Fair.

The day for our trip to the Fair finally came and we were so excited to be in the big city of Phoenix. I couldn't wait to get out of the station wagon that held fifteen bodies and costumes and shoes. When I rolled out my sleeping bag on Aunt Birdie's soft-carpeted floor, my stomach had butterflies in it, thinking about performing the next day. As we left for the Fair the next morning, Aunt Birdie told us, "Now, don't you kids feel bad if you don't win, because there are some really talented people at the State Fair. Real professionals." I didn't care if we won or not. I was just excited to be there.

We were amazed at all the displays, carnival rides and the delicious food. I knew better than to ask for anything. There was no money for that. Mother had packed up a box of eight loaves of homemade bread and twelve cans of tuna. We found a picnic table under a shade tree and spread the bread slices with mayo. I didn't mind another sandwich this time. I was just happy to look around at this different world.

We found the stage where we would be singing and the schedule for the show that evening. We had a dress rehearsal and spent some time becoming familiar with the stage and coming on and off. Then we waited. We ate some more sandwiches and found a drinking fountain. Father came to the table with one can of Orange Crush and popped the top, took a big swig and passed it to Bart. He took a swig and passed it to the right. I was sitting in the wrong spot, the last one at the other side of the table. I knew there wasn't going to be any left when it got to me. I watched Lee take a drink and noticed how far he had to tip the can to get his sip. There was still a chance I might get a small taste. I took the can from Kay, who had barely tipped the can. I knew she was trying to save some for me, because she loved me. I took the can and tipped it all the way up. That one-teaspoon of Orange Crush was a real treat.

Evening finally came. We got dressed in our new clothes and shoes and stood backstage. When the act before us left the stage my heart was racing. Ten thousand people filled the arena and we were about to sing for them. Mother started playing her introduction and we started marching. Father led the first eight of us out onto the stage, left hand held high, singing and marching, looking very much like the Von Trapp Family. We sang the first sixteen lines of the song. Then came the key change and five little girls came marching onto the stage, lining up with the rest of us. Even eighteen-month-old Lillith, who had learned her part, toddled onto the stage, following her sisters. The crowd went wild. They were so loud you couldn't hear us singing. But we just kept marching and doing our actions and the little girls kept up with us. When we finished singing, we marched off the stage in precise order. Everyone, that is, except the baby. She stood there clapping and smiling ear to ear and that made the audience go crazy. Mother went over and took her tiny hand and walked her off the stage. We got a standing ovation. They clapped until we came back onto the stage and bowed and went off again.

The little girls were asleep by the time the judges began to announce the winners. They started with the tenth runner up and by the time they got to the fourth runner up we decided that we weren't going to win anything and Mother started marching us to the car. We were just about to exit the stadium when we heard our name announced over the intercom. "Oh, my heavens. We've won!" shouted Father. "Let's go back. Hurry." Mother, Father and Cheryl were jostling sleeping babies in their arms. We had tied for first place! Take that Aunt Birdie!

We tied with the 1965 National Barbershop winners, the Continentals. They won an appearance on the Jimmy Dean show and we won an appearance on the Ted Mack Amateur Hour. The next day our picture was on the front page of the Arizona Republic. The eight hundred and seventy-five dollar prize money would help us get to Los Angeles. The people in charge helped Mother make reservations at the Hollywood Knickerbocker Hotel, Los Angeles, California. She got frequent calls and letters reminding her to make sure we would all be at the Ted Mack Show on January 24, 1966 for the taping of the show.

I know I was old enough to remember that torturous trip to California, all crammed together in our Pontiac station wagon, but have somehow managed to block it completely out. So the last time I talked to Cheryl, I asked her, "How did we survive that trip in that station wagon to Los Angeles to sing at the Ted Mack Amateur Hour?"

"It was just like all the other performance trips. I always tried to grab a place in the front seat because I knew I would only be holding one little girl. When I sat in the back I had one on my lap and one on the floor at my feet."

Mother had our costumes in garment bags laid out on the bottom of the back of the station wagon, to keep them from getting too wrinkled. The boys got put in the back, stretched out over the costumes, blankets, extra clothes and Mother's bag of music. Mother and Father usually rode in the front with Janice, who was holding a little girl. Kay and I sat in the middle seat with Cheryl, who was holding more little girls.

Mother kept us busy playing games. We played the car game. We had to see who could be the first to yell out the kind of car that was coming toward us. "Chevy! Ford! Pontiac!" We counted telephone poles, sheep, and mile markers. We listened to Father recite "*I think that I shall never see, a poem as lovely as a tree,*" so many times any one of us could have recited the whole poem ourselves. We always asked Father and Mother to sing what we called their 'Church Song' for us, '*Oh, Divine Redeemer*'. With the windows down and the air streaming through the car, their beautiful music was shared with the birds and the weeds and the flowers along the way.

When we pulled up to the Knickerbocker Hotel, I couldn't believe how tall and glamorous it was. The doors of the station wagon opened and we climbed out of the car, stretching our limbs. The people on the sidewalk had all stopped, staring at us. I could hear them counting as more and more of us came out of the car.

"Yeah. There are fifteen!" I said, a little too loud and Mother heard me.

"That was not very nice, Jelene. You need to be kind."

"I'm sick of people staring at us like we're monkeys or something."

"What was I just saying in the car a few minutes ago?"

Mother had been reminding us the last few miles of the trip, "Be polite to everyone you meet and Boys! I mean it. Do not embarrass me". The first thing Roger and Lee did when we got to our rooms, was run up and down the hallway as fast as they could. Bart and Keith got Roger and Lee and the four of them rode up and down in the elevator so many times, they got scolded by the front desk and told to go to their rooms and stay there.

There was gold everywhere. Gold wallpaper, gold curtains, gold fixtures in the bathrooms. I walked around the room with Kay, touching everything. "Can you believe this place? Feel this carpet. It's so soft. I feel like a movie star." I whispered. "I wonder if Annette Funicello ever stayed here? Now we're as fancy as she is."

"Yes, I guess you're right." Kay grabbed my hand and pulled me through the door that connected the two rooms our family shared.

The next morning we heard a knock on the door. A man dressed in a black pants and vest and a white shirt handed some tickets to Father. The Ted Mack Amateur Hour was paying for us to go to Disneyland for the day. On our way through the hotel lobby, Cheryl stopped Mother and pointed over to the big over-stuffed chair where some men were talking. "Isn't that Red Skelton?"

"Why, yes, I think it is," Mother said.

"Wow. We saw a movie Star."

Never in my wildest dreams did I ever think we would get to go to Disneyland. But there we were looking up at Cinderella's Castle. We each took one of the little girls and jumped into the teacups. Next we climbed aboard the train and rode around the park. We stopped in at one of the theaters and watched the automated Abraham Lincoln giving his Gettysburg address. The music playing in the background was a stirring patriotic number and I tried to imagine that he was real. When we walked out into the bright light and onto Disney's Main Street, Father noticed the band playing in the center plaza. We followed him to where the crowd had gathered, listening to them playing a John Phillip Sousa march. Father waited until they were through playing and then he went right up to the band director and asked him if we could sing for the audience. The band director said, "Of course. We were ready for a break anyway." Father motioned with his arm for us to come up onto the stage. The band stepped down and we lined up. There wasn't a piano on the stage, so Mother hummed a note for us and we started singing. The audience smiled and clapped when they saw the cute little girls march on. We sang two more songs and then bowed and thanked the band director for the use of his stage. He said to Mother, "Happy to oblige. What a beautiful family you have." Father beamed with pride.

The small studio at the Ted Mack Show was nothing like the huge stage at the State Fair. A small audience was seated in two rows of chairs at the back of a large room. They were probably the parents of the other acts performing that day. We watched all the acts go on and off before our turn came. Mr.

Ted Mack introduced us and we marched onto the stage. At the key change, the little girls came on. Helen, the leader, turned her head to look behind her to make sure her little troops were all doing their parts. Everyone was amazed and cheered loudly. Lillith kept pulling up her dress and spinning in circles, delighting the audience, who laughed at all her cuteness. I got absolutely no camera time!

We did get an offer after the show, when some talent scouts came up to Father and Mother and offered to star the little girls in a movie. But my parents talked it over and decided they didn't want their children exposed to the wickedness of Hollywood. Suddenly Father was in a hurry to get home and feed the pigs. I'm sure we had someone feeding them for us and there was that thing called a phone but we headed back home to the simple life, back to the things we knew, the familiar: grind the wheat into flour, hang the clothes on the line, milk the cows and churn butter.

Father had worked so hard to get us to this place. He had triumphed. We had just performed for the world on the Ted Mack Amateur Hour. But he couldn't decide what he wanted. The conflict he faced was too great. Father wanted us to be famous but he didn't want us exposed to the world. He wanted to be a polygamist but he knew what would happen if anyone found out his secret. He couldn't give up control of his precious family. We were all he had. He saw no way to balance it all.

Watch the Pearson Family sing on the Ted Mack Amateur Hour.
Go to Youtube and search: Pearson Family 1966

The Academy

At last I was fifteen and old enough to attend the Academy. On the first day of school, I spent extra time pulling my waist long hair into a pearled barrette and making sure my bangs were pulled back into perfect waves. I was wearing the new dress Cheryl had helped me make from a cream-colored fabric printed with brown, tan and green sailboats. We hadn't realized until it was too late that I had cut the bodice with the sailboats upside down. Cheryl tried to make me feel better by telling me, "No one will ever notice unless you tell them. I promise." I loved the way the full skirt, (sailboats right side up) flounced out around my legs when I walked, my tricot slips underneath.

As Bart, Keith, Kay and I approached the Academy it was hard to distinguish the red adobe building from the red sand all around us. When I walked through the front door I could smell the deep earthy smell of the Atrium in the center of the building where the sun shone through the glass ceiling, sending light in every direction. The four large hallways surrounding the Atrium were attached to classrooms on three sides of the building. A large auditorium took three quarters of the east side of the building with a kitchen at the north end.

Everyone who went to the Academy was expected to attend choir every Monday and Friday morning at seven o'clock sharp. My heart was pounding with excitement. We could hear the youthful voices of the Academy Choir coming out of the open windows of the auditorium. "Shoot, I knew you guys were going to make me late," Bart said.

"Well, if we're late, so are a lot of other kids." Keith looked behind him at all the other stragglers coming in behind us. We hurried into the auditorium and onto the stage to join the choir. Kay pointed me in the direction of the alto section just as the song came to an end. Brother Newel Steed, the choir director, called on someone to say an opening prayer and then announced the next song.

Our voices rang out together.

Shall the youth of Zion falter, in defending truth and right?
While the enemy assaileth, Shall we shrink or shun the fight? No!

I felt my heart soar with pride. We were the youth of Zion. We were the future of God's chosen people on the earth.

True to the faith that our parents have cherished.
True to the truth for which martyrs have perished,
To God's command, Soul, heart and hand,
Faithful and true we will ever stand.

The previous Sunday, in church, the Prophet LeRoy Johnson asked us if we were willing to defend the Celestial Law of Marriage. "You young people must be prepared to defend the

Principle. It is a commandment of our Lord and Savior. It will bring you happiness beyond anything you can imagine if you will stay close to the Lord and live it honorably."

I prayed that I would be able to do what my Prophet asked. I wanted so badly to obey God and live the Principle of Plural Marriage because it would take me to the Celestial Kingdom where there would be peace and harmony. War and pestilence would not exist and I was hoping that also meant there wouldn't be any flies, dirty dishes, floors to mop.

Brother Steed brought me out of my daydream. "Welcome to the new students. You are welcome to use a hymn book for a little while, but I expect you to have all the hymns we sing often memorized in the next few months."

Brother Steed was an honored member of the community. He owned a beautiful ranch by Bryce Canyon and came back to his home in Colorado City every weekend to see his families who stayed in town where his children went to school. He led the choir Friday afternoon and again on Monday morning, before returning to his ranch. His first wife was a beautiful woman named Vilate. He then married three of her nieces, all sisters. They made polygamy seem like the perfect lifestyle. They had a house full of beautiful daughters and sons who sang for special occasions in the community. They were one of the only other families in town besides those of the Priesthood Council who were treated like royalty. Our family wasn't royalty: we were more like celebrities. We stood out and made a lot of noise, kind of like Father. We got to do things that kids in our community never dreamed about, like sing on TV.

I realized very quickly that there was a caste system in our polygamist community. The seven Priesthood council members and their families were put on a pedestal. Their wives and children had a sure path to Heaven just by their association with their righteous men. The rest of us would have to work a little harder. The Priesthood brethren seemed to always have the nicest cars, the nicest homes and the most wives. The more wives a man had, the higher his advancement into the Celestial Kingdom, where his wives would be queens. It was the highest honor to be married to one of the Priesthood Council. I was going to have to pay attention and acquire all the traits of a perfect woman so I could be one of the chosen ones. As I stood there singing, Eliza R. Snow's words from the hymn, *Awake Ye Saints of God, Awake!,* I felt the thrill of belonging to Saints of God and believed with all my soul that I could someday be married to a Prophet.

After choir, Kay took my hand and led me into the hall so we could find ourselves a locker. The lockers were wooden boxes without doors or locks, fifteen inches by twelve, set at eye level and hung along each wall and down every hallway. We were on the honor system. One hundred and fifty students comprised ninth through twelfth grades. Each student paid one hundred and fifty dollars a year for tuition. Bart was a senior and Kay and Keith were sophomores. Kay had told me ahead of time which teachers I would like and which ones I would not like. She didn't like Mr. Bradshaw, who was the math, science and biology teacher as well as principal of the school. She just couldn't understand the concept that X plus Y could somehow equal C. Come to find out neither could I. I was happy to receive a C- in algebra, the lowest grade you could get and still pass at the Academy. The only thing I remember about biology is that one day Mr. Bradshaw asked the class why we liked toasted bread better than plain bread. I was the only one with my hand up. He called on me.

"Because toasting it makes it sweeter," I said proudly, remembering the fact that Mother had told us at breakfast that morning.

"Yes, Jelene is right. It's called the Malliard reaction, where the amino acids and sugars unite in a form of non-enzymatic browning giving it a caramel-like taste, which makes the toast taste sweeter." I stopped listening at amino acids. I got a C- in biology too.

I loved my English, history, and typing classes. And I especially loved Veda Johnson's sewing class. Every girl was required to take three years of sewing. A senior year tailoring class was optional. The boys were required to take four years of shop.

I wanted to be just like Veda. She was the Prophet's seventh wife out of fifteen. She carried herself with such elegance and poise. I thought she was the perfect polygamist wife. Sure, she came across as a little uppity. But she was special and she deserved to be uppity. She was also one of the youngest children of John Y. Barlow, a revered Prophet from years' past. Her black hair was pulled into a lovely soft bun and she wore beautifully tailored skirts and blouses, which she made herself.

Kay didn't like Veda because she thought she was mean. She wasn't mean, not really. She was just fastidious and she made us unpick anything that wasn't up to her standards. Any puckers, tucks or crooked seams had to be unpicked and re-sewn until it passed her inspection.

The moment I stepped across the threshold of the Academy's front door, I let go of my childish ways and became very serious about becoming the perfect polygamist wife. I couldn't take lessons from Mother because she didn't live the Celestial Law of Plural Marriage yet, so I watched the polygamist wives around me. If I followed Veda's example, she could show me how to give up all my jealousies and show only love to my sister-wives, the goal of every polygamist wife. It's funny that I thought she was the perfect polygamist wife when actually she was far from the ordinary polygamist wife. She was married to the Prophet who was forty years her senior and too old to give her children. The last five of Prophet Johnson's wives never had children. I'm sure Veda and her young sister-wives were broken hearted knowing they would never have a baby while watching all the other women in the community have too many. Of course they looked perfect all the time because they never had throw up down their backs or breast milk staining their blouses or spent all those sleepless night with sick babies. But I'm positive they would have given almost anything just to have one child of their own.

Fridays were special days in sewing class. We brought our embroidering or crocheting to class to work on. We gathered our chairs in a semi-circle around Veda's desk, and she read us stories that she had written. Thrilling pioneer stories about the Saints crossing the plains, fleeing persecution from the mobs of Missouri. We fell in love with each hero and heroine and their families, each with at least three wives and lots of children. The personal struggles they endured trying to feed their family, as well as find time to be alone with their husband without jealousy towards the other wives, made me wonder if I could do the same.

One Friday after our story, Veda said it was time for us to start preparing for our roles as wives of faithful Priesthood holders by wearing long underwear. They wouldn't have the sacred markings like our parents' long garments, but wearing them would help us be modest and keep ourselves pure until the day when we were given in marriage to the man that the Prophet would assign us to.

Kay and I went home and told mother what Veda had said. I was surprised but pleased that Mother agreed with Veda. The first day I wore my long underwear to school, I felt like I was part of the Righteous Girl Club. The arm-length, long-legged cotton union suit was hot and uncomfortable but I was willing to do just about anything to be considered one of the chosen in Veda's eyes. Now everything I wore had to be long sleeved. My dresses hung to the middle of my calves. I wore my bra on top of the underwear so it could be next to my skin, the armor of God protecting me. I stretched and pulled my girdle over my underwear, up my legs and up to my waist. My girdle had two garters in the front and two in the back to clip to my long nylons I wore over my long underwear. I tried to pull the bottom of the legs of my long underwear around my ankles and only tuck them at the inside of my ankle as I worked the nylons up my legs. It was like wearing a full body chastity belt.

Going to the bathroom was quite a process. Especially when I had my period. I had a notebook in my top drawer with the date of my last period written down. I counted twenty-eight days ahead and wrote down the date, so I was always prepared. Reaching into Mother's bottom drawer, I pulled out an arm full of old white t-shirts she had collected for us girls to use. I could never figure out where she got them all, but there seemed to be a never-ending supply, thank goodness. I took the t-shirts to my bed and spread the first one out, then began to cut it up into eight-inch strips. I cut the softest pieces a little longer than the others and began to construct my pads. Folding some shorter strips together I made the center of the pad and then wrapped the soft pieces over them. The long pieces would be pinned to my panties with safety pins to keep the pad in place. Beside the fact that I spent the first day of every period curled up in my bed writhing with the pain of horrible cramps because Mother didn't believe in using aspirin, these pads were like walking around with a blanket between my legs. At least we didn't have to soak and reuse them like Mother did when she was a girl.

One Saturday, I was on window washing duty with Cheryl. She took the outside and I washed the inside. We were in the girls' bedroom and I was looking out through the glass when I noticed Cheryl was smiling. '*What could she be smiling at?*' I wondered. I kept watching her and she kept smiling, oblivious to my stares. I reached for the latch and opened the window.

"What are you so happy about?" I asked her.

"None of your business," she said.

"Well, you better stop smiling because I can't wash windows with someone who is happy."

"Okay, I'll try." She laughed.

The next day we gathered for Sunday school and Father announced that Cheryl was getting married. The Prophet had assigned her to marry Hyrum Jeffs, the son of Brother Rulon Jeffs, one of the seven Councilors. Father didn't seem too happy about the arrangement. I thought it was because he didn't want to lose his daughter yet. Years later Cheryl told me that the reason Father was unhappy was because she went to the Prophet without him and he felt left out of the whole conversation. Come to find out, Cheryl was afraid to talk to Father about getting married because she was worried he would arrange for her to marry one of his friends so he could negotiate a trade: my daughter for your daughter.

I think Father was feeling frustrated because the Prophet had not given him a plural wife from all the beautiful, available girls in the community. He felt like if he was willing to give a daughter in marriage, he should get a wife in return. And that was not happening. He had to start taking things into his own hands if he was ever going to get another wife. There were other men in the community who were converting girls from outside the community and bringing them home to join their families. I guess Father figured he would have to do the same. I didn't know any of this until after I was married and my husband's friend from a polygamist family in Salt Lake City told us that my father had tried to make a deal with him. He would arrange for my sister Kay to marry this friend, if he would arrange it so that Father could marry one his sisters.

Cheryl decided to be brave and go to the Prophet alone. She was invited into his big white stuccoed home and taken into his office. Cautiously, she asked him if it was okay that she had come without her father. Brother Johnson kindly laughed and said. "Yes, it's okay. Come in. Do you have anyone in mind whom you would like to marry?"

"No, I don't know who I want to marry, I just know who I don't want to marry."

Brother Johnson laughed. "I will go to the Lord in prayer and ask. You go home and wait for me to get back with you."

Two weeks later, one of Brother Johnson's wives came up to Cheryl after church and told her that the Prophet wanted to see her that afternoon. Cheryl made up an excuse that she needed to see a friend and got in the car and drove off. When she was comfortably sitting in a chair across from him, the Prophet told her the Lord had chosen Hyrum Jeffs as her husband. Now Cheryl had to break the news to Father and Mother.

Cheryl told me that the day we washed windows was the first day she had met Hyrum. They had taken a ride out to Berry Knoll, a small hill south of town, where it had been prophesied by our Prophet that one day there would be a temple for our people. Cheryl and Hyrum sat side by side without touching and tried to talk. She was so shy and scared, she didn't say much. Hyrum ask her how many children she wanted and she said, "I guess twelve would be good."

A week later, on Sunday afternoon, we were all sitting in Brother Rulon Jeffs' elegant home in Colorado City at the base of the Vermillion Cliffs. Cheryl and Hyrum stood together before the full-length glass windows that looked out at the red sandstone boulders, as Brother Jeffs married them for time and all eternity. When they broke open the champagne bottles and started pouring everyone a glass, I thought Mother was going to blow a gasket. Her face turned red and she was aghast that they would serve alcohol. Her Mormon upbringing had forbidden alcohol in any form. Realizing that one of the God inspired Priesthood Council drank alcohol cast serious doubts on her testimony. Father gladly gripped one of those delicate, long-stemmed glasses and took a long, loud sip. Mother's face got even redder. I concentrated on the newly weds. They were smiling and holding hands. Cheryl seemed happy. I envisioned myself standing beside a handsome man someday, in love and ready to start our lives together.

Over the next few weeks, we all missed Cheryl, especially Mother. Her ready smile and helpful hands were now someone else's to enjoy. It's weird how someone who is so important to your family just decides it's time to leave. But every time the oldest one gets married, the next in line steps up and takes their place. We all grow up and move on and take control of our own lives. It was time for Kay and I to step up and be the oldest daughters.

One day Father got Mother and all of us kids in the car and we drove two and a half hours north to Salina, Utah. We pulled up to a small house surround by a green pasture, where three Holstein cows and their calves grazed. Mother had been very quiet all the way and didn't join in when Father started to sing and we all followed his lead. She was pale when she followed Father from the car and went into the house. "What do you think they are doing in there?" Kay whispered in my ear.

"I have no idea. But Mother doesn't look too good." I said, worried.

When they came back to the car, Mother looked even worse than when she'd gone in but neither of them said a word to each other all the way home.

Years later, my cousin Clayne, who worked with Father at Hatchco, told me about the woman Father was seeing when he worked for Hatchco Trucking Company in Salina. Sometimes I wonder if that's why Mother didn't have any children for the five years between Lillith and Donna, the same years he worked at Hatchco. Did she cut him off? Of course Mother never said anything to us; we never knew that anything was wrong between them. What could she do anyway? She had agreed to live the Principle of Plural Marriage and Father was just building his Kingdom. But we never went to the house again so I suppose the woman decided to decline the offer of being Father's second wife.

I was excited when Mr. Bradshaw, the principal, asked me if I would like to play the piano for Devotional every morning at eight. Charles Cook, Janice and Jeanie's older brother, had been asked to be the chorister. I was thrilled but also nervous and worried because I was not good at sight-reading. So I ask Charles if he would call me every night to tell me what the hymn would be for Devotional the next day and then I could practice it over and over to make sure I could play it without mistakes. My heart would skip a beat every time I heard his voice on the other end of the line.

"I think we will sing, '*How Firm A Foundation*', on page 56," Charles said.

"Let me grab the hymn book and look at it." I said, as I stretched the chord to the piano five feet away and turned to the page to see how many sharps or flats it had. I hated sharps. One or two was okay but any more and I was in trouble.

"Yes, this one looks good. I can do this one."

"Okay, I'll see you tomorrow."

"Yes, that will be good." I said, blushing. That will be good. Why did I say that? We soon had a list of twelve hymns I could play easily and we sang them over and over. I didn't realize it until I was older but the opportunity to play for Devotional gave me a reason to practice with a purpose. I began to play for other groups of kids who were singing for programs at school or for the community. I memorized some classical pieces that I played for family shows and community programs. Father used to come in the house when I was playing and teasingly say, "Gosh, I thought that was Mother playing the piano, it sounded so good." It was sweet of him to say, but I always knew he was just teasing. No one could play the piano like Mother.

Another reason I was glad to be old enough to attend the Academy was that now I was old enough to go to the Friday night dances. They were held in the church meetinghouse next to Uncle Fred and Aunt Lydia's home. Uncle Fred was in charge of planning a movie night one weekend and a dance the next. The whole community came out to watch an old movie starring Jeanette McDonald and Nelson Eddy every other weekend. We each paid a dime at the door. But the dances were my favorite.

"Are you coming to the dance tonight?" Norman asked me after school.

"Yes, I get to come," I said, grabbing Kay's arm to steady myself. I still got a little weak in the knees whenever Norman talked to me. I thought about the darling wicker purse he gave me for my thirteenth birthday and blushed. (I still have that purse in my cedar chest.)

"Okay, see you there." Norman ran to catch a ride home with his brother.

"What are we going to wear tonight?" I asked Kay.

"Well, I was thinking I would wear the blue dress with the full skirt. You know the one with the double row of fancy buttons down the front."

"Yes, that's pretty. I think I'll wear my favorite plaid skirt and white ruffled blouse. I love the way my tricot slips move when I walk." I grabbed her arm and we began our walk home.

That evening, Bart, Keith, Kay and I, drove to the Hildale side of town to the same, white-stuccoed auditorium where we'd watched a movie the weekend before. We piled from the car and headed toward the dance hall. I could hear Aunt Radie Cook playing the piano and the sound of feet shuffling across the cement floor. My heart was beating with excitement as I took a seat in the chairs that went around the walls of the huge hall. Uncle Edson at the microphone was calling out across the hall, *"Now promenade down to the lonesome sound, of the Whippoorwill in the night, Sashay back, look at old mad Jack, Hugging everything in sight."* Most of the folks had the dances memorized. There were waltzes and quadrilles, each couple weaving in and out of the couple next to them.

When the next dance ended with a bow and a curtsey from each partner and the chairs filled with people, leaving the floor empty, I looked around the room and saw Norman coming toward me. "May I have this dance?" he said with a sweep of his arm.

"I don't know how to dance," I admitted, in a whisper.

"I'll show you." He took my left hand and placed it on his right shoulder. Then he placed his hand around my waist and took my right hand in his. The music started and he said, "Yes, a waltz. You can do this. Just follow me." He began to count out loud. "One, two, three. One, two, three, gliding me onto the dance floor. Suddenly the waltz lessons Mother had given us back in the living room of the Red House in Ogden came back to me. But this time I wasn't in the arms of Kay or one of my stinky brothers. Everything about this experience was lovely.

All of my senses awakened. His after-shave lotion, a mixture of orange and vanilla, delighted my nostrils. I had never smelled anything so wonderful. My skin seemed to burn where his hand touched my back. With such a cute boy so close and smiling at me, I felt light headed. '*This must be what it feels like to be in love*', I thought to myself.

"You're a fast learner. I think you've got it."

I never wanted that dance to end. Norman returned me to my seat, just as Kay was coming back to sit down. Her dance partner was an old man who was losing his hair.

"Are you in love?" I whispered, laughing and tipping my head toward the man who was walking over to sit between his two wives.

"No!" she said, disgusted.

"Well, I am. Norman is the best dancer and his aftershave is...Wow! That was so fun."

"Is it okay to say no, if that old man asks me to dance again?"

"No, you have to dance with anyone who asks you," I said, teasing her. "You don't want to hurt the old man's feeling's, do you?"

The rules on the dance floor were unspoken but there, nonetheless. Don't dance with the same girl too many times unless you are married to her. Married men can dance with as many single girls as they want to. Girls and women must wait to be asked, unless it is a Ladies Chose dance.

How I loved those dances. I had a new crush every year of high school. After Norman, there was Leslie, who all the Cook girls loved. They were so lucky because he stayed at their house during the school months because his family lived in Salt Lake. We all dreamed of marrying him and being sister-wives.

Then there was Heber, Jeremiah and Joseph. I knew we weren't supposed to have boyfriends. We were just setting ourselves up for heartache. When we graduated from high school, we would go to the Prophet and ask him to find us a husband through revelation and we would gladly do what God and the Prophet commanded us to do. But girls will be girls and boys will be boys. It's silly to think Mother Nature can be stopped.

Carter Hammon and Julia Steed weren't setting a very good example. They were seniors who flirted shamelessly with each other in broad daylight. They danced almost every dance together and walked down the halls at school laughing. Carter was the handsome son of a Priesthood Council member and Julia was the beautiful daughter of Brother Newel Steed. They were some of the privileged few that would get to choose their spouses. I envied them but the more I listened to the Prophet and the Priesthood Council in church every Sunday the more I believed it would be better to marry whoever the Prophet called me to marry. It wasn't important that I knew him or loved him before marriage. Building up the Kingdom of God was the whole purpose of marriage and the reason we were here on Earth. I would learn to love my husband, whomever he may be.

One night, after having so much fun at the dance, we came home and tiptoed through the house trying not to wake anyone. We turned on the hall light so we could make our way into Mother's room to tell her good-night. She always wanted us to let her know that we were home. But she wasn't in her bed. We found her on the rug beside her bed with her bum stuck up in the air and her face cradled on her arms. My first reaction was that she was dead. Kay and I leaned over her and listened. She was breathing. "Mother," I whispered softly. She stirred, looking up at her four teenagers.

"Oh, I must have fallen asleep doing my exercises." This was something she did every night without fail, to keep her girlish figure. "I'm glad you are home safe. Good night." And she slipped under her covers and let out a huge sigh. I let out a sigh of my own and my heart quieted down. What ever would we do if something happened to Mother? I didn't want to even let that thought cross my mind. So I didn't.

Every October, Father pulled us out of school and we went to Idaho for three weeks to work for Uncle Robert during his potato harvest. "You can catch up with school when you get back. You're smart," he told us. I didn't argue. I had grown up working for the family. This was just another job. I'm not sure what happened to our earnings and we didn't ask. Questioning Father was not an option. I was either making money for the family or Father was paying off a debt he owed to Uncle Robert, or Uncle Don.

My job was to stand on the back of the potato digger with Kay, throwing dirt clods off the conveyor belt as fast as I could, trying to leave all the potatoes. Then the potatoes would climb up the belt and into the back of a truck that drove along side us. As we took our places on the side of the machine, I couldn't help but notice the handsome young man wearing a cowboy hat and boots sitting on the tractor seat. He was smoking a cigarette.

"Hello, my name is Seth Rigby. What's yer names?" He hollered down from his perch. We told him our names and he reached into his shirt pocket and handed us each a pink jawbreaker, the first of many. "Here, you go. It gets pretty boring back there all day. Somethin' to keep you awake." Oh, I stayed awake. I stayed awake dreaming of Seth Rigby. Oh, the places we would go and the things we would do. Even to this day, when I smell cigarette smoke blowing through the breeze, I remember the taste of those pink jawbreakers. My mouth starts watering and I think of Seth Rigby.

On Sundays, we didn't work so Father took us to Rexburg

to see his brother, Uncle Howard. Father handed Uncle Howard five hundred dollars to pay back a loan had given him years earlier.

"I've got something to show you," Uncle Howard said, turning to Bart and Keith, after Aunt Thelma had given us all some punch and cookies.

Out back at the corral we leaned over the fence and admired the most beautiful Bay with a long black mane and tail and a star in the middle of his forehead.

"His name is Dime. He's an American Saddler. Real high-spirited. But I've got to get rid of him. He won't let me get the bridle on him anymore. I'll just let you have him."

Bart told me later the reason Uncle Howard couldn't get the bridle on Dime was because he had whipped him over the head too much when he raced him. Uncle Howard pointed to Bart. "You love horses. Why don't you take him and see what you can do with him?"

"Can we Father? Can we have him?" Bart knew better than to think he could have the horse for himself. When it came to ownership, Father never gave us ownership of anything. He would have to share the horse with Father. But that was okay. Bart just had to get on that horse.

Uncle Howard let us borrow a horse trailer and we hooked it to our pick-up. "Here's his bridle and saddle. You got to be able to start working him." Uncle Howard patted Bart on the back.

We took the horse back to where we were staying in one of Uncle Robert's hired help shacks and staked Dime out back. Bart ran to the haystack near the potato cellar, brought back a bale of hay, and gave the horse a slice. He found an old bucket and filled it with water.

"Let's see what this horse can do," Father challenged. He brought out the bridle and the fight was on. He struggled and fought, pulling on the horse's ears and eventually got the bridle on Dime. Bart laced up the saddle. Father got on first and Dime began to buck. Father smacked him across the head. Dime reared back and smacked Father in the head. It didn't hurt anything but Father's pride although it scared him a little.

"You get on him," Father said, grabbing Bart's arm. Bart patted Dime on the neck and spoke softly, trying to calm him. He jumped up onto the horse and the horse reared backward. But Bart was used to his old horse Dart who had pulled the same stunt many times. As he came up, Bart could tell what was coming next. He grabbed the reins and pulled them tight against Dimes head and pulled the horse's head back hard toward the saddle. The horse slammed sideways onto the ground. Bart was still sitting on top of the horse. He looked Dime straight in the eye and said. "That's the last time you'll do that. Now let's get up." When the horse got up, he realized Bart was still sitting in the saddle and he never tried to buck him off again. But Bart got careless. He spent so much time riding and training Dime, he didn't have time to change the sprinkler lines he was supposed to and the foreman on the farm fired him. Bart couldn't tell Father because he knew he would lose his horse. He rode Dime up to the office where Uncle Robert and Uncle Don were talking together outside.

"I came to tell you that your foreman fired me because I have been spending too much time training my new horse and I didn't get the water lines turned today. I'm really sorry, but I have to have a job or Father will take my horse away from me." He patted Dimes side. "Is there any way you can get me my job back?"

Uncle Robert looked at Uncle Don. "Well. That's pretty serious, isn't it?" He said, trying to sound rough. "You go back out there and turn the lines on field nine, ten and eleven." He pointed to the south fields. "When I get here at eight o-clock in the morning you will have already been out and checked on them again and you will report back to me. Is that understood? I'll talk to Jim and tell him we're giving you one more chance."

"Yes, sir. Thank you so much. You won't be disappointed, I promise." Bart jumped on his horse. He was getting a second chance, something he didn't get very often in his young life. He fulfilled his promise to his Uncles for the remaining days we were in Idaho.

On our way back home to Colorado City we stopped in Salt Lake City and Bart bought *Barry's Horse Training Series*, a set of books on how to teach horses to walk side-ways and high step and walk backward. He spent hours training Dime to single step. Dime was a natural and took right to the lessons.

Soon they were single stepping all over town. People came out of their houses to see the beautiful horse and his steps. Bart loved the attention. On the 24th of July when the rest of us were marching in the band in the parade, with rivers of sweat running down our backs, Bart was showing off on his horse. Mother said we would just have to get by without him. Riding his horse was more important.

Mother's Band

One Sunday at the beginning of my freshman year at the Academy, Brother Hammon stopped Father and Mother after church and asked Mother if she would be willing to start a band at the Academy and be the director. He handed Father five hundred dollars and told him to go to Salt Lake City and buy the used instruments and the music Mother would need to get started. It was announced in school that band would start in two weeks. Every one was excited, especially Mother. The new band couldn't have been in more capable hands. She had a ready built band already with just her kids. Bart played the baritone and trumpet, Keith, the trombone, and Kay, the alto saxophone, I played the clarinet, Roger the baritone and Lee the trumpet.

Every Tuesday, Wednesday and Thursday morning, Mother came from her room dressed in her Sunday best. Her hair was pulled up into a braided bun on the nap of her neck, a little gray showing at each temple.

"Jelene, have the boys come in from doing the chores? Are you ready to go?" she asked. "We need to leave here by 6:30."

Ten-year-old Helen walked into the dining room rubbing the sleep from her eyes.

"Helen, you know what to do," Mother said, wrapping her arm around Helen and leading her to the stove. "The mush is here staying warm, the bread is sliced and ready to put on the stove to toast and the freshest cream is in the blue pitcher in the fridge. Wake Janice and have her help you get the little girls fed and ready for school. I'll see you when I get home. Okay?" Helen smiled up at Mother. "You sure look pretty, Mother," she said.

"Oh, thank you, love."

We picked our instrument cases up off the living room floor, where we had practiced the family band the night before and headed out the door. Nathan and Isaac Richards had walked from their house up the road and were waiting at the front gate with their trumpet and saxophone by their sides.

"Good Morning!" Mother called out to them as we began our two-mile trek to school.

Mother's musical training from Ricks College and the time she had spent with our family band came to good use. Proficient at arranging music, she could turn a trumpet solo into a duet or add some bass to a song by writing in a part for the baritone.

Mother loved picking the music and planning the spring and fall concerts each year. Every member of the band was encouraged to learn and play a solo if they wanted to.

My sophomore year, when I was sixteen, Mother found out she was pregnant. It had been five years since she had had a baby. When the spring concert came around, she would be eight months pregnant and was too modest to stand up in front of the whole community with her pregnant belly showing. In February, she made an announcement, "In the past, I have been the director at all of our concerts, but this Spring Concert will be different. I don't feel comfortable standing up in front of the whole town in my condition. So this year, you are going to be the directors. There will be twelve numbers on the program. I will be choosing who I would like to direct each piece, with your help, of course. We only have three months to be ready, so let's go over the list of songs we will be doing and decide who is best suited to direct each song." Excitement and terror in equal amounts filled the room.

"I've already studied each piece to make sure your instrument can be missed while you are conducting. Bart, I think we can do without your baritone, if you would like to conduct *The President's March*. Nathan, Kay can keep the alto saxophone going if you want to conduct *Shenandoah*. Jelene, I think Robert can take over your first clarinet part, if you would direct *Pacific Grandeur*.

Over the next few months, Mother taught us how to read and follow the director's music score. We learned when to flip the pages and how to keep up. We practiced using both hands in big sweeping motions to crescendo and hands right in front of us for the soft quiet parts. She taught us how to get the band to start and stop together. How to stand on the podium without falling off. How to bring the soloist in at the right time. How to step down from the podium and take a bow. And most importantly, how to breathe. Don't forget to breathe. She stood beside us the whole time, her arms moving up and down, back and forth, flipping the music for us and giving encouragement and praise at every turn.

After band each day, Mother packed her music in her bag and walked back home. This was her time alone to think and plan and dream without interruptions. I had never seen Mother so happy as when she was leading our tiny little band.

Kay and I wanted to do something special for Mother at the Spring Concert. We secretly asked each band member to bring four dollars so we could make her a new quilt. As soon as we collected all the money, we stopped by the Priesthood store after school. Upstairs in the fabric department, we were immediately drawn to a beautiful purple flowered fabric. It was heavier and wider than regular cotton. Perfect for a bedspread. The lady at the counter helped us figure out how much fabric we would need for a double bed quilt and she sliced through the fabric with her scissors. We took the fabric to our neighbor, Mrs. Black, who made beautiful quilts and asked her if she would quilt it for us and have it done by the April concert. "Yes, I would love to do that for you. What a lovely thing to do for your Mother. "I'll have it done in two weeks."

The concert program listed the names of the songs alongside the names of the student directors. We looked at our names and looked at each other, excited and nervous. Mother was wearing a solid dark pink skirt and a light pink blouse with tiny fuschia flowers that covered her very large pregnant belly. Kay had fixed her hair in a fancy bun instead of her regular braided one. We had secretly double bagged the quilt and stashed it in the back seat of the car so Mother wouldn't see it. When we got to the concert hall we hid it behind the piano so we could bring it out at the perfect time.

As the curtains were pulled, we saw that the house was packed. Our heads and hearts were pounding. Mother walked to the microphone. "Tonight's concert will be directed by the band students themselves. Each of these students has worked hard to get ready and I want to thank them for their hard work. I would also like to thank you all for coming. Let's begin." She handed the baton over to John Barron, one of our trumpet players. He stepped onto the podium and hit the music stand in front of him twice with the baton, then raised his hands out wide. Each player brought their instruments to their mouths and looked at the director. He was white as a sheet and looked like he was going to pass out. Mother gave him a smile and mouthed the word, "Breathe". With a deep breath, he stood up a little straighter and brought his arms down in one big sweep and the concert began.

The next piece was *Pacific Grandeur*. I stood up and took the baton from John. I tapped the music stand with authority. The band started off just fine and I thought to myself, '*this is no big deal*' and then I realized I'd flipped two pages at once but was too busy swinging my arms to try and flip the music back. So I just kept swinging my arms until the band caught up to where I was on the director's score. I was so happy to take my bow and sit back in my seat and pick up my clarinet.

After the last song was played, Kay and I went to the microphone and announced that we had a surprise for Mother from everyone in the band to thank her for all her hard work and dedication. Two girls in the band unfolded the beautiful quilt and brought it forward for everyone to see. Mother stood beside us speechless, surprised and tearful, as she accepted her gift. It was fun to be on the giving end for a change. The quilt looked beautiful on her bed, a constant reminder of the gifts and talents Mother was willing to share with us all.

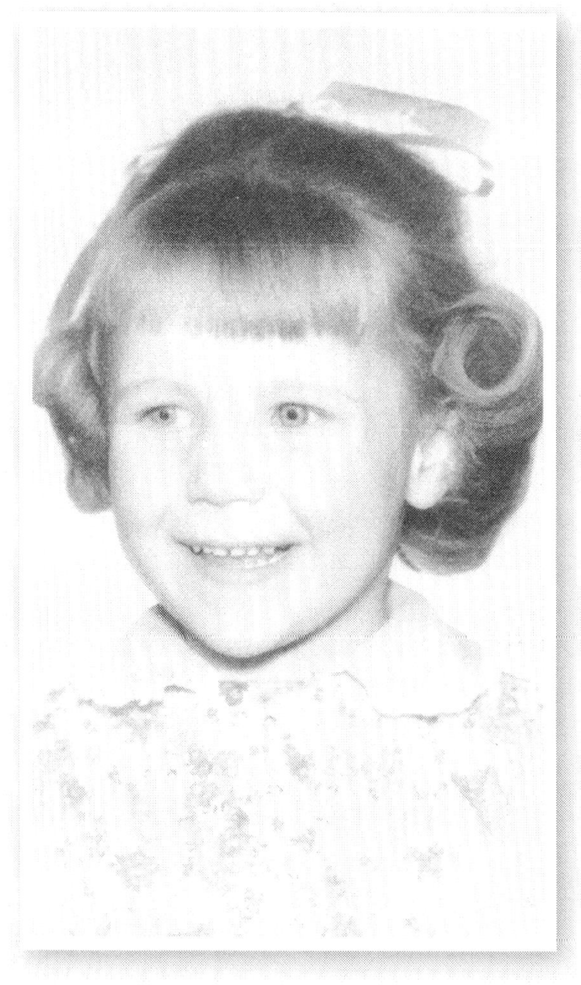

Fara

White Dresses and Blues Satin Sashes

The last day of school for us older kids was the week after our band concert but the little girls wouldn't be out for two more weeks. Fara and Helen were in third and fourth grade. They had lots of friends and loved going to school. One day, Fara's friend, Laura asked her if she wanted to ride home with her on her bike.

"You just sit here on the seat and I will stand up and pump us home," Laura said, patting the padded seat. Fara waved goodbye to Helen and her friends who were standing by the swings. "See you at home."

Helen waved back. Fara's long pigtails whipped her back as she sailed around the corner. Two houses from home, Laura's bike tire hit a hole in the pavement, jerking the handlebars and sending both girls flying. Laura was shaken but unhurt. She jumped up and ran to where Fara lay on the pavement.

"Fara, Fara," Laura said. Blood was coming from a scrape on the side of Fara's head.

"Are you girls hurt?" A car had stopped in the road and out jumped Mrs. Black, our neighbor, who rushed toward them.

"We fell off my bike and Fara is bleeding." Fara opened her eyes and looked up at Laura. "What happened?" She reached up to touch the blood falling down from the cut on the side of her head.

"Here, let's get you home," Mrs. Black said, helping Fara to her feet and into the front seat of her car. Laura followed on her bike.

Laura hurriedly explained what had happened to them as soon as Mother opened the door.

"Oh, let's see here," Mother said, as she looked closely at the bleeding scrap at Fara's temple.

"We'll have you lie down over here, love." She guided Fara to the couch next to the piano.

"Thanks so much for your help," Mother called out over her shoulder to Mrs. Black as she left.

"I'll come over tomorrow and see how you are doing. Okay, Fara?" Laura said, waving good-bye.

"Jelene, get me a bowl of warm water and a wash rag and bring it over here." Mother began dabbing at the dried blood with a wet cloth. "You've got a pretty good scrape there. Now you just lie here and rest. You'll feel better in a minute." She fluffed a pillow and placed it under Fara's head.

"My stomach." Fara sat up clutching herself. Mother grabbed the bowl from the floor beside her and hurriedly put it under Fara's mouth. Fara threw up.

"Oh, dear, that bump on your head has really got you upset. Let me get you a drink." Mother took the bowl to the bathroom and brought a drink from the kitchen.

Fara lay back on the pillow and put her palms on each side of her head. "My head hurts really bad."

"I'm sorry, honey," Mother said. "Let me sit here with you for awhile." She sat down on the couch and placed Fara's feet on her lap. She unlaced Fara's shoes and took off her socks and began gently rubbing her feet. Mother leaned back against the couch and let herself relax, humming softly, trying to sooth the pain. Fara moaned.

"Mother, it hurts so bad."

"I hate to give you aspirin, but I think I'm going to have to this time. Kay, go into my top dresser drawer and bring me the aspirin." When Kay came back into the room Mother took one small pill out of the bottle. "Here, swallow this and see if it will take away the pain."

Fara lay back against the pillow and closed her eyes. "I'll try to be brave, Mother."

"Yes, try to be brave." She began rubbing her feet again. Soon she felt Fara relax under her hands. "Oh, good," Mother said, breathing a little easier. "She is finally going to be able to get some rest." She slid off the couch and went to the kitchen to get supper on the table. When supper was over and homework was done, we all gathered around Mother who was sitting by Fara asleep on the couch. Mother began reading *Swiss Family Robinson*, the book she was currently reading to us each night.

Keith leaned over Fara and listened. "Mother, I hear a gurgling sound."

"Sit her up. Fara, Fara." Mother put her hand on Fara's shoulder and shook her gently. She didn't wake up.

"Fara." Mother felt her daughter's face.

"Jelene, run to the neighbors and call Aunt Lydia. Tell her to come quick"

I ran two houses over to the Broadbents who had the nearest phone. I told Aunt Lydia that Fara had fallen off a bike and bumped her head and she wouldn't wake up. She said she would come as fast as she could. I called Uncle Edson's house and told them to tell Bart to come home immediately. He was living with Uncle Edson's family while he served his two-year mission.

Bart came running up the driveway just as the station wagon that was used as the town ambulance backed up to the utility room door. I pulled him aside and quickly explained what had happened to Fara that afternoon.

Aunt Lydia checked Fara's pulse and heartbeat. We backed away from the couch as they put an oxygen mask over her mouth. Keith and Bart helped Aunt Lydia and Uncle Fred gently pick up Fara and put her into the back of the station wagon on a soft sponge. They covered her with a blanket. Keith climbed in beside her and Mother got in the back seat. Kay and I stood at the door, the little girls peeking out around us.

"She will be fine," I reassured Helen, who looked scared. "The doctors will fix her right up."

As soon as the ambulance pulled away from the house, Bart gathered us all together and said, "We need to pray." We knelt down on the tile floor in front of the couch where Fara had been minutes before and Bart began to beseech God to save our little sister.

My stomach had a bad feeling in it as I put the little girls to bed and came back into the kitchen.

"Do you really think she's going to be okay?" I whispered.

"I sure hope so," Kay said.

I knew the only way to help the sick feeling I had in my stomach was to stay busy while we waited to hear from Mother. While Kay swept the kitchen, I dusted the piano. She mopped the floor with a warm soapy mop and I wiped down the kitchen counters and greased the wood stove. We sat down together on the couch. Kay took my hand in hers and began to pray. "Dear

God, our mother is on her way to the hospital with our little sister. Please bless that Fara will be okay. And please bless Mother with the strength she needs."

We were startled awake from where we had fallen asleep snuggled together on the couch, to the sound of the outside door opening. Mother came into the kitchen. She looked a lot older than when she had walked out the door a few hours earlier.

She walked silently toward us. "Fara didn't make it. She died right before we got to the hospital," Mother said softly. I tried to let the words sink into my brain. How could this be? Just yesterday morning she had laughed and been so happy when I put pigtails in her hair for school. How could she be gone?

I went into Mother's arms. Tears rolled down our cheeks. Mother's body began to shake. Her pregnant belly moved up and down with each silent sob. I couldn't tell if she was holding me up or if I was keeping her from falling. No words came. Only the sounds of sadness. The morning sun was dawning over the red mountain, pouring light into the big family room. A new day. How do you live when someone you love dies?

Kay went to the refrigerator and got a glass of milk and brought it back to Mother.

"Thank you, dear." Mother wiped at her tears.

"Let's start breakfast. The little girls will be up soon," Mother said.

"Kay, will you get the fire going and the toast made? Jelene, separate the cream and bottle last night's milk."

Mother sat down at the table and I wondered how she was going to ever have the courage to tell Helen. Fara was Helen's best friend, just as Kay was mine. I imagined trying to live without Kay. Who would I tell all my secrets to? Who would I talk to about everything important? How could Helen bear the loss of her closest sister?

Mother went to the sink to wash her hands and when she turned around, Helen stood before her, her eyes full of questions.

'Please don't tell her. Don't ever tell her.' I wanted to scream.

Mother wrapped Helen up in her arms. Tears glistened in her eyes. "I'm so sorry. Fara died on the way to the hospital."

Helen shook her head back and forth. "No, no." Each no got louder and louder, until she was screaming. "No, she can't be dead. No! No! No!"

"Come, let's sit down." Mother led her to the couch. She pulled her close and ran her fingers through her long red hair. Helen clung to Mother's big belly and sobbed. Ruth, Beth and Lillith came from the bedroom and sat beside Mother. "I have something very sad to tell you," she said, pulling the little girls close. "Fara died last night. When she fell off the bike yesterday, she bumped her head really hard. That bump caused her to have a brain concussion. Her brain swelled up in her head and started to bleed. And that is what caused her to die. I didn't know that until the doctor explained it to me at the hospital last night. There was nothing anyone could have done. We are going to miss her so much. She was the sweetest, most precious girl. Now she has gone to live with our Father in Heaven. She will be happy there. It's going to be very hard to live without her. We will cry. But we can't cry forever, so we will have to be brave." Mother pushed away the tears that ran down her cheeks. We all sat in silence and wondered if we would ever move off the couch. "Helen, it would really help me if you could go in and get the little girls dressed for the day. Bring me the brush and I'll get their hair braided. Breakfast is almost ready."

After lunch, Mother called Kay and I to her room where she had gone to rest. "We are going to need a nice dress to bury Fara in. Can you think of anything she has that would work?" Mother asked.

"Can we make her something new?" I asked "Maybe a white dress with a wide blue sash."

"That would be lovely." Mother said. "I am also going to need you girls to go with me down to the mortuary to dress Fara, and Kay can fix her hair nice. I would really appreciate it and I'm sure Fara would love to have her sisters take care of her instead of a stranger."

I had been taking sewing classes for the past two years in school and had been sewing my brother's shirts and the little girls' dresses. I found a pattern for Fara's dress. I lay the soft white fabric out on the table and started cutting. The dress would have a dropped waist, blue sash, a square collar trimmed in lace, and long sleeves with a cuff. I worked feverishly on it all day and was glad to have something to keep my mind busy.

The next morning, Kay and I went with Mother to the mortuary in St. George. A man dressed in a navy blue suit met us in the front office. He introduced himself as Mr. Spilsbury. Mother explained that Kay and I were there to dress our sister and do her hair and that she would be taking care of all the paper work. He seemed surprised that girls so young would be ask to do such a task. He called his assistant, Mrs. Stucki. She would be the one helping us. We followed her through a large room with gold-framed pictures and mirrors on the walls. Red and gold velvet chairs were placed in groups around the room. We continued down a long hallway and then down ten steps to a metal door. Mrs. Stucki pushed against the metal door and the smell of sulfur washed over me. Light came from three long windows high up on the left side of the room that seemed to be at street level. A single light fixture hung from a cord over the long metal table in the center of the room.

There was a body on the table covered with a sheet. Kay took my hand. We walked over to the table and Mrs. Strucki looked again at our innocent faces. Without saying a word, she slowly pulled the sheet back. It was Fara, lying on the cold metal slab. She looked much longer than I thought she should be for a nine-year-old. I had to close my eyes for a minute. I took a deep breath and opened my eyes again. Her skin looked like wax. I touched her arm. She was cold. How strange for her to be cold. She had always been warm, happy, alive. On the right side of her neck there was a three-inch gash. The skin was overlapped and stitched up with black thread. I looked up at Mrs. Stucki.

"That is where we put in the medicine that preserves the body," she said, almost apologetically. "We'll have it covered with make-up next time you see her." I touched Fara's blonde hair and the poem Mother had helped her memorize, the one she said every Sunday in Sunday school came to my mind.

"My Mother says she doesn't care
About the color of my hair
Or if my eyes are blue or brown,
Or if my nose turns up or down.
It really doesn't matter.
My Mother says she doesn't care
If I'm dark or if I'm fair,
If I'm thin or if I'm fat.
She doesn't fret over things like that.
It really doesn't matter.
But if I cheat or tell a lie,
Or do mean things to make folks cry,
If I'm rude or impolite,
And do not try to do what's right...
Then that does really matter.
It isn't looks that makes one great;
It's character that seals your fate.

It's what's within your heart, you see,
That makes or mars your destiny.
And that's what really matters.

Kay took a hairbrush from the drawstring bag of hair supplies we had brought from home and began brushing Fara's thick, long blonde hair. She handed me the first brushed strand and I rolled it onto a curler. We worked together in silence until there were pink sponge curlers covering every inch of her head.

"Let's see if we can get this pretty dress on her now." Mrs. Stucki took some scissors out of the desk drawer and cut the slip I had sown so carefully, all the way down the back. She took the dress and cut it open from where the buttons ended all the way to the hem and then put the slip inside the dress. "Because we can't lift her arms, we will have to start down here at her hands, put her hands in the sleeves first and then up the arms, pulling it up, up to the neck, like this." She began to pull and tug the dress onto Fara's stiff body. "Now you can help me. We are going to roll her over to face this way and tuck the dress around her back. Yes, very good. And now we will roll her over the other way and tuck it in just like that. Very good. You girls are great help." I reached down and pulled up the lace collar that was stuck under the shoulder seam. The dress fit perfectly. '*Fara would have loved this dress*', I thought. She hardly ever got a new dress. I wished that I had made it for her while she was still alive. In my mind, I could see her beautiful smile and her twirling and twirling around and around in her new dress.

I looked across the table at Kay. She licked away the tears that were falling down her cheeks. I swallowed hard and pressed my lips and eyes together tight. '*I can't cry now*,' I told myself. '*I'll cry later*.'

The metal door opened and Mr. Spilsbury ushered Mother

into the room. She came forward and Kay and I instinctively put our arms around her waist, holding her up. After a long silence, she said, "Beautiful."

"Yes, they did a great job," Mrs. Stucki said softly. When Mother turned to leave, Mrs. Stucki led us toward the door and we retraced our steps through the big room and out into the sunny May day. On the long ride home, Mother was silent, but I could hear her saying, *"If that were you lying there, who would you want to get you dressed and do your hair? Your sister or a stranger?"* And I think Fara was happy.

Father was home when we got back from the mortuary. The morning Fara died, Mother had sent Keith to the neighbors to call Father's boss and tell him there had been an accident; we needed Father home immediately. I found him in Mother's bedroom crying. His huge shoulders shook as he tried to control his emotions. I wrapped my arms around his burly chest and squeezed him tight.

"It's my fault. I should have been here," he sobbed. "Maybe I could have done something. She might still be here if I had been home."

"No, it's not your fault. The doctor said there was nothing anyone could have done. It was just a terrible accident. There's nothing any of us could have done." I had never seen my father cry. I didn't know before that day that men's hearts were breakable too. He turned away from me and wiped his eyes. There were dark, tired circles under each eye. Eyes that fought to stay open mile after mile, driving the diesel truck across the country to feed his kids. Eyes that had seen the world, but now longed to see his little girl once more.

The morning of the funeral, the long black hearse pulled up in front of our house. They rolled the casket in through the front door and pushed it up against the built-in bookcases on the north wall in the living room. We all gathered around the casket as the attendant opened the lid. There she was. So pretty and peaceful. Her long blonde curls fell over her shoulders and her hands were folded together at her waist, holding a single pink rose. Five-year-old Lillith looked into the casket. "I thought you said she went to Heaven," she said, looking up at Mother. "Her spirit went to heaven, the part that made her alive," Mother whispered softly.

"Oh," Lillith said and ran outside to play. Mother sat down in a soft chair, her pregnant belly taking up most of her lap. Father came and stood beside her, resting his hand lovingly on her shoulder. Friends and neighbors brought food and filed by the casket for the next two hours to pay their respects to Mother and Father.

Mother's father, her brother Don, with his wife, Vera, and her sisters, Mary Lou and Lola, had all come from Idaho to show their love and support. Father's brother, Lee, and his wife, Dorothy came from New Mexico. When it was time to go to the funeral services held at the church, we were called to gather for family prayer around the casket.

Father asked Uncle Don to say a prayer. We each came forward to say our final good-byes to Fara. It dawned on me that this would be the last time I would see my little sister in this life. It had been a strange comfort to have her lying there through the morning. Whenever I walked by the casket, there she was. She wasn't gone. She wasn't really gone. But now the man from the mortuary was closing the lid to the casket. This would be it. I would never see her again until we met in Heaven. A sob started deep in my stomach and came up to my chest. It moved up my throat and out my mouth in a loud wail. I was surprised by the sound and the ache deep inside me. '*So this is how death feels.*' A kind of loneliness I had never felt before. '*Good-bye, little sister. Until we meet again.*'

In Mother's journal she wrote, *"I have never suffered such torture as I did sitting through Fara's funeral. Our children sang, "I Think When I Read that Sweet Story of Old" and how they did it, I will never know. We thought our hearts would break."* Mother never said those words out loud. She never shared her grief and neither did we. She was just too sad to talk about it. Her motto in life was never whine about what you don't have, be grateful for what you do have; always move forward. Helen told me years later, that after Fara died, she often cried herself to sleep at night over the loss of her best friend and wondered; if she died, would anyone remember her or talk about her? Or would she just vanish and be forgotten? You never know what little people are thinking unless you ask them. Yes, we all thought our hearts would break.

Two days after the funeral, Father went back to work. The relatives went home. Mother said she wanted to walk up to the cemetery to see Fara's grave. Kay and I gathered the little girls and made sure they had their shoes on. We walked in silence. I was worried about Mother walking all the way up to the cemetery in her pregnant condition. Kay had Lillith riding piggyback most of the way because she complained that she was tired.

We stood around the small mound of deep red sand. We didn't have a headstone and didn't know if we would ever be able to afford one. I walked over to the fence that ran along the south border of the cemetery and brought back two red rocks and laid them at the top of the mound. Helen and Ruth ran back over to the fence and began collecting rocks to add to mine. Soon we had a small marker a foot high, made of rocks. We would know where Fara was now. We would not forget her.

At a sister weekend not long ago, Ruth told us a story about Fara. One day the little girls were getting ready for school and

Ruth was throwing an ever-lovin fit. She was sprawled out in the hallway screaming bloody murder. Mother said, “Fara, go in there and see if you can find out what is wrong with Ruth.” Fara went to Ruth and asked her what was wrong. Ruth told her that her tights had a hole in them and she was not going to wear holey tights to school. Fara took the tights she was wearing off and handed them to Ruth and told her to give her her tights. She put Ruth’s holey tights on, and wore them to school. Ruth stopped bawling and everyone was happy. I guess some people are just too good to be here.

A Baby From Heaven

The day after our trip to visit Fara's grave, Mother had her baby. Number seventeen. After five girls in a row, the boys were determined to have a little brother. They had been calling the baby Charlie for months. Surely, there was no way any woman could have six girls in a row. What were the odds?

Cheryl had talked Mother into going to Aunt Lydia's birthing clinic to have her baby instead of having a home birth. Janice and I were excited because Mother told us we could come with her and witness the birth. After watching Mother deliver Lillith with little more than a soft moan, I was surprised to hear her cry out in pain during transition. She later told me she wished she had just had her baby at home, where she would not have been flat on her back. It was hard to see her in so much pain especially since she had already suffered so much in the last few days. Her efforts were finally rewarded with the birth of a beautiful red headed baby girl. And Charlie became Donna.

She was a beautiful distraction from the pain of the loss we had just suffered. Seven older sisters were there to spoil her and to see that she never cried. We took turns holding and kissing her. We fought over who got to change her diapers, give her a bottle or put a pink bow in her wavy red hair. We dressed her up in cute dresses two or three times a day. Sometimes I crept softly to where she slept in her bassinet in Mother's room and put my ear close to her mouth to listen and see if she was still breathing. We were still so close to knowing death. So afraid that our new baby might die, too.

Everything she did was precious. Every smile and burp was celebrated. We held our breath for the first few months, until the pain of loss left us and the joy of Donna became our daily reality. She was a precious gift from God, sent to heal a whole family. She never crawled because we kept wrapping her tiny fingers around our fingers and making her walk from the time she could stand on her tiny chubby legs. She walked alone at nine months old. And with every step she took, we followed. Then she ran and we ran with her. Away from death. And Mother smiled again.

Falling in Love

Saturday chores were done and the house smelled fresh and clean. The front door to the living room stood open, welcoming the cool October breeze. I sat across the quilting frame from Kay pricking my left middle finger on the underside of the quilt every time I went in and out with my needle. Looking across the soft red, gray and black wool squares and triangles Mother had sewn together; I recognized most of the pieces. There was the gray and red plaid wool skirt I had worn and grown out of, the black wool pinstriped suit that Father's belly had grown out of. The red square in the center of each block came from a pretty red dress Aunt Mary Lou had given Mother. Mother loved it and wore it until the seams under the arms couldn't be patched anymore.

Mother was from an older time when quilts were made from wool. None of this modern, pretty, light weight stuff. The whole purpose of a quilt is to keep you warm, the heavier the better. Father brought home wool army blankets from the surplus store and we used them for the batting. If we had money, Mother would buy some flannel to put on the backside of the quilt. If we were poor she would piece together old shirts or skirts or whatever she could find. No wonder Kay and I never really mastered the art of small stitches. The quilts were three inches thick.

"Would you girls like me to read some more of our story?" Mother asked, as she came into the room.

"Yes, please. Read," we said.

Mother picked up the book she had been reading to us for the last couple of weeks while we quilted. It was a love story about a knight and his lady in a faraway land. As she read, our imaginations took us with the two lovers as they battled through a war, a corrupt Catholic Priest and the heroine's conniving father. I wondered what it would be like to be in the knight's arms and wished I could take the heroin's place. I could almost feel the wind whipping my long hair, my arms wrapped around my knight's waist, as I held on tight. Our trusty steed galloped through the storm toward the safety of the castle walls. I was sixteen and full of romantic nonsense.

Love at sixteen should have been easy and silly but in my world love was very complicated. Polygamy complicated everything. How could a man love you and someone else at the same time? How could you show love to another woman who also loved your husband? It didn't look fun but if you could pull it off you were some kind of saint. If you could smile and be happy while your husband was sleeping with another woman you could have your calling and election made sure.

Later that evening Mother gathered us around her where she sat on the warm oven door rubbing Donna's back with olive oil after her bath.

"It makes her sleep better." Mother smiled down at Donna's chubby belly. "She's had a busy day, haven't you, baby?" Donna's red curly hair bounced as she laughed and giggled when Mother tried to rub her under her arms and down her sides. A fresh cloth diaper covered her bottom, probably one of the ones Janice had taken off the clothesline today and folded up neatly in the basket beside Donna's bed. Mother slipped Donna's nightgown over her head.

"Okay, Jelene, it's getting late. Open your bible and let's begin.

The chastity lesson we were about to receive was mostly for Kay and I. I suspect that Mother was feeling a little guilty after reading to us about knights saving damsels in distress and what that might have done to our young impressionable imaginations. But a little bible study and chastity lesson would be good for the boys too. She needed to reinforce the lessons we learned in Church the Sunday before when Brother Hammon had banged on the pulpit and raged on about the importance of "all you young people being virgins when you offer yourselves up to the Prophet for assignment in marriage". Mother turned the pages of her notebook to where she had all the chastity reference numbers written down.

"Jelene, start with Timothy, Chapter two, Verse 22."

"Flee also youthful lust: but follow righteousness, faith, charity, peace, with them that call on the Lord out of a pure heart." I passed the Bible to Keith.

"Keith, read Psalms, Chapter 119, Verse nine and ten."

"Wherewithal shall a young man cleanse his way? By taking heed thereto according to thy word. With my whole heart have I sought thee: O let me not wander from thy commandments." The bible was passed around the circle and Kay finished with 1st Corinthians, Chapter six, Verse nineteen. *"What? Know ye not that your body is the temple of the Holy Ghost which is in you, which ye have of God and ye are not your own."*

"Okay, time for bed," Mother said. The sex talk was over. She never asked, "Does anyone have any questions?" Heaven forbid. That would have been awkward. Mother never even said the word pregnant. It was '*expecting*'. The word bra was '*brassiere*' and breast was '*bosom*'. We were left to figure out the sex thing all on our own. After all, if you had a brain in your head you could figure out by watching the animals in the barnyard how babies were made, no need to dwell on the subject.

Years later, I was at the library and picked up a book that looked like just what I needed, a romantic love story. As I got into the story it seemed very familiar to me. I soon realized it was the same book Mother had read to Kay and I while we quilted years ago. When I came to the first very steamy love scene, I knew I didn't remember that part. Then I realized Mother had left out all the love scenes. I wonder how many more Bible verses we would have had to endure if she had read us the good stuff.

My junior year in high school, when I was sixteen, I had a crush on Michael. Of course, I wasn't supposed to have a crush on anyone. It was against the rules, the rule that said someday I would go to our Prophet, LeRoy Johnson and let him talk to God. Between the two of them they would choose me a husband. That's what we were all supposed to do. But that's not the way it really was. I was a flirt. I always had a secret crush on someone and when they became unavailable or I got tired of them, I would just get a crush on someone else. My friends were just as wicked as I was. We talked about boys and flirted with them. By flirting, I mean arranging to trade lockers so we could be next to our latest crush or looking up and smiling at them in study hall, or if we were brave, walking by their house after school, hoping we would see them and get to say hi. Interestingly enough, I don't recall any of us ever having a crush on someone who already had a wife.

Michael and his best friend, Nathan, took geometry, calculus and trigonometry classes and always had their heads together in study hall, trying to figure out their math lessons.

They had a fun group of friends who frequently came over to my house, music in hand, to ask if I would accompany them on the piano. We spent hours around our piano laughing and singing together. Their group sang at school and community programs. I especially remember them singing, *'Those Were the Days My Friends'*. Michael was the leader. His blonde curly hair framed his handsome face and oh, that smile!

One night after we practiced their songs, I thought I would show off the fact that I had my new drivers license. Mother was nowhere to be seen. I grabbed the keys to the car and followed Michael and Nathan out the back door. "I can give you guys a ride home."

"Okay. That would be great not to have to walk all the way home," Michael said.

"I just live up the street." Nathan said. "I can walk."

"No. I'll take you, too." I smiled my prettiest smile. Just as I started the car ignition, I turned to look out the window and there was Mother, motioning for me to roll down my window.

"Where are you going, Jelene?" Mother asked.

"Well, I thought I would just take these guys home." I stammered, thinking, *'Wait till I get my hands on Helen. She was the only one who saw me leave and she ratted me out.'*

"Yes, and that's just what you will do. You will take them home and come right back," Mother said, ever so politely.

"Yes, Mother. I'll be right back." I was grateful she didn't embarrass me. She could have, but she didn't.

The summer after my junior year, I got a job working at the Priesthood Grocery Store. There was a small fabric department upstairs. It was the perfect job for me because I loved to sew. I was the only employee working upstairs and I spent most of my time daydreaming about the curtains I would make for the tiny romantic cottage Michael and I would build together. I ran my fingers across the fabrics choosing this one for the bedspread we would cuddle under. And this soft, silky fabric for the nightgown I would wear.

Michael had gone to work at one of the Priesthood farms for the summer. As the hot summer days began to cool I knew that he would soon be back for our senior year of high school and we would pick up where we left off, chatting in the halls, catching each other's eye in class and giving each other a quick smile. Only two weeks until school started again. I could hardly wait to see him.

There weren't any customers in the fabric department at the moment so I walked over to the big window that looked out over the parking lot and the service station across the street. I heard a car door slam shut and was completely surprised to see Michael and some of his brothers getting out of the car. He was back early! My heart skipped a beat! What would he say when he saw me? Then to my shock and horror, he reached into the car and brought out a girl! Lisa, my friend from school? She sat beside me all last year in band and played the clarinet. We had shared a music stand! I couldn't believe my eyes. Then Michael pulled her to him and kissed her squarely on the lips and I knew if they were kissing, they were married. Married? I stepped back from the window barely able to breathe. My heart felt sick and I wanted to disappear between the bolts of corduroy and calicos. Michael was barely sixteen and Lisa was only fifteen. This didn't make any sense at all. Why would the Prophet marry them so young? Mother said you should at least finish high school before you get married.

At this moment of crisis, the lessons I had been trying so hard to learn from Veda, my sewing teacher, about how to calm my jealousies and be the perfect sister-wife, failed me. I held onto the fabric counter and prayed that Lisa wouldn't come upstairs to buy fabric for curtains or silky nightgowns. Funny thing, I never once thought, "*Jelene, you could be his second wife.*" No. It was time to get a new boyfriend. So when school started, I started flirting with Nathan, Michael's best friend. I knew Nathan already. He and his brother had walked to band with us for the last two years. He was kind and smart and played a mean saxophone.

The first week of school, Mr. Bradshaw, the principal, called me and three other students into his office and appointed my friend Peggy as the girl's councilor, me as secretary, Jeremiah was the boy's councilor and Nathan was the treasurer. We gathered every morning in Mr. Bradshaw's office to schedule student activities. This gave me even more time to spend with Nathan and when he wasn't there, I flirted with Jeremiah. Every week, in between my flirting and my classes, I managed to hang a new schedule on the office window telling the student body whose turn it was to clean the bathrooms, sweep the halls, and empty the garbage cans.

Among our responsibilities, the senior councilors were in charge of the "Harvest Hay Ride" every October. Nathan and Jeremiah would make sure there were enough tractors and trailers with hay bales for seating to bring us home following the party. Peggy and I were in charge of getting enough hot dogs, buns, chips and drinks. We rode buses and cars up the canyon to the park where the Vermillion Cliffs rose like giant red guardians over our town. The boys started bonfires so we could roast hotdogs while Peggy and I got help from the other girls to set out the food. After supper, we settled into a huge circle around a big bonfire for the program. The Steed sisters sang, '*Whispering Hope*'. Nathan and Michael and their friends sang, '*Those Were the Days My Friends*'. Then Brother Steed, the choir director, moved into the center of the circle and told us again how lucky we were to be the chosen few who had been called of God to be here at this very moment in time to live the Gospel of Jesus Christ. We all sang together *'The Spirit of God Like a Fire is Burning'*. As the sun set, the bottom half of the canyon turned a deep red. Our voices rang off the canyon walls and I felt the thrill of belonging to the Kingdom of God.

I leaned toward Debra, my best friend. We had spent many sleepovers in her basement bedroom talking about our futures and the boys we liked. We were two innocent girls, excited for the future, so willing to give our lives to the Principle of Plural Marriage. I could feel the carefree lives we had been living for the last seventeen years coming to an end. Soon we would leave the protection of our homes and give our lives to our husbands. What kind of husbands would they be? There were all kinds of men in the community, men with lots of happy wives and men with lots of sad wives. Where would we be in the next year or two?

The tractors and trailers carrying hay bales around each edge were lined up ready to take us home. I grabbed Debra's hand and ran down the row until I found the trailer Nathan was riding on.

"Let's get on this one," I said. We started to climb up onto the trailer, trying to keep our dresses from fluffing up and exposing a leg, when suddenly there was a hand reaching out toward me.

"Here, let me help you up," Nathan said, grabbing my hand and pulling me onto the wagon. Then he helped Debra up. "Sit here if you'd like. There's plenty of room." We sat down leaving a couple of bales of hay between us.

I like Nathan, I thought, *and I think he likes me. Nathan would be a good husband. He loves music. We always have fun dancing together at the community dances. He's smart. He's cute, a little short, but you can't have everything. But most of all he is always kind and respectful to Mother in band.*

The hayride procession began and Nathan's brother, Isaac, shouted above the noise. "Let's sing*! 'Oh, give me a home, where the buffalo roam'.* Our voices echoed through the mountains. I listened for Nathan's tenor voice and harmonized along with him. We glanced at each other and smiled.

By the time we got to the river bridge crossing, Debra and half of the kids had jumped off to go home. There was still one lonely bale of hay between Nathan and I. Every time another person got off we moved a little closer. By the time we got to the top of our street we were sitting next to each other. I thought that if we moved together slowly no one would notice. We didn't touch each other on purpose. But the tractor lurched every time another person got off, throwing us together and I could feel the warmth of his body next to mine, drenching me with pleasure and excitement. We arrived at my house first. "I think the whole evening was a great success," I said.

"Yes, I agree. I think everyone had a great time," Nathan's eyes met mine. He jumped from the wagon and held out his hand to help me down.

"Oh, thank you," I said.

"You are most welcome," He bowed, and I could almost hear his armor clanging in the dark.

That night in my bed I wondered if Nathan and I would be some of the lucky ones who got to marry someone we knew instead of strangers. Would we be happy together?

I felt like I could do things to contribute to any family I might marry into. I could sew a man's shirt. I could play the piano. I could read music and sing any part you ask me to. I could play the clarinet. I could gut and clean a chicken and I could drive a diesel truck. I couldn't cook but that's why you had sister-wives.

I saw that Mother was happiest when she was giving to her community through her band. She showed everyone that women could use their talents and still run a family. She was the perfect example of what a woman should be like and I never wanted to feel invisible like I felt so many of the women in my community seemed to be.

One of the best things about attending the Academy were the service projects the student body did together. One Saturday we hoed weeds around the schoolyard and then walked down to the community park and cleaned up the leaves. With so many of us, it didn't take long to get a job done.

Our favorite time together, involved piling into the school buses and cars to travel to Brother Steed's ranch near Bryce Canyon, where, for a week in October, we harvested potatoes. The harvester dug down into the Earth and left hundreds of big fat potatoes on top of each row. We each grabbed a gunnysack and dragged it behind us as we filled it and then another and another.

Each night we climbed exhausted into our sleeping bags. The girls slept on the top floor of the huge shed next to their house, while the boys took the bottom floor. The farm fresh food the Steed mothers fed us was almost worth the trip by itself. There was fried chicken, slices of roast beef and all the creamy potatoes and gravy you could eat. We left feeling satisfied that we had performed a needed service and were rewarded with good food and fun friendships.

Other school trips to harvest corn took us to New Harmony and to Brother Harker's potato farm in Beryl, Utah. In the spring we gathered at the community garden to weed the first crops of vegetables. We were free labor and we were having too much fun to care. Without us even knowing it, the Brethren were building the next generation of faithful followers and instilling in us a love for our community.

At the start of my senior year, Mother began learning a new piano piece. Every morning we woke up to her playing scales to warm up her fingers. It was five in the morning. We were allowed to stay in bed for half an hour while she practiced and then it would be time to get up and do chores and head off to band. The piano piece, *Impromptu Op142/2 in A Flat Minor* was part lullaby and part-frenzied runs up and down the piano keys. During the lullaby parts I would try to go back to sleep for just another minute but then the wild runs would come and wake me again. The runs were hard and Mother would go over and over them until she had them perfect. She told Father she wanted to go visit her family in Idaho for Thanksgiving and she was going to play her new piece for them.

I was trying to find the perfect piano solo to play at my graduation program. I started with *Romance Op.24, No. 9*, by Jean Sibelius. I added a showy, fast *Rustles of Spring* by Christian Sinding. I also chose Tchaikovsky'*s Piano Concerto in B flat minor* just to be ready. Every day after school I practiced for hours. When Helen had had enough of my banging, she started singing opera, following my notes up and down the trills of the song, until I complained. "Mother, make her stop." Helen was probably saying the same thing to herself, "*Mother, make her stop*."

We hadn't been to an Archibald Family Thanksgiving for years. It was awkward. All the cousins we once played hide-and-go seek with, who had been cute and little and friendly, were now pimply, insecure teenagers. My brothers were wearing long-sleeved shirts, collars buttoned at their necks, and Kay and I wore dresses down to our mid-calves, with our long hair in braids. It was the 60's. All the cousins our age were wearing bell-bottoms, perms, and shirts with big cuffs.

The Thanksgiving feast was delicious but in the Archibald

family, the food was always upstaged by the program. Aunt Lola's little kids sang some church songs and our family sang a couple of our show songs. Then Leon, who was my age, got up, stood by the piano in his platform shoes and announced that he would play, *Prelude in C# Minor by Rachmaninoff*. And he did, flawlessly. I was blown away.

Then Terry, who was also my age, went to the piano with his red hair premed into an afro and said, "I shall also play, *Prelude in C# Minor by Rachmaninoff.* But he rolled his r's on Rachmaninoff and everybody chuckled. And he also played it perfectly. I didn't know either one of them played the piano and here they were playing like concert pianists.

I was next on the program. I stood by the piano and said, "And I will also play, *Prelude in C# Minor by Rachmaninoff* and after everyone laughed at my joke, I said, "Not really, I will play, *Romance, by Jean Sibelius.* They loved it.

Uncle Ronald's little girls played their violins and then Mother finished off the program with her new piano piece. I was so proud of her. And I was proud to be a part of this big beautiful family who ate music with their food.

Before we knew it, it was May and the end of the school year was fast approaching. Mother and her band students had worked hard to give the community another grand band concert. I think she probably knew it would be her last band concert. Father and Mother were starting to question their belief in the Prophet and the group. In the eleven years we had been a part of the Group, Father had never been given another wife. The kingdom he imagined he should have by now, with many wives and children and the pride and glory that would be his reward, had not come to pass. He had given his oldest daughter in marriage to one of Brother Jeffs' sons. He had paid his tithing faithfully all these years. He had shared his beautiful family and their talents with the community at every opportunity. He began to question why the seven Priesthood Councilors had large finished homes, lots of beautiful young wives and expensive cars, while most everyone in the community struggled just to feed and clothe their large families. His friend, Harold Blackmore and his family had left the Group a year earlier and Harold had invited us to attend Sunday meetings the first Sunday of every month with a group of Independent Polygamists Families.

I was torn about this new turn of affairs. I had this horrible feeling that life as I knew it was about to change. I kept asking myself, '*What about the Prophet? Is he not the Prophet any more? What about being part of the Kingdom of God? What about me? And Nathan?*'

I was hoping no one was noticing the fact that we were skipping church with the Priesthood Council and the Saints, the first Sunday of every month and going instead to church with a bunch of apostates in St. George, Hurricane and Bunkerville, Nevada.

At home I worked hard on my graduation dress. It was blue satin with a white chiffon overlay. A large collar was edged in lace. The cuffs on the sleeves were also edged in lace that went from my wrists to my elbows. The tiny pleats around the waist gave it a fullness that made me feel like a princess going to the ball. '*This dress is pretty enough to be my wedding dress.*' I thought as I looked at myself in the mirror. I couldn't wait to get to the Academy on graduation night and see the look on Nathan's face when he saw me in all my glory.

So it was, that on graduation night, when we got to the school, I was horrified to see Steve Kirkland Jr. and his three sisters walking toward us through the parking lot. We had met them at one of the Independent Polygamist Sunday meetings that Father and Mother had dragged us to and unbeknownst to me Father had invited them to come to my graduation. How could this be happening on my special night? I didn't want anyone to know that we had been going to the Independent Polygamist Meetings! Now everyone would find out! What would Nathan think if he discovered we were going to meetings outside the group? I looked around to make sure no one could see me talking to outsiders. I hurried and said hi to our visitors and then told Kay I needed to go and get ready. Of course, Kay was nice to them because she didn't know how to be any other way. She ushered them right in to sit with her and the family and when I looked out across the congregation and saw them sitting with my family, I hoped and prayed everyone would think they were Mother's relatives.

The program began with the graduates singing, "*God of Our Fathers*." Brother Hammon gave the commencement address which was so long I thought I would throw up by the time my turn came to play my piano solo, *Tchaikovsky's Piano Concerto in B Flat Minor*. I was able to keep my fingers on the right keys even while shaking like a leaf and was so relieved when it was over.

I made sure I was standing under Nathan when we took graduation pictures of the seventeen graduating seniors. The boys were on the top step of the three step bleachers and the girls were under them, which as I think of it now, was symbolic of how it would be for us girls from that day forward.

After the ceremony, Mother invited Steve and his sisters to our house for baked chocolate pudding and whipped cream, my favorite dessert. I was annoyed that my two worlds had collided. I don't know why I thought I was going to be able to keep them separated. How was I going to marry Nathan if my Father and Mother and my family left the Group. The people we were meeting at the Independent Meetings were nice people. But

I wasn't ready to give up my other family, the big community family whom I had grown to love over the last seven years. I tried my hardest to be polite to Steve and his sisters and wish I had been more gracious when they handed me a black velvet box with a beautiful necklace inside. It was the only graduation gift I got.

Nathan and I had never talked to each other about marriage because that was forbidden, but deep down inside I hoped and prayed that The Gods would make it happen. Right after graduation, Nathan went to his father, one of the Seven Council members, and told him that he would like to have me as his wife. His father said he would go to the Prophet and get his approval and then go to my father and ask for his permission. Although everyone else in the community was supposed to go to the Prophet to get a spouse, it was well known that many of the Seven Councilor's children got to choose the person they wanted to marry. Because they were revered almost like Prophets themselves, the people figured the Seven Councilors could have a revelation for their own children.

Nathan's father came to the house one day when I wasn't home. Father told me later that he had invited him inside. They shook hands and sat down in the living room. "Well, I was thinking it would be a good idea if my son Nathan and your daughter Jelene got married."

"A good idea? Father questioned. "I thought every marriage appointment was given by revelation? Did you talk to the Prophet about this marriage?"

"Yes, and he thought it was a good idea too."

"So my daughter doesn't get a revelation. She gets a good idea?" Father was not happy.

"No, no. It's not like that. It's like an arranged union between two families that will bless us both. All of us, " Nathan's father stammered, throwing his arms out and back, in a gathering gesture.

"Ilene and I will discuss it and get back to you in a week or two."

"Yes, that will be good. Very well then." Nathan's father jumped up and walked quickly to the door.

That night Father and Mother took me outside to talk. "Nathan's father came to see us," Father said.

"Oh?" I stammered, my heart racing.

"Yes, Nathan has asked for your hand in marriage. But your Mother and I would like you to wait a year to get married. We know you like Nathan and we like Nathan, too. He's a good boy. We just don't want you rushing into marriage. If you still want to marry Nathan in one year, then we will give you our blessing."

I nodded slowly. "I'm not in any hurry to get married, I'm only eighteen. I can wait a year."

"That's what we were hoping you would say," Mother said, "You're going to get a lot of pressure from his family to get married right away. So be prepared to stand up for yourself."

"I can do that," I told them. I felt the deep love and concern my parents had for me. I was grateful for their concern and, looking back, I'm impressed with their wisdom. They cared enough to step in where they felt they needed to, but smart enough not to forbid me to marry him, knowing that's exactly what happens when you tell an eighteen year old girl she can't do something.

The next Sunday we all piled into the station wagon to go to a meeting with some Independent Polygamists in Bunkerville, Nevada.

Father stopped the car in front of Nathan's house. He said, "You need to go in and tell Nathan that you have decided to wait a year to get married."

"Okay, I'll go tell him." Excited to see and talk to Nathan, I jumped out of the car and went around to the back door and knocked. Nathan's mother answered the door with a smile. "Is Nathan in? Could I talk to him?"

"Of course. Come on in," she said. She seemed happy to see me.

Nathan saw me from the kitchen and came toward me. "We need to talk," I whispered. He led me to a bedroom off the dining room and closed the door. I sat down on the bed and he sat beside me. "I've come to tell you that I would love to accept your proposal of marriage but I am also here to tell you that my parents would like me to wait a year to get married and I told them I would."

"Wow. I wasn't expecting that." Nathan stood up and faced me. He looked confused. "That's not how it's done. The prophet wants us to get married right away. I'm leaving to go to the University of Utah in a few weeks and I want you to go with me as my wife. Can't you talk to your parents and get them to change their mind?" I could tell he was trying to stay calm but his face was getting red.

"I believe my parents have my best interest at heart and they are older and wiser than I am. So I am going to do what they ask me to do."

Nathan looked frustrated. I was surprised by his reaction. I had never seen him upset before. I had only seen him in the fun times and we had never even had a real conversation about our likes and dislikes or our dreams of the future. That was all expected to happen after we were married. After the Prophet had chosen you an eternal partner, you would have plenty of time to get to know each other.

"You want to follow your parent's advice over that of a Prophet of God?" He chastised me.

Suddenly, we could hear a great commotion coming from the kitchen. Someone was yelling.

"Where is she? If I don't see her out here in two seconds some heads will roll! Get her out here now!" Nathan's mother opened the bedroom door and swiftly ushered me out to where my father was standing in the center of the kitchen. He looked relived to see me. "Come on," he said, taking my arm. "We're leaving."

As we got closer to the car Father said, "I don't trust them. I was worried that they might kidnap you and marry you off to Nathan and we might never see you again. That happens all the time here. A girl is at church one week and the next; married off to someone in Salt Lake City or Canada and you never see her again. I don't want that to happen to you."

As we drove out of town it occurred to me that Nathan and I might never happen. I would hold on to hope that we could still be together. But we were leaving Colorado City. I knew we were. I couldn't deny it any longer. And I also knew that wherever my parents and brothers and sisters went, I would follow. We did everything together. We always had. They were everything to me. When you grow up standing beside your brother and hear him sing the same notes you are singing, a thick rope of trust grows between you. If you forget, he remembers, and if he stumbles, you've got his back. Even in the car today, all squished together like Mother's wheat biscuits, rising in the sun, I loved these, my people.

A week had passed since the scene at Nathan's house. I was hoping and praying he had forgiven me and would still want to marry me in a year. The thought kept me awake. The clock on the bureau read 4:00 a.m. If I hurried, I could catch Nathan before he left with the crew to go work at Brian Head. I slipped silently from between my warm sheets and hooked my foot to the bottom bunk, where my little sisters slept. I quietly pulled my brown cotton stockings up over my long white underwear and hooked them at the top of my leg with the garter belt hook. Then I did the same thing with my shiny tan nylons. I wiggled my thin, five-foot-five body into my favorite plaid dress. It had a band sewn on the bias around the middle that emphasized my twenty-four inch waist. Grabbing a bobble, I twisted my waist long hair into a ponytail and tiptoed through the kitchen, not knowing which step would me give away and bring Mother from her room. I stepped into the cool morning and wrapped my arms around my body, wishing I had brought a sweater. It was scary being in the dark alone. I never went anywhere alone. Nathan's house wasn't too far up the road. He is going to be surprised to see me.

My heart raced as I ducked behind his garage to wait for him to come out the back door. Fifteen minutes passed and then I heard the back door creak. Nathan came walking down the path, carrying his coat and a sack lunch. I stepped out from the darkness and came toward him slowly so I wouldn't frighten him, but he still jumped when he looked up and saw me.

"I'm sorry. I just had to see you before you left for work."

He laughed softly. "No, it's okay. I was just thinking of you, too."

We walked to the front porch and sat down on the cement steps. I was shivering with cold and excitement. He threw his coat over my shoulders and we slid close together, our shoulders touching. Gathering my courage, I asked him, "Do you still want to marry me?"

"Of course, I do." He took my hand and we sat in the perfect morning listening to the crickets greet the day.

From far away we could hear a diesel truck engine humming up the road, getting closer. "Dang. That's my ride. Will you ask your mother if we can go on a horse ride down the creek on Saturday?" He pulled me up and we walked to the garage so that no one would see us together. "Sorry, I have to have my coat. It's cold up there."

I took his coat from my shoulders and handed it to him. "I would love to go on a horse ride with you next Saturday."

"Okay, one o'clock, here, Saturday." He walked backward to the street, smiling at me.

Saturday at noon I went to the barn and took the brush from the nail on the wall and began to brush Meg's bronze coat. She was a small Morgan horse and most of the time we used her to pull the little red, two-seated cart built especially for her. I loved the smell of her and the oil that came from her coat, making my hands brown. Her mane grew softer with each brush stroke and soon she was pretty enough to go with me on my ride. I whispered to her that I was going to marry Nathan, telling her how perfect he was and how happy we would be together. Then I heard kissing sound coming from behind the bales of hay.

"Oh, I love you so much," Lee said, trying to make his voice go up high like a girl.

"No, I love you more, buttercup," Roger said, in his deepest male voice.

"You two go to Hell!" I shouted, throwing the brush as hard as I could in their direction. I heard them laughing as they ran toward the corrals. I grabbed Meg's saddle and threw it over her and strapped her in tight.

Nathan was waiting on his horse in front of his house. We headed through the sagebrush to the sandy shores of the creek. There were other horse tracks making a trail down the steep incline. The rain from the storm the day before had given the sand a solid firmness. When we reached the flat open creek bottom, Nathan kicked his horse into a gallop. Meg followed.

We raced west down the creek bed and under the highway bridge that took everyone out of town. We were free of worry for a few minutes. Two kids who didn't know what was going to happen next but were ready and willing to take a chance on life.

We finished racing and came back up the embankment. "How's work at Brian Head?" I asked trying to start a conversation.

"It's great," Nathan said. "I need to save as much money as I can for school. Not too many people from here get to go to college." I was about to say something to encourage him to talk more when he said, "Since I'm leaving soon, I was wondering if I could have a kiss?"

"Well, I guess that would be okay." We were breaking all sorts of rules by being together, but what could it hurt? A simple little kiss. We brought our horses side-by-side and I leaned in to kiss him just as Meg stepped sideways, braced her back legs and started to pee. And my very first kiss landed on my ear. I turned red, mortified. We were both too embarrassed to try for another kiss so we headed back home. There would be plenty of time for all that lovey-dovey stuff later.

We were almost back to Nathan's house when he stopped his horse and I pulled Meg up beside him. "My mom wanted me to invite you to a family picnic on Wednesday. They're all going out to Pipe Springs. Can you go?"

"Sure, I'd love to."

"I'll tell her," Nathan called out as he turned toward home. I watched him go down the lane. *What a sweet boy*, I thought.

Nathan's mother made sure I rode with her to the picnic. I think she knew I would be a little overwhelmed by Nathan's large family. There were four older wives in their fifties and sixties and three wives in there thirties and forties, which included Nathan's mother. And then there were three new young additions. The youngest wife, Kathleen, was Kay's age.

We had taken the same math and science classes. The caravan of cars drove ten miles east to Pipe Springs National Monument and we spread our blankets out on the grass by the picnic tables. Each wife came from her car loaded down with babies and coolers of food. The kids raced to see who could get the first swing. I gravitated over to the table where the three new wives were spreading out a tablecloth.

"I think you and Nathan make such a cute couple," Kathleen said.

"Oh, thank you. I'm very happy about it," I said, softly.

"When is the big day?" she asked.

"Well, my parents want me to wait a year to get married and I told them I would."

"Boy, won't that be hard, going against the Prophet's suggestion that you get married immediately?" She paused, looking concerned. "Maybe you should go somewhere quiet and pray to God about giving you a sign that you and Nathan are supposed to be together now. You know, a burning in your bosom, like it says in the *Doctrine and Covenants*. In fact that's what I did when I was told I was supposed to marry Nathan's father. I prayed and got a distinct burning in my bosom that made me feel calm and clear about my decision. Maybe if you got an answer about Nathan, your parents would let you get married sooner."

"That's a really good idea. That's exactly what I will do."

Nathan's mother announced that the food was ready. The young wives ran to the swings to pick up the kids, tickling and laughing with them as they walked back to help them get a plate of food. Each mother helped the child next to her without seeming to notice whether they were hers or not. There was a feeling of love among them that was wonderful to see.

The next day, I told Mother I was going for a walk and

headed north through the sagebrush toward the creek. I found a huge cottonwood tree with branches that leaned out over the deep sandy embankment. I took off my shoes and sank my toes into the cool red sand. Then I turned to face the tree and got on my knees. I started right off beseeching God with all my might. "God, I need your help." I stopped and looked around at the blue sky and the Vermillion Cliffs north of town, feeling funny about praying out loud. I was alone. I needed God to hear me. I was desperate.

"God, Kathleen said that she got an answer to her prayers and I need one too. Am I supposed to marry Nathan? If I am, can you give me a sign? A really big sign, so big I can't miss it? A burning in my bosom, like in the *Doctrine and Covenants*. Please. I realize that this is the most important decision I will ever make, choosing my eternal companion. Even with the Prophets help, I would like to have my own confirmation that Nathan is the one. Thank you, God. I really appreciate it."

I sat back down and slid all the way down on my back, making a bed in the sand. I rested my arms under my head and waited. A few white wispy clouds drifted through the sky heading east. I wished with all my might that they would come together and spell out the words, "Marry Nathan!" That would truly be a sign from Heaven. But that didn't happen. So I waited some more. My mind went back to the house and Kay. She was on the same shaky sinking raft I was on. Should she ask Father for permission to go to the Prophet to ask for a husband, or should she look outside the group. How could she ask the Prophet if he wasn't the Prophet anymore? We were meeting lots of new people at the Independent Polygamists monthly meetings. There was a nice couple from Enterprise, Utah, who had left the Mormon Church for polygamy and who had come to the house to see her. Had she gotten a burning in her bosom about him and his cute wife and their little family and if so, was it a big enough burning for her to become a second wife?

Ten minutes later I still hadn't received my revelation so I headed back home, talking to God as I walked. "I don't mean to be impatient God, but anytime you want to give me a sign, you know where I live and I'll just be here on earth waiting. I've got stuff to do. But, honestly, it can be anytime, anywhere, God. We'll stay in touch."

Back at the house I headed for the sewing machine. Bart was getting married and we all needed matching yellow dresses. The bride's favorite color.

Where You Go, I Will Follow

The first time Jean saw Bart it was love at first sight. I don't know if it was quite the same for him. He was still mourning the loss of Lorraine, his high school crush. Bart had lived with Uncle Edson, Lorraine's father, and his family while he served his mission. This gave him even more opportunity to fall in love with her. After his two-year mission he went to the Prophet and asked him if he could marry Lorraine and he got his answer the very next Sunday when she walked into church on another man's arm.

So he went to the Prophet again and asked for Lorraine's younger sister, Noreen, but got the exact same answer the next Sunday. He began to realize he was going to have to look for a wife among the Independent Polygamists. And it just so happened that a friend invited Jean and her family to the Independent Polygamist picnic in Cedar City. She brought Jean over and introduced her to Bart. He couldn't help but notice her tall slim body and long jet-black hair pulled back from her pretty face. There was an instant connection.

Jean spent the summer with us. Bart wanted to see what she was made of. He took her hauling hay, cutting loads of wood and building houses. She proved she could work as hard as he could. Bart had become completely indoctrinated into what he thought was the polygamist male role. Years later, Jean told me that he made her agree to certain things before he would marry her. Jean had to agree to be the peacemaker if they ever had any arguments. She had to promise to give him a virgin as a second wife, because she wasn't one. She had been married before and had a two-year-old son. Jean grew up in the 50s and 60s in Orderville, Utah. She remembered Sunday sermons at her LDS Ward where the brethren talked about polygamy and the fact that we would all live it in Heaven. Polygamy was not new to her. She felt she loved Bart so much she would be willing to live polygamy with him. I made her a wedding dress.

On a hot August afternoon, Father married them in our living room. The Blackmores came from La Verkin to show support to the bride and groom. They understood the transition these two young people were about to make. They were leaving their homes and their families. Harold offered them a place to stay after their honeymoon and a lot to build a home on.

Father stopped by Harold's home every chance he got to discuss our exit plan. Father and Mother had to decide quickly. Kay, Keith and I were now of marriageable age and this intensified their dilemma.

Father knew every polygamist and wanna-be-polygamist from Montana to Mexico. One of those polygamists was Steven E. Kirkland from St. George, Utah. Father had met him back in 1962, before we moved to Colorado City. He warned Father about *'that bunch of power mongers, living off the saints of Colorado City'* but when Harold Blackmore moved there, Father had ignored Steven's warning and followed Harold.

Among the Independent Polygamists we met at the Sunday Meetings, the Kirkland's were my favorite. They had three girls near my age, Evelyn, Fennella and Linda. Everyone in St. George knew Mr. Kirkland was a polygamist but admired him and his family because they were honest and hardworking. He didn't belong to any polygamist group. He studied the Bible and Book of Mormon faithfully. He had his own beliefs and would tell anyone who had the inclination to stop by his house on 400 North in St. George, all about them.

He and his sweet wife, Mary, were from Georgia. They had converted to the Mormon Church in 1942, when two young missionaries came knocking at their door. As soon as they were baptized they packed all their belonging and two children, leaving their large Baptist families, who had disowned them. They had heard about St. George, Utah and its mild winters but the thing that attracted them the most was that there was a LDS Temple in St. George. They planned to live there long enough to get married in the temple and do some temple work and then they would go back home to their beloved South.

Mr. Kirkland got a job as a policeman and took turns working the nightshift. He had expected that the good Mormons of St. George were as devoted to their religion as he was. However, he realized that some of the folks in town would say one thing when they bore their testimony in church on Sunday and do something else at the local hotel on Saturday night.

Steven was a purist. He believed your word was your bond and he lived his life that way. One Sunday during Sacrament Meeting the Stake President got up before the congregation and introduced the man who would be their new bishop. Steven had seen this man on his late night watch at the local hotel and knew he could never in good conscience raise his right hand and sustain him as his new bishop. His was the only hand that went up when the Bishop ask for any opposing votes. The new bishop took Steven aside later and told him he was going to ruin him and run him out of town. Steven didn't let that frighten him at all. In fact he began to wonder whether callings made in the church were truly inspired. He dug deeper into the teaching of Joseph Smith and Brigham Young and the teachings of the Principle of Plural Marriage and he started sharing what he was learning with Mary.

Sylvia Barton was a beautiful, shy twenty-seven-year old girl who attended church in the same ward building as Steven and Mary. She had a good job working as a court recorder. She told her daughters years later that you wouldn't believe the shenanigans that went on in little tiny St. George, Utah, when the population was only eight thousand people.

Sylvia considered herself an old maid and had been praying with as much fervor as she could muster that God would send her a sign and tell her who she should marry. One Sunday in church she saw Steven Kirkland and his family and a voice told her "*that is who you will marry*". She was not happy with that premonition. Meanwhile, Sylvia's father had a dream and in that dream a voice came to him three times and said, '*Steven Kirkland is going to come to you and ask for Sylvia's hand in marriage. What will your answer be?*' Her father talked with his wife about it and they decided that if the dream came to pass, it would have to be Sylvia's decision and hers alone.

Steven and Mary had received a testimony of the truthfulness of polygamy and believed that God had told them to live it. Mary spent hours on her knees praying for the strength to do Gods will. She began to look around her at Church and she noticed Sylvia. Mary prayed and felt that Sylvia should become their second wife. "What about Sylvia Barton?" She asked her husband. Steven prayed about it and then he went to Sylvia's father, who was waiting for him.

There were many trials. Steven and Mary had a daughter, Ruth, who was seventeen, followed by six boys, ages fourteen to four and would have five more children after Sylvia joined their family. They were all crammed together in a very small house. Over the next twenty years Sylvia bore six children who lived and six who died because of the Rh factor.

The kids were called plygs and worse, but all grew up to be strong and resilient. Steven bought a forty-acre farm in the neighboring town of Washington, Utah, so the boys would have a place to learn how to work. They had cows, chickens, sheep, and horses. They raised hay to bale and corn for silage. Up at five-thirty every morning, they jumped in the truck and went to the farm to milk the cows. Then they went home, went to school and came back to the farm to work. There was no time to play sports or participate in school activities.

The summer after my graduation, Bart and his hay crew, which included Keith, Roger, Lee, Kay and I, were hauling hay in Enterprise, Utah. Kay and I pushed and pulled and rolled the hay bales with our knees and arms and every other muscle we possessed into a long row so that the loader could scoop them up, and the boys on the back of the truck would stack up the bales nice and snug. I drove the truck when Bart needed me to because I could get the truck over the dikes without throwing the boys and the bales off the truck. Bart was a perfectionist when it came to his hay loads. They had to go down the road without being roped, although we roped every load for safety. He loved it when some old farmer would say, "That's the purddiest load of hay I ever seen."

We headed to St. George to drop the load off at Cox Dairy and then we stopped at Kirkland's to get a drink. Mrs. Kirkland invited us in and we sat around their large kitchen table where their eighteen children had to eat in shifts at mealtime. I was enjoying my tall glass of cold water when in walked a very handsome stranger. He took his hat off and went around the table and shook everyone's hand. "Hi, I'm Linton, one of the older boys." He had brown eyes and dark hair and a drip of sweat rolling down his sideburn and into the slight stubble on his chin. He was so handsome he took my breath away, a little.

Nathan hadn't even left for school yet and here I was breathless over this person. *What was wrong with me?* I quickly reminded myself that I was getting my husband from a Prophet of God and I was not interested. Linton didn't seem interested in me either. Of course, I had my best plyg look going on, with my long dress over my pants, my plyg waves smashed against my sweaty head and a straw hat hanging from my neck.

When Linda walked us out to the truck, I asked her about her brother.

"Oh, Linton? Yes, he just moved back home from Salt Lake to help Dad and Mama Mary in the Kirkland Nursery. All the brothers are going into business together. John and David are going to do the fencing and Linton will do the landscaping. When he's not busy planting somebody's lawn, he drives truck for Rocky Mountain Trucking Company."

"Oh, okay." I said, trying not to seem too interested.

I saw Linton again at a camping trip in the hills east of Fillmore, Utah, later that summer. All the Independent Polygamist families had headed to the mountains for a fun camping weekend. Linton brought his new green Ford truck and all the teenagers jumped in for a ride up the canyon. On the way back down Kay and Linda and I were sitting on the tailgate. The truck bounced over a rock and Kay fell off, landing on her tailbone. Linton stopped the truck, got out and ran back to help her up. She said she was fine but he apologized over and over and then proceeded to ask her if she would like to come up front and sit with him. She smiled sweetly and said, "Sure, I guess." I watched them through the back window as we bumped back down to the campground. *Was this jealousy I was feeling*?

The longer Nathan was gone and the more I associated with the Independent Polygamists the freer I felt. Just the idea that I could choose my own husband felt right to me. Although I had kind of chosen Nathan, the fact that he would still be attached to a Prophet who controlled him, worried me. That we would have to do everything the way the Prophet wanted us to for the rest of our lives felt stifling. I watched the girls in the Independent Polygamists families wear stylish clothes, cut their hair and choose for themselves whether they would live polygamy in the future.

The last day of the camping trip we all gathered around the picnic tables to listen to Harold Blackmore give the Sunday sermon. He was talking about the vows that are read at a covenant wedding. He said that he or any other man who held the Priesthood handed down from Joseph Smith the Prophet could perform a marriage, even a plural marriage. He began reading the vows from the book and I looked across the table at Linton and whispered, "Hey, do you want to get married? Just say 'I do' when he gets done and we'll be married." I winked. We smiled at each other and I think he could tell I liked him.

In February, we invited the Kirkland's to come to Colorado City for my nineteenth birthday party. Linton came with his sisters and his brother, Steve, who was newly divorced and interested in Kay. She was not impressed. After the party, the girls invited me to come to St. George and stay with them for a few days. Linton stepped into the living room with Father and asked him for permission to take me on a date while I was in St. George. Father told him he could date me but we had to have a chaperone. Linton was pissed.

Friday afternoon Linton called his mother's house and Linda, handed me the phone. "If you need a chaperone, you better get one. I'm coming to pick you up at seven."

I was excited and nervous.

We went to out eat and to the movie. We went the next night, too. Linton reached for my hand as we walked to the car. I felt warm all over.

There was a monthly polygamist meeting at Kirkland's that Saturday evening. Mother and the family were waiting for me when we got back from our date. She had expected me to be at the meeting and not out running all over town with a tall handsome man. I could tell she wasn't happy with me.

The next day, I was sitting in the living room enjoying the sun shining in the big picture window, dreaming about the last two nights and my dates with Linton, when the little girls came running into the house. "Jelene's boyfriend is here." There was Linton, tall and good-looking as ever, in his jeans and white t-shirt, the cuffs rolled up over his biceps.

"I just thought I would stop by and see how you were doing," he said.

I blushed.

"I was wondering if I could come out and get you in two weeks and we could go on another date?"

Dreams really do come true.

Linton and I dated steadily all summer. Neither one of us had much experience on how to engage in conversation. We were both from large families where 'Children should be seen, not heard.' Linton would drive for an hour to Colorado City to get me. Then we would drive back to St. George to go to dinner and a movie or bowling. Then he drove another hour to take me back home and another hour back home to St. George. The two hours we were together in the car were spent listening to the radio and sitting close. Not talking.

I did get brave enough to tell him that I didn't want to kiss anyone until I was married. He respected my wishes and never tried to step over that boundary. I thought that if a couple had enough in common and always had the other person's best interests at heart, they could make a marriage work. Linton was old fashioned. He believed that women should be in the home raising the children while the husband worked to provide for them. I had been raised to believe the same thing. At twenty-seven years old, he had proposed and been turned down twice by two Mormon girls because of his polygamist beliefs. He truly believed in his father's polygamy and wanted to do the will of God.

Of the six Kirkland brothers who were already married, Steve and Linton were the only ones who wanted to follow in their Father's footsteps and live the Celestial Law of Plural Marriage. Linton was hoping that by finding me, he had finally found someone who would be willing to live polygamy with him. Although I looked every bit the part of a girl from Colorado City, bun in my hair, dress to the middle of my calf and three layers of stockings, he never made me feel embarrassed for who I was. I always felt beautiful around him. Sometimes he invited his brothers and their wives to join us on our dates. We went bowling or played pool and went to lots of movies together. His brothers and their wives showed me how young couples look and act, how to carry on a conversation, and how to laugh and have fun.

One September Sunday afternoon, Linton came to my house in Colorado City. He was in a grumpy mood. He saw a picture of Bart and Jean on the quilt we were making and picked it up to look at it. "There's a marriage that will never last," he said, almost under his breath. I was shocked by his rudeness. In the nine months we'd dated I had never seen him be so negative. In our family we lived by Mothers rule, *'If you can't say something nice, don't say anything at all'*. After Linton left that day I became more and more upset at him for being so rude. I decided to write him a letter telling him that I could never date anyone who didn't wish the best for my brothers and sisters. *How dare he*! I would say how I thought this must be a sign that we were never meant to be together and that we should cease all communications. I was being a little dramatic but I was sure that when he got the letter he would come to me all repentant and apologetic. After all, how could he live without me? I wrote the letter and mailed it. Then I was shocked when he never came to see me again and never called. Not one word.

I hadn't seen or heard from Nathan for a year and now I had told Linton we were through. I hadn't been without a boyfriend since fourth grade and now I was at the mercy of my Father and the weirdoes he brought into my life. Maybe God would intervene. I prayed with all my heart that He would.

When word got out that I wasn't dating Linton anymore, Aunt Florence Blackmore made arrangements for me to go out on a date with her son, Shawn. I agreed to go but only if I could take Kay and Keith with me as chaperones. I didn't trust Shawn because he had already been married and divorced. The evening Shawn came out to get me, he was a little taken aback when all three of us climbed into his car. But he was cordial all the way to town and he told us he had the perfect movie he was taking us to. At the theater, we got our popcorn and drinks, Shawn graciously insisting on paying for everything. About a half hour into the movie, I became a little nervous with the story line. It went downhill fast when the girl in the story took the boy up into the attic and began undressing him. I should have known by the name of the movie, '*Girls in the Attic*', and the sly smile on Shawn's face, that I was being paid back for bringing my brother and sister with me to the movies. I hadn't noticed that it was R rated and I wouldn't have known what that meant anyway. I just trusted that Shawn would make sure he took us to a good movie.

Keith, Kay and I hurriedly got up and walked out just before the girl got the boys pants off. We waited outside on some benches for Shawn to finish watching the movie. When he came out he was almost laughing. "How did you all like the movie?"

I gave him a dirty look and we all endured a long, silent ride home. All I could think of was that in all the nine months Linton and I dated he had never taken me to a movie like that. How I wished I had never sent that letter.

Father had been looking all over Utah and Nevada for a cattle ranch he could buy. And because the world was still going to hell and he had to protect his family from the wicked world, he found a ranch that was fifty miles from the nearest sign of civilization; four hours northwest of Colorado City and fifty miles north of Pioche, Nevada; the last twenty-five miles on a winding dirt road that went on forever, disappearing into pine-covered mountains.

Three Donohue Brothers had owned the ranch since 1890. One of the brothers had recently passed away and the last two didn't want to find each other dead some morning in their beds, so they had decided it was time to sell.

Father took us all out to see the ranch and meet the old bachelors, who looked at least two hundred years old. They were very shy and awkward and acted like they hadn't seen another human since D-Day. They stood against the fence, listening to Father talk.

The ranch house was small, maybe twelve hundred square

feet. It had a tiny living room and kitchen and two bedrooms on the main floor. You had to go through one of the bedrooms to find a tiny, steep stairway that led to two more bedrooms upstairs. The bathroom stood fifty feet away, up high on the hill just north of the house. Water came from the spring up in the canyon and flowed down a small creek that ran by the back door of the house. There was no electricity and no phone. If we thought we were going back in time to the 30s and 40s when we moved to Colorado City in 1964, it was nothing compared to this. It was 1971 and we were moving back a whole century.

After the family toured the mansion, I linked arms with Kay and walked with her up to the cranny so I could relieve my bladder. I pinched my nose and went inside and turned the wooden latch that locked me in while Kay stood guard. "Well, when the world comes to an end, at least we'll be safe from the armies of the enemies," I hollered out to her, as I hovered over one of the two holes.

"You're right. There's absolutely no way anyone will find us up here." Kay called from the outside. "Our prospects of finding a man up here don't look very promising either."

Father made a deal with his sons that if they all went in together to buy the ranch they would be equal partners. If they worked hard, they would have it paid off in ten years. The ranch cost $90,000 for 650 acres. It only had thirty-five head of cattle on it, but they would build that up over the years. They had saved $10,000 building condominiums at Brian Head Ski Resort. Father had a friendly banker in Cedar City who would let them use the cattle for $10,000 collateral, so with the $20,000 as a down payment, the sale was finalized. But we still had to leave our home in Colorado City.

In September, Roger and Lee went back to the Academy and the little girls, Helen, Ruth and Beth, and Lillith went back to grade school. The little girls loved school. They were popular because they sang together and Mother always made sure they had the best birthday parties in town. But word had spread through every household in Colorado City that our family was going to Sunday meetings with apostates and that we were moving away.

One night I woke up to the sound of one of the little girls whimpering. I got out of bed and went to their double bed pushed up against the wall under the window. I listened to see who was crying and climbed over two bodies and squeezed myself between the wall and seven-year-old Lillith. "What's the matter?" I whispered. Lillith sniffed and wiped her nose on her long sleeved nightgown.

"My teacher told me I was stupid because I misspelled a word on my spelling test."

"That's just awful. Doesn't she know stupid is a bad word?" I tickled her under her ear, trying to get her to smile. "What word did you misspell?"

"America." She sniffed again.

"America is a really hard word," I told her. "There are too many A's in it." I tickled her again.

"Why does everyone hate me now?" She asked. "None of my friends want to play jump rope with me anymore. They won't even sit by me at lunch or walk home with me. Yesterday when we were walking home Helen said that her teacher poked her with a needle and called her an apostate. What's an apostate?"

"They call us apostates because we don't believe in their Prophet anymore. I'm so sorry that you have to go through this."

"Why do we have to be apostates? I love my friends. I love my home. Are we going to move away?"

"It's not your fault. You didn't do anything wrong. Father has decided that we are moving so we will move. I'm sorry sweetheart." I snuggled up closer and rubbed her back until we both fell asleep.

The little girls began waking up screaming with nightmares every night. Father went to the school and told the principal he better put a stop to the persecution. Twelve-year-old Helen, ten-year-old Ruth, nine-year-old Beth and seven-year-old Lillith met under the weeping willow tree after school and walked home a different way every day so the boys chasing them with rocks couldn't find them.

Soon after school started, Father and Mother told us that moving day was set for November 1st. On Halloween we packed up most of the house and trudged the boxes and furniture up the ramp into the two ton Dodge truck and Father's diesel packing everything in tight. We woke early next morning to a cloudy, cold day. I helped Mother pack up all the music from the top of the piano and the piano bench into a cardboard box. Father and his boys put their shoulders up against the piano and rolled the heavy oak upright up the ramp and into the truck.

The beds went in next. Kay had the vacuum roaring back in the bedrooms, cleaning up. There wasn't room in the ranch house for the round table with the Lazy-Susan so we sadly left it behind. I ran a sink full of hot soapy water and started washing the empty kitchen cupboards. It was one of Mother's rules. You always leave your old house clean for the new people who will move in after you.

"As soon as you are done there, I think we are finished," Mother said, breathing heavily after lugging a box to the car. Donna, now three, came to Mother with her arms outstretched and whined until Mother picked her up and sat her on her hip. "Janice and Helen are cleaning bathrooms. Father is ready to leave, so be quick. We have to get all the way to the ranch today and get some things unpacked before dark."

I looked out the kitchen window and remembered the night Jeremiah, our neighbor and one of my boyfriends at the time, put his face up against the window in the dark while I was doing dishes, he scared the heck out of me. He laughed and I yelled at him and told him he was terrible, which was exactly what he wanted to hear. I smiled at the memories. So many I couldn't count. It had been a great place to grow up.

My reverie was interrupted by Father hollering from outside. "Everybody in the car. Now!" I drained the water from the sink and left the raggedy cloth hanging from the faucet. I looked around me and saw an empty house. It would be lonely without us and Mother's piano.

None of us realized until years later, the effect we had had on this tiny community. Whenever we ran into old friends from Colorado City, they said things like, "How's your Mother? I've never met anyone so talented." Or, "It was like a light went out in our town when your family moved away."

Music can bring joy where there is none. And Mother and Father certainly brought the music.

As we drove past Nathan's house I thought of the night I'd sat with him on the front porch. The way I had scared him when he came out of the house. His sweet smile of relief when he saw it was only me. I hadn't seen or heard from him since our horse ride and that failed kiss. That was over a year ago. A lot had happened since then. I had dated Linton for nine months and then wrote him a Dear John letter. I was leaving my home with no sign of any future love.

Father pulled the diesel up to the stop sign at the highway leading out of town. Keith pulled up behind him in the Dodge. They waited for the car with Mother and the rest of us inside to catch up.

"Pull up beside the truck," Mother instructed me, as we got

closer. She was letting me drive so I wouldn't cry. When Father saw us pull up beside him, he opened his door and climbed out. I put the car in park and turned off the engine.

"Let's all get out and gather around. I know it's cold," Mother said, opening her door and helping the little girls out of the back. She grabbed Donna and set her on her hip. "We forgot to pray," she said to Father, who was still wondering why we had stopped the car.

"Boys, get out here," Father yelled, motioning with a sweep of his arm.

"Everyone join hands," Mother instructed, as she grabbed Ruth's hand in hers. Ruth grabbed Helen's and Helen grabbed mine. The boys joined the circle and we stood there at the stop sign and bowed our heads as Mother prayed. "Dear God, thank you for each of these children and their goodness. Please bless us as we go on another adventure together. Help us to always be kind to one another and be grateful for each other. Amen."

I opened my eyes and looked around the circle. Everyone looked lost.

A Long Winters Walk

The cold increased as we drove further north, leaving the red rock mountains of Southern Utah and crossing into the sagebrush and pinyon pine covered hills of Nevada. Twenty miles north of Pioche, Nevada, just after the tiny town of Ursine, I gripped the steering wheel and hugged the inside edge of the winding road that dropped off one hundred feet to the water of Eagle Valley reservoir. Twenty-five more miles of dirt road and we would be there. The fields were crowded with cattle brought down from the mountains for the winter and they stood heads down, feeding on the dry golden grass in the crested wheat fields. We were leaving civilization behind. There were a couple cabins, hiding up against hills but they looked abandoned. The cows were the only other living things around.

As we pulled up to the ranch house, it started to snow. We worked as fast as we could to get the trucks unpacked. Mother had a fire burning in the kitchen stove trying to warm up the house.

The first thing Father did the next day was replace the tiny wood stove in the kitchen with the big black Army stove we'd used in Colorado City. Then he hooked up a water heater to the stove so that in the spring when it stopped freezing, we could dig a trench and pipe the water from the creek into the house. Then we would have hot water every time we had a fire. But for now, every cold frosty morning we had to break the ice covering the stream, before we could haul water to the house. Sometimes the water ran crystal clear and clean. Other times there were all sorts of tiny bugs and algae swimming in it and we had to strain the water through a dishtowel and boil it before we could drink it. Once again we heated our water on the stove so we could bathe in the big number ten tub, while someone held up the curtain, like we did in Idaho.

Father, Keith, Roger and Lee had jobs in Brian Head building condos so they were gone all week and came home on the weekends. Mother kept us girls busy cleaning the house. The walls were covered with eighty years of soot and smoke from the wood stove. A family of mice had taken up residence in the pantry, so everything had to be taken out, thrown away, and the shelves painted with white, oil-based washable paint. For the next few weeks we all huddled around the stove and tried to stay warm. Kay and I wrapped up like Eskimos every morning and evening when we went out to the rickety old barn to milk the cow, feed and water the horses and coax an egg out of the chickens who had decided it was way too cold to lay eggs. Kay warned them that if they didn't start pooping out eggs soon we were going to have to chop their heads off and eat them. The next day there was one egg. We had a good laugh about that and a more exciting reason to do the chores.

Kay and I shared a cold double bed upstairs. Janice had a single bed next to our double. We had so many wool blankets covering us we could hardly roll over. Kay tired to cuddle up to me to get warm but I hated anyone touching me. She confessed to me, years later, that she waited until I was asleep and would then snuggle up against me to get warm. The five younger girls slept in two beds in another small bedroom upstairs.

One day, we went exploring into the closets that lined each side of the upstairs bedrooms and found five boxes of old books. The heat from the stove never seemed to reach the upstairs bedrooms, so we put on our coats before we went up again to look through the treasures we had found. We sat around the boxes and sorted through them like we had discovered boxes of gold. Mother was excited when she found the *The Hue and Cry,* one of her favorites books from her childhood. We found *The Silver Chalice* and *The Robe,* which later became two of my favorites. That night, Mother opened *The Hue and Cry* and read to us by lantern light through the long evening hours.

Whenever I got an extra minute I had my face buried in one of the books I found upstairs. I wasn't a reader like Kay, but I had to find something to occupy my time before I went mad. I don't remember the title of the romantic novel, but it was about a handsome king who married a young princess and then had multiple affairs. It was quite an education. I learned a lot from that book and I wondered if I was going to be stuck in this hellhole forever or if some knight in shining armor might accidently get lost in the middle of nowhere and rescue me. I wondered if I had done the wrong thing by letting Linton go. He had been so kind. So what if he was grumpy? Everyone gets grumpy sometimes. I was grumpy myself about having to live out here in the boondocks.

I thought about Nathan and wondered if he still wanted to marry me. Maybe he had been assigned to someone else by now. Did I want to be married to him, trapped in a world governed by the Priesthood Brethren? But I was trapped here, too. Which was worse? Our escape from the Priesthood Brethren had not brought me freedom. It brought me loneliness and isolation. I needed to take matters into my own hands and find me a husband. Finally, I broke down and confided in Mother.

"Why don't you write Nathan a letter and tell him your feelings and see what he writes back to you? Maybe it will help you make a decision," she said.

I wrote to Nathan, telling him I didn't think I wanted to live a life that was controlled by the Priesthood Brethren. I didn't want my daughters to marry old men and I felt that people should be able to make their own decisions about whom they marry and where they should live. He wrote back, "I think it is a privilege to have a Prophet who can give you counsel from God and I would hope you would want that, too."

I didn't write back. I was a different girl than I was a year ago. *Good-bye sweet Nathan. I really liked you. I might have even loved you.* But what did I know? I was only nineteen.

Mother was anxious to get Helen and the younger girls doing some school lessons. She would be their teacher from now on. One day, when she and Janice were busy with the laundry, she called me from my room.

"Jelene, get the girls around the table and help them with their math. They mustn't get too far behind." The girls gathered around the table and opened their writing tablets.

"Hello, students," I began cheerfully. "Helen, why don't you start out with a page of long division? Write down four numbers divide it by three numbers. Make more up as you go." Helen started writing down numbers as fast as she could. "Ruth, why don't you start with your four times tables."

"I know more than my four times tables," Ruth said, with disgust. "I know clear up to my twelve's. I learned them last year in school. I don't know why you think you can boss me around. You are just going to get married and leave us out here all alone.

I hate you!" She screamed. "I want to go home. I'm going to run away. I'm going to run away and go back home!"

Mother dried her hands on a towel and came to the table. "Ruth, you can't talk like that," she said, calmly. "We don't hate anyone, especially not your sister, who is only trying to help you." Ruth came out of her chair and threw her arms around Mother's waist and sobbed. "I'm sorry. I just miss my friends so much and I don't want to live here. I don't."

Mother missed her home too. She held her sad girl and I'm sure she was thinking back to the years she led the band in Colorado City and how much joy it had brought her. The air seemed lighter there; the sunshine brighter. The ranch in the mountains of the high desert had been covered in clouds since the day we arrived. But it was winter now. In the spring it would be better. It just had to be.

Every weekend Father and the boys came home with supplies to start building an addition onto the ranch house. It would include a large living room and two bedrooms above it. They tore down an old service station in Salina, Utah, and brought the used lumber out to the ranch.

It seemed we had only been at the ranch for a month before men from other polygamist groups started showing up at the house to lend a hand and hammer to the building of the new addition. Really, they came looking for wives. They were all Father's friends and he told them, "Come on out and look around." It felt to me like he was telling them, "*You have daughters, I have daughters. Maybe we can make a trade.*"

I wasn't interested because they were all old and not that good looking. Maybe if they had been handsome, I would have been nicer to them. But I did my best to discourage them and after their second visit, I would let Father be the bearer of bad news and tell them I wasn't interested.

At the December Independent Polygamist meeting at the Teerlink's home in Bunkerville, Nevada, I was happy when Linton's sister, Ruth told me that he asked her to ask me if he could come and see me at the ranch.

"Yes. I would love to see him again." I told her. I thought back to the fun nights we had spent at the movies and going to Paula's Mexican Restaurant for my favorite burrito. Linton was young and handsome and he smelled good. Unlike that last old geezer with his sad wife and fifteen snotty nosed kids that kept showing up at the ranch, all smiley.

It had frozen hard every night since we'd moved to the ranch but on December 24th we had a winter thaw. It warmed up to sixty degrees, turning the dirt road into a slick muddy mess. That happened to be same day Father headed out to the ranch with a load of windows for the new addition. The truck tires made ruts two feet deep in the road, causing the truck to lurch back and forth. Every window was broken by the time he got home.

Unbeknownst to me, on December 25, Linton decided it was high time he came to see me. He brought his sisters, Evelyn, Linda and Trudy, with him, thinking they were just going on a nice Sunday drive. They got to the crested wheat fields ten miles from the ranch house and started to sink into Father's truck tire tracks. Linton took off into the field, thinking he could get better traction in the grass. Down he went into the mud. He was stuck. He had no idea how much farther it was to the ranch, or even if he was on the right road. So he told his sisters to get out and walk a little farther up the road and he would go back to where he had seen a two-ton truck at a ranch house they had passed. "Don't go too far," he warned them. "If you get cold, come back and turn on the truck and stay warm." They walked up about a mile and didn't see any sign of life. They came back to the truck and waited.

Linton kept walking south. It started to snow at mile seven. It was getting darker and he was getting colder. There was a large sagebrush bush beside the road and he climbed under it for shelter. *I just need to rest a minute*, he thought, shivering with cold. *Once I rest, I'll have enough energy to get to where I saw that truck*. He was just about to drift off when he remembered a story his brother had told him about an old rancher who got stuck out on the Arizona Strip in a snow storm. The rancher knew it was just two miles to his neighbor's cabin but he got tired and decided to get under a tree and rest. That's where they found him the next morning, frozen to death. Linton forced himself out from under the bush and started walking again.

It was fifteen miles back to the house where he had seen the truck. He couldn't feel his feet anymore but he knew he had to get back to his sisters. Thank goodness for the half moon that gave enough light to show him the way. He knocked on the door of the house where the truck sat in the driveway, but no one answered. Luckily the keys were in the truck. He started it up and drove back to the girls, picked them up and took them back into town where he called his brothers.

Father had come home that weekend with news that he had found Kay and I a job cleaning condominiums in Brian Head so we were all heading into work Monday morning when we came around the corner and saw three men hooking up a chain to a green truck. That truck looked very familiar. Then I saw him, a blanket thrown over his shoulders, my tall, handsome, skinny man.

"That looks like Linton." Lee said, from the front seat.

"Looks like he got himself good and stuck." Roger said with a chuckle as he rolled down his window to wave. Father pulled the car to a stop along side the edge of the road and they got out to see if they needed help.

"Well, I see I was at least in the right part of Nevada," Linton joked, as he saw Father walking toward him.

"Yeah, you were almost there. Just ten more miles and you would have run right into the house."

I hadn't seen or talked to Linton since I wrote that Dear John letter in September. I slumped down in the back seat, my heart pounding. Here was this beautiful man I hadn't seen for three months, a man who I told I never wanted to see again. Then changed my mind and now I did want to see him. And here he was, stuck out here in the freezing cold, all because of me.

"What do I do?" I asked Kay.

"Well, he came all the way out here to see you. You have to at least go over and say hi," she said.

"Do I have to? I look terrible."

"Yes, you do. You look fine. "

"You have to come with me then." I begged.

We got out of the car and walked over to where Linton was in the middle of his story, telling Father and the boys about his long winter's walk. Our eyes met and I felt the heat rise in my face. I stood behind Father, listening and when he was through with his story I stepped over to Linton. "Hi. Are you okay?"

"Well, I can't feel my feet, but other than that I'm okay," he laughed.

But what I heard was, I'm your knight in shining armor and I have come to take you away from this hellhole.

I smiled up into his beautiful brown eyes and said, "I'm so glad."

"When you get this truck out, you all go on up to the house," Father said. Mother will fix you some breakfast. You can't miss it. It's just up the road a bit."

"Yea, we'll do that," Linton said and winked at me.

The January monthly meeting was at the Kirkland's house

in St. George. It was so good to be back in town. Stores, cars, people.

Linton grew more handsome every time I saw him. When he walked into the meeting he was wearing jeans and a royal blue shirt. I could hardly believe that someone that beautiful wanted to date me: a girl from the Creek who dressed like a plyg. After the meeting, Linton asked me if I wanted to go with him across town to see his brother. Steve was newly married to Susan, a pretty girl from St. George, with long black hair. When we walked into their cute basement apartment, they were holding hands and I looked at them with envy. I wanted what she had. A man of my own. A kitchen of my own.

After we'd eaten the sandwiches and cupcakes Susan had made for us, Linton asked if I would go for a ride with him. He took my hand when we got outside and I felt the world shift under my feet. The skin on my hand began to feel extremely warm and I felt the warmth go up my arm and into the rest of my body. *What was happening*? I had never had this happen before. We scooted into the driver's side of his 1963 brown and gold Mercury Sedan and I leaned into his shoulder so I could keep that warm feeling coming.

We turned and drove up Flood Street. The radio was playing '*Stand By Me*', by Ben E. King, when out of the blue, Linton asked, "Will you marry me?" The question I had hoped and prayed he would ask me took me by surprise. I didn't know what to say. I wanted to say yes, right then and there, but I knew I had to consult God first. I couldn't just make a decision this big on my own. I had never made any big decisions by myself in my life. I was just a girl. I didn't have any business making decisions like this on my own.

"I'm going to have to go home and pray about it," I said, honestly. Linton smiled back at me.

I think he was glad I was taking it seriously. At least I hadn't said no.

"We'll be coming into town again in two weeks and I'll give you my answer then." Linton drove up to the "Dixie" on the red hill and parked the car. We got out and leaned back against the car and looked out over the city. He put his arm around my shoulder and felt the warmth coming from him. *Was this the sign from Heaven I'd been waiting for*?

When I got home I fasted and prayed. I begged God to give me a revelation. I had to know without a shadow of a doubt that Linton was the one. I picked up the *Doctrine and Covenants* and read in Section 9, Verse 8,

> *"If it be right I will cause that your bosom shall burn within you; therefore, you shall feel that it is right. But if it be not right you shall have no feeling, but you shall have a stupor of thought that shall cause you to forget the thing which is wrong."*

There was a burning in my chest every time I thought of Linton followed by that overall warm feeling I had felt the day he ask me to marry him. After days of worry, sore knees and no food, it was just going to have to be enough. My other choices were old men with unhappy wives who gave me real stomachaches.

I got off my knees and went downstairs. I put some shortening on an old rag and oiled the top of the black army stove. Mother brought the pancake batter over to me and I put a cup of dough on each of the four round black lids of the stove. The dough sizzled and bubbled as they cooked into golden brown saucers. Mother came back to the stove to take the plate full of pancakes back to the table. I put my arm through hers and pulled her toward me. "Linton asked me to marry him Sunday after the meeting," I whispered.

She looked surprised. "Oh."

"And I'm going to say yes," I told her.

"Well, I think that's wonderful." She said, nodding her head in approval.

It had been two weeks since I'd seen Linton and I asked Father if I could go to town with him. "I'm not going to St. George today. I'm only going into Cedar City. Sorry," he said, as he hurried to his truck. Linton would just have to wait until the next monthly meeting to get his answer.

The February meeting was held at the Teerlink's home in Bunkerville, Nevada and I was so nervous waiting for Linton to show up that I paced back and forth in front of their living room window. Finally, I asked Ruth, his sister, if Linton was really coming. "Yes, he's coming." She looked at me and laughed as she rushed her toddler to the bathroom. A few minutes later, I saw a diesel truck pull into the yard and realized it was Linton and he must be taking a load to California after the meeting. I watched him get out and go to the passenger side and open the door. He helped a girl out of the truck. What? Did Linton want me to share him already? I just had to breathe and smile until I could get him alone and ask him what was going on. I waited until he brought the girl in and introduced her to everyone.

"This is Becky," Linton said. "She's a friend of mine from Salt Lake."

I smiled sweetly, but felt the contents of my stomach rising up to my throat. Becky went around the circle and shook everyone's hand. When she held out her hand to me, I wanted to scream, but I took her hand, swallowed hard and graciously said hello. Then I slipped out the back door as quickly as I could. Linton followed me.

"Let's go for a walk." He grabbed my hand and pulled me after him to the top of the small hill that looked out over the house and the Virgin River wandering though the valley. We sat down on some large rocks.

"Could you please explain to me who Becky is?" I said, trying hard to control my jealous heart.

"She's one of Lloyd's sisters. He's a friend of mine from Salt Lake. I met his polygamist family when I was going to LDS Business college. Becky and I went out a couple of times but we just didn't click. She showed up yesterday at my parents house so I invited her to the meeting," he said, his face the picture of innocence. He pulled me close and I could smell his aftershave. "So, are we getting married?"

I made him wait a half a minute. "Yes," I whispered. "Let's get married."

"I have one more thing I have to do." He grabbed my hand and practically dragged me down the hill and into the house where we found Father and Mother in the crowded living room talking to Mr. Teerlink. We walked over to them and Linton said, "I'm here to ask for your daughter's hand in marriage." The room became completely silent. Father looked at me and said, "Is this what you want?"

"Yes," I said, smiling.

"Well then, you have my permission to get married." Everyone, including Becky, congratulated us. I went to Mother and hugged her. She squeezed me back. I was kind of surprised that it had gone so smoothly. In my heart of hearts, I knew Father would never let me marry anyone unless it was to his advantage.

After the meeting I took my place on the passenger side of the diesel truck. I was staking my claim and I wanted everyone to know Linton was all mine. At least for now. I drove with Linton down to the exit where I got out and into the car with my family to go home. We had set a wedding date. Two weeks from today.

Linton surprised me and braved the ranch road the very next weekend. He came to get me so we could go to town and pick out my wedding ring. It was lunchtime so Mother invited him to sit down to eat with us.

With hot pads in hand, Mother opened the oven door and brought out one half of a baked banana squash on a cookie sheet and set it in the middle of the table. Lunch. She asked Helen to bring the butter and salt and she began cutting everyone a slice of squash. I couldn't eat squash without gagging so I said I wasn't hungry. Linton graciously accepted his slice, which he salted and began cutting it into small squares. Besides squash, we had been living on pinto bean soup made with two quarts of Mother's bottled tomatoes. Luckily the bottled tomatoes, applesauce, and peaches we had canned last fall had survived the trip from the cellar in Colorado City to the ranch. I was wishing we had some of that soup to serve Linton today.

Later, Linton told me he was shocked. He thought that if we were rich enough to buy a cattle ranch we could surely afford some groceries. He thanked Mother for lunch as he finished his last square of squash.

"We should probably get going so we can get to town in time to look at rings today," he said, sliding his chair back from the table. "I'll make sure she is safe at my mom's house tonight and we should be back here tomorrow afternoon." I gave Mother a kiss on the cheek, grabbed my coat and bag and ran after him out the door.

I couldn't believe I was going to get to pick my own wedding ring. After we stopped by Dick's Café in St. George to get a hamburger, which I practically inhaled, we headed to McArthur Jewelers on Main Street. Linton picked up a boring gold band from the glass case. "I was thinking maybe something like this."

I pointed to a beautiful diamond solitaire under the glass,

with a diamond pattern carved into the gold bands. "I was thinking about something like this," I said, looking up at Linton with a smile.

"Okay, that's the one," he told the salesman. It cost him $150 dollars.

I spent the night at Linton's mother's house. It was always fun to see his sisters. At supper Mr. Kirkland sat at the head of the table and everyone gathered around and waited for the blessing. There was an oval plate filled with fried chicken, a bowl of rice, a pitcher of gravy and another bowl of butter beans swimming in butter and cream. Mr. Kirkland's booming voice thanked the Lord for the bounty. Then he broke a piece of whole-cake cornbread from a plate beside him and spread it generously with more butter. There was a small lump in my throat as I tried to swallow the delicious chicken, thinking about the squash my sisters were eating at the ranch.

The next day Linton picked me up and we began the three-hour drive to the ranch. When the family saw us pull up to the house, the girls, all bundled up in their coats, ran to meet us.

"We're going out to feed the chickens," Ruth said.

"Can you help me with something first?" Linton asked, heading to the back of his truck. He climbed up into the back and opened up four large coolers. He started handing everyone bags of groceries. "There's a turkey in that first bag you'll want to cook right up," he said. I'm sure he was thinking about our lack of a refrigerator. "There's some canned goods and different kinds of crackers and cheese I thought you might like. And there's even some broccoli. " He laughed, as he handed down the last of the food and smiled at the girls, wide eyed with wonder at the miracle they had just witnessed. I gave Linton the look I've given him many times since, the one that said, '*thank you.*'

The boys worked every day to get the new living room ready

for my wedding. They laid linoleum and carpet, covered one wall with some old barn wood and built cabinets along the north wall. Mother gave me enough money to pick out some white fabric and lace for my wedding dress, and Kay and I went into Cedar City with the boys when they went to get the roofing material.

Father had arranged for us to do a family show at the Caliente Detention Center for Girls in Caliente, Nevada, three days before my wedding. He wanted to show off his family and let everyone in the county see how well we could sing. I couldn't believe he expected us to do a show on top of everything we had to do to get ready for my wedding. We had been so busy we hadn't practiced enough to do our parts perfectly and I hated to perform when I didn't feel ready. But the show must go on.

It was the first show without Bart because he was married now. So the boys couldn't sing their quartets. But Mother pulled us through. She was at the piano playing and it seemed that with every introduction we went on autopilot. We sang our family numbers, got out our instruments and played the family band numbers, and the younger girls filled in the rest with songs and poems and piano solos. The girls from the school enjoyed every minute of it and gave us some rousing applause.

When we walked out to our car Linton and his sister Linda were in the parking lot waiting for us. I had informed Linton about the show in Caliente and he said he would bring Linda out so she could go to the ranch with us to help Kay make our wedding cake.

But that's not the only thing he had on his mind. I didn't know he wanted to take me with him to Las Vegas and get married legally before we got married at the ranch on Sunday. I walked over to where he was talking to Father and I heard him say, "I'll bring her back the same day."

"Absolutely not!" Father said firmly. "The priesthood ceremony is the only one that counts. You can get married legally anytime you want after that."

Linton was pissed. I followed him to his car and sat down in the passenger seat. "Please, I'm begging you not to make this an issue. He'll call off the wedding. He will. Please."

He reached over and took my hand. "Okay. It was worth a try, I guess. I'll see you Sunday."

I finished sewing my wedding dress using Mother's old treadle sewing machine because there was no electricity. As I sewed the buttons on to the cuffs, I hoped and prayed that Linton wouldn't show up on our special day with another old girlfriend.

My wedding day, Sunday, February 20, 1972, was sunny and warm. There were patches of snow in the fields and up on the hills. Linton showed up around 11:00 a.m., alone. I didn't want to bring us bad luck by letting him see the bride before the wedding, so I stayed upstairs while he hung out with my brothers.

The cake Linda and Kay had made was on the new cupboard counter in the living room. It was a white three-layered cake with yellow flowers and green leaves. The center cake had drooped a little in the middle after it came out of the oven, causing the whole cake to tilt to the right. The new living room was finished just in time and it still smelled of new carpet. There was a rectangle mirror hanging above the piano and a new brick fireplace on the east wall. I was so happy to have a nice place for my wedding.

Linton's father and mothers brought the kids who were still living at home and his married siblings began arriving with their spouses. They traveled 150 miles to the ranch, 25 of which were dirt roads, to be with us on our special day.

Kay was upstairs helping me get ready. "Let's see. We need something old, something new, something borrowed, something blue," she said.

"Let's look in Mother's top drawer and see what we can find." We walked to Mother's room. "Here's a hanky with blue flowers. And it's old. And you are borrowing it. Wow! That was easy," Kay said, laughing. "You will come and see me, won't you?" Kay took me in her arms and gave me a warm hug. Tears came to her eyes. "I'm going to miss you so much. I don't know what I'll do without you."

"I'm sorry to leave you in this place. But you will find someone soon and then you will be an old married lady like me." I hugged her harder. "What about something new? There's nothing new here."

"You have new wedding shoes and a new wedding dress," Kay said. "That will have to do. I'm going to go downstairs and see if everything is ready for you to come down. Are you so excited?"

"I'm nervous," I told her. She went down the narrow steps and came right back.

"They're ready for you," she whispered, squeezing my hands. She helped me down the stairs in my long dress and when I got to the kitchen, she went ahead to the living room and gave Mother the signal to begin the wedding march. My dress caught on the nails holding down the old linoleum in the kitchen and had to back up and start again. I could see Linton standing there in the living room waiting for me. He was smiling. I just concentrated on getting to him.

I was so nervous I didn't even think about how sad Mother had looked that morning. I had noticed her red eyes but didn't say anything. *Why would she be sad on my wedding day*? I wanted her to be happy, as happy as I was. We had been through a lifetime together. I had been by her side while she was leaving her beloved church, joining the polygamists, and leaving the fundamentalist group. I had watched her have babies and bury many of them. I didn't understand until I had daughters of my own what Mother already knew: that when your children say *'I do'* they are not yours anymore.

Linton took my hand and we stood before Father, who opened the *Doctrine and Covenants* to the Marriage vows and began. When we finished saying our vows, Linton grabbed me with such gusto that my veil came off with our first kiss. Everyone got a chuckle out of it.

The Teerlink family had come to our wedding and brought a set of blue plastic bowls, our only wedding gift. Actually Linton's brothers and their wives gave some money to his mother and she gave it to us in an old cookie jar that I still treasure today. When we got home from our honeymoon we opened it up and there was one hundred and fifty dollars inside. Linton asked me what I wanted to do with it and I said I really had to have an industrial sewing machine. He added another two hundred dollars to the jar and we went out to Colorado City and bought Hannah Pledger's used Bernina that I still sew on today, forty-five years later.

After our wedding ceremony, we headed to Salt Lake for a three-day honeymoon. It was dark by the time we got to Wendover, Nevada, so we decided to stay there. I was so nervous when Linton opened the door to the room at the Wendover Cozy Inn, I didn't know if my heart would make it through the night. I went into the bathroom and had a long luxurious bath, something I hadn't had since we left Colorado City, three months ago. I climbed into the long white flannel nightgown I had made especially for this night. It had long sleeves gathered at the wrist and stand up collar that went almost to my ears. I brushed out my waist long hair and let it fall in waves down my back. When I finally mustered the courage to open the bathroom door I stood at the foot of the bed and waited. In my fantasies, my new husband always came to me and wrapped his arms around me, saying, "You are the most beautiful bride in the world." Then he took me in his arms and we made passionate love together. In real life, without looking up from his paper, Linton patted my side of the bed and I walked over and lay down beside him. Then he continued to read the Salt Lake Tribune that he had picked up when he checked us into the motel. And I fell asleep.

The next day we went to Salt Lake City and got a room at The Little America, the nicest hotel in town. As soon as we got settled in the room, Linton stretched out on the bed, leaned back against the headboard, and unbuttoned the first two buttons on his shirt. He was acting a little nervous. "So, what do you want to do?" he smiled, shyly.

"Well, I would love to go to a fabric store."

He chuckled and jumped off the bed and buttoned his shirt. "Then, that's what we'll do." The fabric store was located in one of the big malls down town. I had never seen so much fabric. Linton followed me around the store holding the bolts of fabric I handed him. I picked out some white, lightweight fabric with tiny yellow roses on it for a blouse and some black polyester to make me a pair of bell-bottom pants. At the time I didn't think there was anything wrong with going fabric shopping on my honeymoon. But my sisters and my kids love to make fun of me when out of the blue, someone will say, "Who went fabric shopping on their honeymoon?" Then they all bust up laughing at my expense.

That night in bed Linton started to French kiss me and I wondered what he was doing. Why would anyone stick their tongue in another person's mouth? Disgusting.

Years later, I asked Linton why it took us three days to consummate our marriage, and he said, "I was scared to death and I had absolutely no idea what to do with you and that nightgown."

The next weekend we took Linton's brother, Steve, and his new wife Susan, to be our witnesses and drove down to Las Vegas and got married legally at the county court house. After the quick ceremony we went to the casino and took pictures under the million-dollar horseshoe and ate at a buffet with more food than I had ever seen in my life.

I was looking forward to the ride home and getting to know my new brother and sister-in-law. They had only been married two months. But all they did was fight all the way home over who forgot to pay the electric bill. I had never seen a married couple argue and I told myself that I would never talk to my husband like that and was determined that my marriage would be perfect. The good news was they were so busy arguing they didn't notice us making out in the back seat.

My Blue Heaven

The Kirkland farm in the neighboring town of Washington, Utah, was lined on the south with old cottonwoods that drank from the muddy Virgin River. The top twenty-five acres were planted with alfalfa and corn. The bottom fifteen acres, where the sheep and cattle grazed the short grass, were meandering lands that would occasionally flood when the river came up over its banks during the spring and fall rains. This is where the twelve Kirkland boys spent every morning and evening milking the cows and all their summer days building fence, stacking hay and chopping silage.

Linton's oldest sister, Ruth and her husband Tom, lived in a tiny house that Grandpa Kirkland had moved onto the farm. They offered to let Linton and I move in with them so we could save money to build a house. She moved their five kids over into bunk beds in their bedroom, so we could have the only other basement bedroom. Upstairs, there was a small kitchen and dining area and a tiny living room with a tiny bathroom in between.

We had a double bed, a chest of drawers and of course, my wonderful new sewing machine wedged in. Linton was unpacking some boxes and discovered a tin can full of change. He laughed and handed it to me, "Here, take this and buy what ever your little heart desires. It won't be much, but I'm sure you can think of something you just can't live without." I went to the store that afternoon and bought a box of raisins. My own box of raisins. I stuck it in my drawer and any time I wanted a raisin or two or even a hand full, I would eat some. I didn't have to share. Growing up, raisins were like gold. They would show up in cabbage salad with bananas, in oatmeal cookies or boiled raisin cookies, but we were never allowed to just eat them out of the box. Now I could. My kids love to tease me about that story. "A box of raisins, Mom?"

One of the things that surprised me when I got married was how much money everyone had. I had worked for Father all my life and had never seen any of the money. I felt lucky to be married to someone who was always so generous.

Kirkland's Nursery was growing fast. Mr. Kirkland and his six oldest sons decided to expand the nursery to include landscaping and chain-link fencing. Linton's brother Ben, left his job as a lab technician in Salt Lake and moved down to help. I went to work for Linton's father at Kirkland's Nursery, helping transplant tomato starts. We gathered for lunch everyday and it was fun getting to know my new family.

In the lonely evenings when Linton was gone driving truck, I walked up the dirt road to the top of the lane where Ben and his wife Rachel lived in a trailer house beside John and Rose's trailer. On one visit, Rachel had invited John and Rose over for supper. When I knocked on the door, Rachel hollered, "Come in."

As soon as I walked into the kitchen, John said, "Come on in and have some spaghetti. It'll make your boobs grow." I blushed bright red as they laughed at me. Was he talking about bosoms?

I wondered. When I got back to the house, I asked Ruth, "What are boobs?" She chuckled and pointed to her breasts.

"Why do you ask?"

"Well," I told her, "John just told me that eating spaghetti would make my boobs grow."

"Don't pay any attention to him. He just loves to tease," she laughed.

Every time I made spaghetti after that night I secretly hoped it was true.

Ruth's husband, Tom was from Georgia and I had a hard time understanding his Southern accent. One night when Linton was gone and I was eating supper with Ruth's little family, Tom teased me, saying, "So, Linton's gone out to find hisself another '*wowman*', ay." I was so homesick and heartsick I wanted to cry, but I waited until I got downstairs to my room.

The next day I got a letter from Kay:

> I love to saddle Meg every evening and ride up to the 320 to change the water. I tie her up to the pine trees and sit very still to watch the deer come into the meadow to eat. It is so beautiful and peaceful up here. But I miss you so much sometimes I sit here and cry. I have started a journal so I bring it with me and write in it. I bet you are having so much fun being married. I can't wait until I get married and start my life, too.
>
> Love your Sister, Kay.

I wrote back:

> I miss you too. Sometimes I lie in my bed at night when Linton is gone and cry because I miss you and Mother and

the little girls so much. But I do I love being married and working at Kirkland's Nursery. They have been so kind to me.

It's been fun to get to know all my new sister-in-laws. ReVoe is my favorite. She is so modern. She rats her hair up in the front and smoothes it over and pulls it back in a pretty silver barrette then she sprays it with lots of hair spray. She is six months pregnant and wears the cutest maternity clothes. On the days I don't work at the nursery I walk over to her place and visit. You wouldn't believe how cute her trailer is. Every thing matches. Even her hot pads match her curtains. She is a really good cook and always has cookies or a cake on her kitchen counter for her husband. Every time I go over she pours me a big glass of Coke over ice so we will have something to drink while we watch 'Days of Our Lives'. You wouldn't believe how scandalous that show is.

She believes in using birth control and says she is going to use the Pill after she has her baby so that her children aren't so close together. I would never take the pill because I believe God wants us to bring as many spirits to the Earth as we can. But I still love her and I can ask her any question about husband and wife and baby stuff and she doesn't make me feel stupid. She has made me feel so loved and welcomed.

How is Mother? When will I see you all again? I hope you come in to the fundamentalist meeting next month. I think they are planning to meet up at Oak Grove Park in Leeds. Please come. I love and miss you all."

Immediately after we returned from our honeymoon, Linton wanted me to start taking a prenatal vitamin and go to the doctor and get a physical to make sure I was healthy enough to get pregnant. I made an appointment with the doctor and after the exam, I said. "We would like to get pregnant soon."

"Well, you're completely healthy. How long have you been married?"

"Two weeks," I said, completely serious.

He tried to keep a straight face and proceeded to tell me that he was almost positive I would be pregnant very soon.

He was right. We were excited.

When the Kirkland brothers decided to go into business together, they also decided they would put 10% of their paychecks into a family fund each month and when they had enough money they would start with one house and build until each of their families had a new home on the farm, all paid for. It was a great plan. There was already a basement foundation built next door to Ruth and Tom's. A friend of the family had started to build there and then got mad at Grandpa Kirkland and left. The other boys didn't want to build on that basement so Linton said we would take it. Every Saturday Linton and his brothers worked on our house. The wooden floor went in over the basement walls and the gray cinder blocks went up from there. Holes where windows and doors would go were waiting to be filled. The house grew and my belly grew.

We moved into our new house eight months from when we started building. The only rooms with sheet-rock were the bathroom and the bedroom. I did dishes in the tub until Linton built a makeshift cabinet to hold a sink in the kitchen. His parents gave us an old refrigerator and stove. I finally had it all. My man and my kitchen.

Linton did all the plumbing and electrical himself. He wanted electric heating so he read a book to learn how to do it and then spent every night tacking up the tiny electric wires across the first pieces of sheetrock, then mudded and hammered another piece of sheet-rock over that without hitting any of the wires. Every night we built, stained or painted something. Our bedroom was painted and carpeted, all ready to bring home our new baby on December 26th, my due date.

December 20 was Grandpa Kirkland's birthday and I was looking forward to the party that evening where the whole family would meet for cake and ice cream. Around three o'clock that afternoon, Ruth came over to borrow an egg. I was standing with my back pressed against the cupboard visiting with her when water started running down my legs. I looked over wide-eyed at Ruth. "I think I just peed my pants."

"No silly, your water just broke. You are going to have a baby today."

"Should I head to the hospital?" I asked her nervously.

"Oh, no you have plenty of time. Find Linton and tell him to come home and then call your doctor and tell him your water broke. He'll tell you what to do next." She smiled at my innocence and tried to reassure me. "You'll be fine, I promise. Women have been doing this for a few years now."

"How far apart are your contractions?" my doctor asked when I called.

"I don't think I'm having contractions," I said.

"Come to my office and we'll give you a pitocin pill to dissolve under your tongue and that will get the contractions going." I called Kirkland's Nursery and luckily Linton was there. He came home and took me to get the pill. I happily put in under my tongue and we went home to wait.

"That was a good one," Linton said, looking at his watch two hours later. "They're getting closer."

"Good for who?" I asked, scrunching up my face.

"Well, you can't keep that baby in there forever."

"Can't we just be pregnant for a couple more months and then we can have it." I laughed but I really wanted to cry. It really hurt.

"I'm worried that I won't be as good a mother as my mother is." There, I had finally expressed my biggest fear.

"I'm not worried about that," Linton said as he leaned over and kissed me on the cheek. "You'll be a great mother."

The next two contractions came five minutes apart so we headed to the hospital.

The nurse admitted me and gave me another pitocin pill to put under my tongue. The harder the contractions came, the more scared and out of control I felt. I remembered what Ruth had said to me only a couple hours earlier. "Women have been doing this forever." I wanted to scream, "*WHY*! And then I wanted to scream, "*How did Mother do this seventeen times*!"

The only thing that saved me was Linton's hand, holding mine. He stood beside me for the next five hours. When he was about to faint for lack of food, he said he needed to get something to eat, I said "No, you are not leaving my side. I can't do this without you." And just when I knew I couldn't take it anymore I wanted to push. And just when I thought I couldn't push anymore, sweet baby Lillie was born.

I was positive that there had never been a sound as beautiful as Lillie's first cry. My body and heart were changed forever. The girl who came to the hospital to have her first baby would go home very different. I was a mother now, something I had always wanted to be. What a difference a few hours can make. Our story was about to begin.

The nurse wrapped Lillie up tight and handed her to me. Linton leaned in and ran his finger across her forehead. "She has hair," he said, surprised.

Lillie was trying to open her eyes. "Hi, pretty girl," I said.

"You are just beautiful aren't you? Wow, isn't she just amazing?" I whispered to Linton.

Too soon, the nurse held out her arms. "Okay, it's time to get her all cleaned up. We'll take her to the nursery and bring her to you a little later."

I was helped into a clean bed and rolled into the recovery room that I shared with four other new mothers. The bathroom we all shared was down the hall. I said goodnight to Linton and he went home to rest.

A few hours later, I woke to the sound of a baby crying down the hall. I looked around the room where all the other mothers were sleeping soundly. The baby sounded frightened. I lay there for a minute listening when suddenly I knew, *'that's my baby crying'*. I started to get out of bed. Every muscle ached, remembering the struggle of just a few hours earlier. Gently I brought my legs over the edge of the bed and reached for my bathrobe. Slipping it over my arms, and stepping into my slippers, I walked as quickly as I could to the sound of those cries.

The nurse saw me at the nursery door. "Are you Mrs. Kirkland?"

"Yes."

"Your baby just won't stop crying. I've given her a bottle and changed her diaper. I think she wants her mommy. Come sit here in this rocker and see if you can get her to settle down."

As soon as I sat down I heard my mother's voice, "There is nothing like holding your new baby, smelling its breath and nuzzling its neck. These are the best days of your life. Cherish every moment."

The nurse placed my screaming baby in my arms. I brought her up close against my face and smelled her. "Come here," I whispered. "I missed you too. Everything will be okay, I promise." Her sobs grew further and further apart as her tiny body began to relax. Rocking back and forth, I leaned back and closed my eyes and softly started to sing the first song that came to mind, "When Whippoorwills Call, and evening is nigh, I'll hurry to my Blue Heaven."

Afterward

In November of 1971, when we moved to the ranch, I think Mother was excited for the new adventure. She had the ability to always see the best in people and situations that she found herself in. I think she was hoping that now that Father had the cattle ranch he had always dreamed of he would settle down and stay home. She should have known better. This wasn't the first time he had dumped her in a godforsaken place and then left her to do all the work. He was a people person and couldn't stand the isolation of the ranch.

In the early 70's, Las Vegas was booming and my brothers got construction jobs and Father followed them leaving Mother and the girls to run ranch. Father and the boys came home on the weekends with food and the supplies to build a bathroom and remodel the kitchen. One Saturday morning, they were busy hammering up the new bathroom walls when the Lincoln County School Superintendent pulled up in his truck. He told Father the girls were required to attend school in Pioche, fifty miles away. Father told him Mother had a two-year teaching certificate from Ricks College and that she would be home schooling them and the state of Nevada could pay her to do it. Seeing that he was not going to win that argument, the superintendent agreed. Mother went to the school district office and took two tests to become certified to teach in Nevada.

The ranch years were filled with adventure for the five youngest girls, Helen, Ruth, Beth Lillith and Donna, age's twelve to three. When they weren't studying around the kitchen table they had cows to milk, horses, chickens, and rabbits to feed. They also became the ranch hands. They jumped on their horses and brought the cattle down from the hills in the fall and pushed and shoved them back up in to the mountains in the spring.

There were winters when the snow was so deep that Father and the boys couldn't make it home. The county road crew finally came out and cleared the road almost up to the ranch house, but not quite. The girls longed to see another human being and prayed that the grater operator would stop and trek through the snow and come and tell them news from the outside world. He didn't. Helen told me years later that as she watched him turn the grater around she wondered it anyone cared if they lived or died.

Father invited a steady stream of weirdoes to the ranch who seemed to have no trouble finding the middle of nowhere. Some of them stayed weeks, and some stayed months. He once brought out a young mother with her six children, who had left her polygamist husband. Father told her if she lost fifty pounds he would marry her but in the meantime he would collect her welfare checks and Mother could teach the children so he could get a bigger check from the State of Nevada. The children slept in their sleeping bags on the carpet in the living room and their mother took the downstairs bedroom. The kids peed the bed at night, which soaked into the carpet, sending Mother and the girls to their bedrooms upstairs for fresh air. Almost a year later, after the mother had lost fifty pounds, the school year came to an end and everyone had had enough, she packed her bags and left.

Besides Father's polygamist friends who came to the ranch looking for wives, there was the artist who came and stayed all summer in his camper and taught the girls art lessons every afternoon. After he left another wanna-be polygamist moved out to the ranch with his cute wife and family and started building a rock house up the north canyon. After six months they decided they had had enough of ranch life and moved to town and got divorced.

One of their most in-famous visitors was Ervil Labaron, the leader of Church of the First Born of the Fulness of Times who dropped by the ranch just two weeks before he had Dr. Rulon Allred, leader of the Allred Group in Bluffdale, Utah, killed. Ervil was on the run from the law, having already been accused of ordering the killing of another polygamist group leader. Helen remembers being grateful Father was home that day. Mother looked worried and told the girls to stay upstairs in their rooms and not make a sound. They were glad when Ervil got in his truck and pulled out of the driveway.

Father made it clear that when we left Colorado City and moved to the Ranch, we would be bringing polygamy with us. Father reasoned that just because the men leading the FLDS Group were wrong didn't mean plural marriage was wrong. He was still determined to live the Celestial Law of Marriage.

The summer after I got married, Father did take another wife. This was his last ditch effort to build his kingdom. She was a lady from the Allred Group in Salt Lake City. She had three teenage kids and was in her early forties so I guess they thought she could still pop out a kid or two. They were married at our ranch. Bart had sufficient Priesthood so he officiated.

Mother stood beside Father and placed the other woman's hand in Fathers as a sign from the first wife that she freely gives this woman to her husband in marriage. After the marriage ceremony the lady went back to her home in Salt Lake City and the marriage only lasted five months.

Many people have wondered what happened to each of us after we all got married and moved away. So I will try to recap according to birth order.

When Cheryl was twenty-years-old she married Hyrum Jeffs and they moved into a tiny pioneer home on Rulon Jeff's compound in Little Cottonwood Canyon in Sandy, Utah. Cheryl had nine children when Hyrum took a second wife. They found a large home in Lehi, Utah with enough land for some cows, horses and chickens. She has a beautiful family of fifteen children and many grandchildren.

Janice was Mother's helper all her life. Janice's life changed dramatically in 1999, when Beth graduated from high school and she and Helen moved to Las Vegas to work. Mother worried that her girls were not living in a safe place and decided they needed her protection. Against Father's wishes, Mother took Janice, Lillith and Donna and moved to Las Vegas, thinking that if they all got jobs and worked hard they could afford to rent an apartment and eat. Mother got a job at Dunkin Donuts. The day she dropped Donna off at Woodbury Elementary, she got back in her car and cried her eyes out. *What have I done,* she wondered, *bringing my sweet baby to this wicked place.* Mother soon got a job at Cannon Junior High as the Orchestra Director's assistant. She was back in her musical element again and loved it.

Janice got a job at the Salvation Army Thrift store. One of the handicapped workers took a shine to her and they spent time getting to know each other in the broom closet. She was forty years old when she got pregnant. She had always wanted a baby; a dream encased in a cedar chest full of things she had collected throughout her life: baby clothes, bottles and diapers. Father was furious and made Janice identify the sperm donor.

When Janice delivered Jeremy, Mother reached out with her arms and her heart to help Janice be the best mother she could be. Jeremy was born handicapped and Mother kept him alive through the ravages of many sicknesses. Mother rubbed him with olive oil everyday and exercised his legs and arms. Just as her mother had done so many years before with Bart's broken arm, Mother insisted that her grandson become strong. Jeremy learned to walk and talk and play but in his mind and emotions he would remain a seven-year-old.

Mother took Janice and Jeremy and they went back to the ranch to live, after her youngest child, Donna graduated from high school. When Jeremy was old enough to go to school she drove fifty miles into Pioche everyday, so he could have the teachers he needed. While Jeremy was in class, Mother practiced the piano in the school auditorium. The teachers at the school still remark how much they enjoyed having their own concert every day.

Janice and Jeremy started going to church with Lee and Ellen, who had moved back out to the ranch when Mother did. Janice was baptized a member of the Church of Jesus Christ of Latter-Day-Saints and loved to go to the temple with Lee's wife, Ellen. Janice was thrilled when the Relief Society President asked her to lead the music in Relief Society. This was torture for anyone who knew what a downbeat was, but total bliss for my sister who smiled from ear to ear through every hymn.

After Mother passed away, Keith and Lacie took Janice and Jeremy into their home in Panaca, Nevada. They had a small house they had lived in before they built their new home next door, so Janice and Jeremy moved in there. Janice loved living in the small community of Panaca, where everyone knew and loved her. She often walked down to the market to buy all the donuts and candy she wanted.

The summer of 2016 she started feeling weak and the doctors found a stomach ulcer that was sitting right on her main artery to her bowel and was inoperable, but the doctor said he had a drug that would either heal her ulcer in three days or it could make it worse. The ulcer healed in three days and she was happy to be going home.

Helen came to town and took her back to the Caliente hospital, where they could watch her closely. She loved it there. She knew all the nurses from church and they took good care of her. She started walking up and down the halls and said she wanted to get better so she could go home. But on Tuesday morning the ulcer started bleeding again. The doctor said she needed a blood transfusion. Helen called a few minutes later. Janice's veins had collapsed. I knew then that we would be saying good-bye.

The next two days were filled with love for Janice. Lillith, Helen and I sat and laughed with Janice and sang to her and brushed her hair. Lee and Ellen and their kids came from the ranch to see her. On the evening of the second day, Keith and his boys came and sang to her for a while. After everyone left, we ask the nurses to come in and help us move her to a more comfortable position because her breathing had become labored. Ten minutes later we watched as her sweet spirit left her body. It was the same day Mother had passed away six years earlier.

What a journey Janice had! I envisioned Mother meeting her with open arms and both of them swinging around in a circle, laughing. We did it! We did it!

❧

In 1971, when Bart married Jean, he believed in living the Principal of Plural Marriage. He and Jean were living in Cedar City, Utah, when they met a cute blond girl named Elizabeth; a mormon girl from Texas who was attending Southern Utah University. Jean gave Bart permission to court Elizabeth and things progressed swiftly. They were married a few months later. Bart's family grew fast; Elizabeth had two babies and Jean had four when a friend gave Bart a book by Ron L. Hubbard on Scientology. Bart felt inspired to investigate. Scientology offered the same dictatorial dialogue he was familiar with from the FLDS Group. Every step of your exaltation planned out for you by Hubbard. If a person completed all the steps he would be a God and could then dictate his eternities. Jean joined Bart wholeheartedly in his pursuit of Scientology Godhood, but Elizabeth did not. She took her babies back to Texas where her mother lived.

Over the next thirty years Bart and Jean ran a successful construction company in Las Vegas. He was very ambitious and work was always on his mind. He was also serious about personal growth and spent thousands of dollars on Scientology's prescribed steps to "get clear" on every level. The problem for Bart was like that of many others, he gave his money and did all the required work only to be told by his superiors that he still was not clear. Eventually, he decided he had paid enough and he told them to go to hell.

As Bart got older, he started taking time off work to spend time with his brother and sisters. I loved it when he stopped by my house. We had long talks about forgiveness and gratitude. On one occasion, we gathered up Helen and Lilly and the four of us went on a trip to Idaho together. We laughed and cried and remembered the good old days. It was our last adventure together. Bart died of a massive heart attack at the young age of sixty-seven, just when we were really getting to know each other again.

*

Keith married Lacie Ward, the second daughter of Mary and Roger Ward, an independent polygamist from Pahrump, Nevada. Lacie grew up with a strong conviction of the truthfulness of the Principle of Plural Marriage but only five months into her marriage when she was pregnant with her first child, Keith started dating a sixteen-year-old girl who was living at the Ranch with the family.

Lacie learned first hand the despair and heartache that every wife feels when her husband begins to think of taking another wife. Keith told this girl that they would have to wait until she was eighteen to get married and she soon moved away and became disinterested. Lacie was so relieved. After they had their first two girls, Keith started courting another woman. This time Lacie went to the Lord in fasting and prayer because she had the same foreboding feeling she had had before. When she didn't receive an answer she went to Keith, believing that her marriage would be over when she told him that if he needed to live polygamy he would have to do it without her because she felt like if she tried to live it, it would destroy her. After some silent moments, Keith said the thing that she needed to hear. "Well, it isn't worth living polygamy if it means losing you." Later, he admitted he was relieved because he noticed he had never met a happy polygamist. Keith and Lacie joined the Church of Jesus Christ of Latter-Day-Saints and have six beautiful children, who are all grown. They live and work in Panaca, Nevada and still take good care of Jeremy for Mother. Keith has carried on the singing tradition and sings with his three sons. The boys love it and their dad loves it more.

ゐ∽ஒ

Kay became a second wife. She met the love of her life when we were getting ready to leave Colorado City. He and his wife had left the mainstream Mormon Church to join the Allred Group. After we moved to the ranch he kept coming out to visit with his darling little family; Kay eventually fell in love and agreed to become his second wife. She and her husband have thirteen children. Kay did a marvelous job of instilling the love of music in her children. Her oldest son sings in a quartet and her daughters sing trios and quartets together. She is a wonderful mother and her seventy plus grandkids love her dearly.

ゐ∽ஒ

Linton and I had seven children, six daughters and one son. When we got married, we planned on living polygamy. After my sister Helen graduated from high school, she came to live with us in St. George to attend Dixie College. I loved having her there. She was so sweet to the kids and I thought she might want to be part of our family. I imagined that living polygamy wouldn't be so bad if I could live it with one of my sisters. I told Linton he should ask her to marry him but when he popped the question, she said no. She told me later that she had no interest in ever living polygamy.

Linton and I moved to Salt Lake City with our five little kids in 1980. One afternoon I was canning green beans and opened the pressure cooker too fast and burned me across my breast and stomach. I called Mother to see if my sister Ruth could come and help me with the kids. While Ruth was with us, Linton asked her if she would be interested in marrying him but she told him she was already interested in someone else, who became her husband one year later.

Linton was working for a polygamist friend at the time and I think he felt some pressure to get on the stick and get another wife. And whom should he think of next, but Becky, the very same Becky who came riding up with him in his diesel truck that long ago Sunday in Bunkerville, Nevada. She had been married, but was now divorced with a little boy. Linton came home one day after work and told me he had taken her out to lunch. I think I had about three heart attacks and turned to him and said, "You need to look around you at these six little kids," and I spread my arm in a sweeping jester to add flare, "because they and their mother will be gone if you ever do that again." And that was the end of our fantasy dance with polygamy.

Linton and I moved our little family back to St. George, in 1984. When my oldest girls were twelve and eleven they started wanting to go to Young Women's meetings at the Mormon Church with their friends. We felt it was important for them to feel they were a part of their community and that going to the Mormon Church would be good for them. When we moved to Bullhead City, Arizona, in 1990 I started going with my kids to the LDS Church because I needed to meet some nice people and introduce my children to some good friends. Two years later when we moved back to St George I continued taking the kids to church.

When the kids started attending church, Linton told them they had to wait until they were eighteen to get baptized. He also let them know that he would never join the church because he still believed in polygamy and figured he was going to Hell because he had never lived it.

Our first three girls got baptized and started getting married in their early twenties. When our first two girls got married in the LDS Temple, Linton and I had to stand outside because we weren't members and couldn't even attend our own daughter's weddings. In 2000 when my last two girls got baptized I decided I would get baptized too. Because of our families' polygamist history we had to go up to Salt Lake City and visit Elder Worthlin in his office. He was very kind and welcomed us into the Church. My son had just returned from his mission so he baptized all three of us. I started going to the temple so I could attend my third daughter's wedding later that summer.

My father and mother never told me not to join the LDS Church. After all, they had been through a few religious changes themselves. In 1995 they were initiated into a group called Science of the Soul. They had a Master, became vegetarians and meditated two and a-half hours everyday. Among their thirteen children there are Polygamists, Scientologists, Mormons and Born again Christians.

Many times over the years, when Mother and Father came into town to visit, Father sat at my table and told me about the Master and how he taught that the only reason we are here on earth is to learn to love.

At one of those visits, Father told me what his Master had said about the power of forgiveness and that we all had people in our lives we needed to forgive so we could be forgiven for our own trespasses. It was almost Father's Day and I found a nice card and wrote to my father and sincerely thanked him for giving me life. For feeding and clothing me all the years I was in his home. There were a lot of mouths to feed and I'm sure he did the best he could. I needed to forgive him so that I could be forgiven for the ways I had failed my own children. Even though they would have to think really hard to find any, I'm sure.

I love the Mormon people but I left the Mormon Church in 2010. I guess it was a combination of things that caused me to question my reason for getting baptized in the first place. I always wondered about the mysteries of the Temple. I wanted so much to be at my daughter's weddings and was grateful for that experience. I might have wanted to be accepted by my Mormon friends and neighbors too much.

Certainly, my leaving the Mormon Church was influenced by events that happened in Colorado City, Arizona. About the time Warren Jeffs became the Prophet of The FLDS, I still had family and friends in Colorado City whose families were being torn apart because Warren felt his authority was being threatened. He sent Fathers (and Mothers) away from their families telling them they needed to repent of their sins and their wives and children were given to other men. I wondered what caused a man to believe he had the authority to control people's lives like he did. I heard my father's voice from my childhood reciting the 121 section of the *Doctrine & Covenants*, verse 39: '*We have learned by sad experience that it is the nature and disposition of almost all men, as soon as they get a little authority, as they suppose, they will immediately begin to exercise unrighteous dominion.*' My heart ached for my family and all the other families whose lives have been ruined by men who call themselves prophets. I began my quest to find my truth and make sense of Mormonism, as I knew it. I read, *No Man Knows My History* by Fawn Mckay Brodie, *Rough Stone Rolling* by Richard Lyman Bushman *and In Sacred Loneliness, The Plural Wives of Joseph Smith* by Todd Compton, and after much prayer and study, I decided I had lived enough of my life in fear. Fear of hell and damnation if you don't belong to the right church, dress right, eat right, act right and say the right things. It felt like a breath of fresh air to finally be free. Just me and God.

I believe that no one has a right to tell another person what to believe. I believe that God loves all His Children, everywhere. I believe that most of us try to guide our children in righteousness so they will raise up another generation of beautiful, kind people.

Five of our children and their families are Mormons and two are not. They all love each other very much and prove it by playing March Madness together every year. The seventeen beautiful grandchildren they have given us are the reason we take each breath and shower, so they will come and see us.

Roger married Kady Ward, Lacie's older sister. Roger and Kady have eight grown children. Roger runs a backhoe and construction company in Las Vegas, with his son. All of their children were band majors in high school. Mother loved to go see them perform whenever she could.

Kady was from a polygamist home and figured she would someday welcome another woman as her sister-wife. But after fasting and praying many times about it she gained a testimony of the truthfulness of the Church of Jesus Christ of Latter-day Saints and told Roger that she was going to join the Church and that she would not be living polygamy and that if he felt he had to live it he would have to do it without her. Roger started to think seriously about the Church of Jesus Christ of Latter-day Saints and he began fasting and praying. Kady waited patiently for Roger to gain his own testimony and two years later Roger was able to baptize Kady and their three oldest boys. Eventually all eight of their children became members. Roger has a beautiful cabin built at the ranch and loves to spend his weekends at his mountain retreat.

Lee married Felecia Ward, who is also Kady's and Lacie's sister, the oldest daughter of Mr. Ward's second wife. Lee and Felecia built a beautiful home three miles down the road from Mother's ranch house. They had three young boys when they divorced. Lee was single for seven years when he met Ellen, a returned missionary. They fell in love and got married. When Mother moved back to the ranch with Janice and Jeremy in 2000, Lee and Ellen moved into his house on the ranch and are still raising the last of their eleven wild and crazy ranch kids. Their last son became Father and Mother's 100th grandchild. Mother and Father enjoyed having Lee and Ellen's children around them during their last years on the ranch. Mother taught the girls to play the piano and sing together, and Father spent his last days on earth with Lee.

Helen is married and has five girls and one son. They have a batch of cute grandbabies who are the pride and joy of their life. She was a schoolteacher in Las Vegas for fifteen years, then moved to Panaca, Nevada, where she teaches in the Adult Education program. Life is Good!

Ruth became a second wife. She and her husband have twelve children and lots of grandbabies. She raises a huge garden every year and helps teach at their private school in her community. She is a great mother and so busy I don't know how she does it all.

❧

Beth lived in Chino Valley, Arizona while working and raising her two wonderful children. She had the opportunity to go to Alaska where she adventured for four years after her children were grown. Beth enjoys her grandchildren and is currently engaged in helping her sisters write their story about living on the ranch.

❧

Lillith went to Beauty School in Rexburg, Idaho, while she waited for her handsome missionary to get home. They were married for thirty years and then divorced. They have five wonderful children. Lillith worked in her home beauty salon while her children were growing up. Lilly is on a journey to find love and happiness and keeps her sisters beautified and grounded in gratitude.

❧

Donna has owned a successful accounting firm in Kentucky for the last twenty-five years. She has three beautiful children who were encouraged by their mother to participate in band throughout high school just like she did. They all enjoyed it, but Donnas youngest daughter must have inherited some of Grandmother Ilene's talents because she is pursuing a degree in music education and plays the piano and trumpet beautifully. Donna and her husband divorced and after a few years of finding her own path to happiness, she has found love again and is looking forward to the years ahead.

So that's all thirteen of us. What a life it has been. We were all together last June for a Pearson Family reunion. The food was delicious, the babies were plentiful and the songs went on and on. I'm sure Mother, Father and Janice and Bart would have loved it immensely.

I want to thank my parents for the wonderfully rich and interesting life they gave us. And even though Father was quite a character, it's like my friend said, "if you hadn't had the father you had, you wouldn't have a story to tell." So true.

As Father got older he began having heart trouble. I was working at Hurst Ace Hardware when he stopped by to see me. He looked very pale and it seemed like he was going to fall over. "It's just my heart giving me a little trouble," he said. I quickly found a chair for him to sit on and told him to stay there and I would clock out and take him to my house until he felt better. I ran to the office and told my boss I needed to leave but when I got back Father was not there. I called his cell phone and he answered. "I'm just up the rode in Dameron Valley. I decided I would just go on home. I'm starting to feel a little better." I went back to work. He was his own man and always had been and there was nothing I could do to change him. He kept his heart ticking with cayenne pepper and garlic for a few more years. The year he turned eighty he was still running to Cedar City to get equipment parts for Lee or sauntering into the Café in Pioche for coffee and gossip. One night he came home and ate a small bowl of vegetable soup and complained to Mother that it had been 'too hot' and went into the living room to rest in his chair. Mother needed to use the phone at Lee's house but before she left she gave Father a nitroglycerin pill and took off his shoes and massaged his feet. He began to feel better and told her, "I think I can sleep now. You go ahead and use the phone and hurry back." Mother left Janice with Father and took Jeremy. When she got home Mother went to check on Father and she knew he was gone. She didn't want to upset Janice and Jeremy so she sent them to bed and when she was alone she pushed her chair close to his and sat with him through the night.

Many times when we were with Mother after Father's passing, she told us how much she missed him. I wondered how you could miss someone who had caused you so much sorrow. Then I recalled the poem from The Prophet by Kahlil Gibran that Father had memorized and recited to us often over the years, "Your joy is your sorrow unmasked. And the selfsame well from which your laughter rises was often times filled with your tears. And how else can it be? The deeper that sorrow carves into your being, the more joy you can contain." So it was with Mother and Father.

Mother left notebooks over flowing with records of her grand children's birthdates, who attended the family reunions and how much money down to the last cent she spent on her trip to Kentucky to see Donna. One notebook was labeled "The Homes I Have Lived In" and she told about every home she had lived in from her birth to her death. But many times as I was writing this book I wished she had written more.

On January 24, 2010, she wrote, "I drove into Pioche Sunday for church and when I got home I got my blanket and went and sat in my big chair. I was so tired, I said, "This is it. I am through." That day she had picked up a bad cold and spent the next three months at Lillith's home in Las Vegas getting better. There were nights when we didn't think she would make it. All five thousand of us descended on Lillith's house to love on her and tell her she couldn't die.

On May 1, 2010, she listed the things she was grateful for:

I am grateful for this new day.

My bright mind

My brothers

My strong heart
My wonderful children and grandchildren
My good home
My friends

My goats.... (Roger brought out two goats after Mother moved back to the ranch from Las Vegas and they eventually turned into hundreds over the next twenty years.)

On August 2, 2010 Mother wrote: "We had our best rain of the summer last Saturday. Janice had made a fire under the big tub outside and was all ready to jump in for her bath but we had to wait until 9 p.m. because of the lightning. We watched the storm go north over into Hamblin Valley and then we had our baths." (Soon after the family moved to the ranch, Father bought a big caste iron tub that was made for scalding pigs after they were slaughtered. He built it up onto cinder blocks so they could build a fire under it to heat the water and that is how the younger girls grew up bathing. It became the highlight of the grandkid's stay at the ranch, to get to bathe in the pig pot!)

Mother was faithful to her Master's teachings, meditating two and a-half hours every morning. Science of the Soul followers believe that being vegetarian helps them not build up any more Karma. And if they meditate every morning, the Master can help them get rid of the Karma they already have. They believe that this earth is the Hell of Hells and that if they are faithful they can go to a better place in their next life.

I felt sad thinking that she might be disappointed with all her trying when she wrote: "The Master has not come and told me it is my time to go. I have really tried hard to live a good life and do what is right. If I should go tonight, I would like to say "Thanks" to each of my children. Thanks for being brave enough to come down here and live with your father and me. I know it has not always been easy, but I have loved you all dearly.

It has been fun. Thanks for loving to sing. That has been a great joy to me."

Mother jokingly told Helen one day that she was quite sure she had gotten rid of all her Karma with this life because she had lived it with Father. The life she had lived with him had been nothing like the life she had envisioned for herself as a young girl. So even if she had to come back here again she was quite sure it couldn't be any harder than this life had been.

After Father passed away, every Sunday morning, Mother took Janice and Jeremy and joined Lee and Ellen and their family at the Mormon Church in Pioche, Nevada. She loved playing the piano for primary. She bore her testimony telling the congregation that they were not standing up for the Constitution and they were not teaching their children to fight for the truth. "You parents must get rid of your TVs and video games and read to your children from the bible and the Book of Mormon." She would become full of the spirit, like she had finally found her voice after all these years and wasn't afraid to use it. I'm sure the bishop worried every time she got up to bare her testimony that he may have to tug on her jacket and suggest that she stand down!

The fall of 2011 Mother started having a hard time breathing at night and wondered if it might be because she lived at 6000 feet above sea level. We brought her in to Dixie Regional Medical Center in St. George and learned that she had congestive heart failure. The doctor could put her on some medications to help her but she said no. She had never used drugs, even for a headache, and she wasn't about to start now. She let them put her on oxygen, which helped her breathing and we brought her home to my house.

Every weekend family showed up to see Mother. One weekend we invited the whole family to a barbeque and it rained so hard I had eighty people standing in my house and garage trying to eat and stay dry. Helen and Lillith lived in Las Vegas and drove up every weekend to cook and clean and take over for me. Mother loved it when they took turns reading, *The Seven Miracle that Saved America* to her. One afternoon she started playing the piano for us but only made it through one piece before she grew too tired and needed to rest. We tried to hide the tears in our eyes as she finished because we knew that it could be the last time we would hear her play.

When Mother's toes started turning black from lack of oxygen I told her I needed to call hospice to help us decide what to do and she agreed. I let her know that just because I was calling them it didn't mean she was dying. She just smiled at me.

She had been living with us for six weeks when Keith and Lacie and Jeremy came in to see her one evening. We were sitting around the table eating and she was trying to get a little soup down. She had been having a hard time eating the whole time she was with me, but that night was worse. She got up to go to the bathroom and Jeremy got up to help her. She suddenly went stiff and almost fell over but Jeremy caught her and Keith helped get her to the bedroom. She had had a stroke. Her left side was paralyzed and she couldn't speak. Keith and Lacie sat with her and I called hospice. They came and helped us get her settled in her bed. At 11 pm she closed her eyes and drifted into a coma. The next morning Helen and Lillith drove up from Vegas and we spent the next three days singing and playing the piano for her. Lee and Ellen brought the kids in from the Ranch to say good-bye. They would miss her the most. Piano lessons every week and Sunday dinners together. Roger came from Las Vegas and the grandkids who lived close stopped by to say good-bye.

On the third day there was a break in the flow of company and Helen put on a CD of piano music. *Traumerei*, the piano piece she had played at her brother Blair's funeral the year before was playing and Lillith came from the bedroom and whispered, "I think she just left." We gathered around Mother and wept. What a woman. It wasn't until she took her last breath that it really hit me that she could actually leave us... that I would never hear her voice again... that I would never hear her play her piano again.

A few month's after Mother passed away, Lee told me that he and Ellen were visiting their bishop one day and he told them that Mother had come into his office, asked for and was given a temple recommend. After all she had been through why would she think she needed a temple recommend? Was it because she saw truth in everything good? Were her beloved brothers calling her to come back home? Maybe you can't take away what is woven into a child's soul? I don't know the answer. But every Sunday morning when my husband and I sit down to watch 'Music and the Spoken Word' with the Mormon Tabernacle Choir, I feel like I am sitting next to Mother. The music that she loved so dearly, that was part of every cell of her body, might have been reason enough to call her back to her beloved family and home.

We held a celebration of Mother's life in the Panaca LDS Church auditorium. It was a grand day with music and stories from the life of an amazing woman. Mother's brother, Ronald, the last of her brothers and sisters alive, played *Fantasy Impromtu*, one of the piano pieces we fell to sleep to as children. All of Mother's grandchildren and great-grandchildren came forward to sing *America the Beautiful* for their dearest Grandmother.

As I write this, I look again in her notebook and find she has written, "Never give up. Trust in the Lord." Yes, Mother, we will do our best. And thank you.